AF006148

Pink Hell

Mari Sea

New Delhi • London

BLUEROSE PUBLISHERS
India | U.K.

Copyright © Mari Sea 2024

All rights reserved by author. No part of this publication may be reproduced, stored in a retrieval system or transmitted in any form or by any means, electronic, mechanical, photocopying, recording or otherwise, without the prior permission of the author. Although every precaution has been taken to verify the accuracy of the information contained herein, the publisher assumes no responsibility for any errors or omissions. No liability is assumed for damages that may result from the use of information contained within.

BlueRose Publishers takes no responsibility for any damages, losses, or liabilities that may arise from the use or misuse of the information, products, or services provided in this publication.

For permissions requests or inquiries regarding this publication, please contact:

BLUEROSE PUBLISHERS
www.BlueRoseONE.com
info@bluerosepublishers.com
+91 8882 898 898
+4407342408967

ISBN: 978-93-6452-728-6

Cover design: Shivani
Typesetting: Sagar

First Edition: July 2024

PINK HELL

Memories of rape victim

Contents

Preview 1
Invitation to the Hell 4
So, You Want to be a Flight Attendant? 15
Theory of Hell 26
Hell Corporation Industries Induction 36
Rabbit Issues 42
Naye Saal Ki Shubhkamnayein 55
Rabbit in a Stuck 63
Rabbit in a Cage 73
Heresy 86
Entrance 102
Day 1 106
Day 2 115
Day 3 124
Slavish Humility 148
Groundhog Day 173
1.01.1 189
Don't Sleep on the Frontline. 210
Stage of Despair 228
Get the Price of Freedom 236
Walls of Silence 245
Your Fight is Over 254
Wakeup Call 259
Day Limits.. 270
Night Limits 280
The Bloodstained Pink... 290

Preview

Dear reader, I don't know why you took my book from the shelf of this store or opened the preview link. I'm unsure if I'll still be alive when you open this page. Or if you are aware of who I am and what happened with us in India.

My darling India, how many changes you brought to my small woman life...

This book isn't written by a seasoned author or a literary giant. It's the heartfelt work of an ordinary woman driven by a desire to make a difference within herself.

The book won't whisk you away to a fairy tale world where evil always loses.

The book represents the memories of a rape victim caught in human trafficking by a Senior Large Company in an Indian State in 2022.

The book is an expanded version of the first part of the complaint filed with the Indian Police Station and Court in April 2023. All names and abbreviations are changed as the trial is still ongoing, and the accused "criminal gang" is not fully identified. All chats mentioned here as an "Exhibit" are real evidence and part of the investigation process.

Some of you, after finishing the book, can think that this is the end, but that was just the beginning of a big story that has the potential to leave a lasting mark on India's legal system and change the mindsets of countless individuals.

This is just the beginning of the fight, which already changed hundreds of minds. As I delve deeper, I encounter more women approaching me for help. These women, like me, have been victims of rape, their cases silenced or dismissed casualties of a corrupt system that prioritizes bribes and inflated statistics in the state over genuine safety for women.

This is the beginning of a powerful story – a story of real life, filled with support, pain, betrayal, hope, challenges, persecution, and even two attempted murders within a single year, which I will show you soon.

A story about simple Indians and their inner demons.

A story about me facing a period that would become the most challenging and complex of my life: this wasn't just turbulence or a difficult passenger; it was an experience that sent my world into a tailspin.

It's a story of hitting rock bottom but also of the strength I discovered within myself to rise again.

There's no doubt that changing the system won't happen overnight, but your honest review and acknowledgment of the situation can be a robust foundation for your daughters' future.

***

Why did I shatter the mold of my life and hurl myself across the globe to India? This relentless question bleeds into my consciousness every dawn, a crimson stain on the pristine canvas of morning. Do I curse the day I made this audacious choice? Perhaps it's a crucible, a fiery trial meant to forge me anew, but the flames lick ever higher, threatening to consume me entirely. Do you hear me?? Whoever or whatever sits upstairs. I am utterly broken, a hollow shell cast upon the shore of this strange land, incapable of even the semblance of the life I once knew.

Invitation to the Hell

Limbo

I was preparing a new applicant who had finally decided to join an Israeli factory near a border city when I received a call from hell. No, my darling, that day, I didn't know how it would change my life and bring me death…

-Good afternoon, Ms. Mari! This is Annikki, a recruiting manager from "Job One." I'd like to discuss a potential job opportunity on a private jet with you if you're available.

"Again, under the open sky! I can't help but think about last week when I received more than five offer letters to rejoin my beloved clouds. But I decided to take a chance on earth, just to see if my adventurous spirit could handle staying in one place for at least six months….. So much I missed this feeling of the next flight, the next takeoff and landing. That feeling can only be understood by a stewardess. Ask any flight attendant what she loves most about her job, what makes her wake up that early Sunday morning at 4. To start the ritual of preparing her hairstyle, makeup, and perfectly ironed uniform - and that shawl, oh God, the shawl! If it doesn't look right after she ties it, she'll remove it, iron it one more time, and even give it a spritz of hairspray for good measure before tying it up again. This meticulous ritual will continue until she's satisfied with her reflection in the mirror."

-Hello?

-Yes, sorry… Sure.

-Ma'am, I have an Indian family interested in hiring a personal assistant for their private jet, a G550. Would you be interested in learning more about this opportunity?

-Yes…- I tried not to show my strong interest.

"India - I've never been to India, not even the popular Goa. Who are they? The only thing I knew about India came from a movie with fantastic alien heroes and beautiful women dressed in colorful saris and gold ornaments. Also, some angry passengers were pissed off that we didn't have nonveg food on board. But flight is different! From my vision, I had the impression that Indians dance and sing all day, on the streets, at work, and home, and that they have masala in their blood. It seems like a fairytale country with princesses and elephants."

-Ma'am?

-Yeah, I am so sorry it's a bad connection. Can we discuss details in WhatsApp, please?

-Sure, I will text you.

After the talk, I returned to my office table, a fire burning in my chest. This might be the reason I'll throw in the towel and return to my lovely sky. I was typing the Hebrew name of my future employer, but now I can't help but imagine landing in India and the aroma of masala tea.

I was absolutely in love with my job, the amazing country I lived in, and the people around me. There weren't any conflicts with my boss or at my rental home. Every day, I finished work at 4 pm and relaxed with my bestie on beach chairs overlooking the magnificent Mediterranean Sea. If you've never visited Israel's beaches, it's hard to explain the extraordinary energy of the Holy Land.

Traveling around the country, I was constantly amazed by the natural wealth packed into such a tiny landmass. Imagine this: just a 9-hour drive separates you from desolate Martian landscapes and dense mountain forests. You can experience the Dead Sea, the saltiest body of water in the world, surrounded by rocky dunes and seemingly endless stretches of lifeless sand. And then there's Jerusalem, the ancient and spiritual city considered a holy center by major world religions, divided for the past 70 years between two countries with a troubled history. You don't need to be a believer in Jesus, and it doesn't matter what religion you follow; you'll still feel it - that divine spirit in the Land of Israel.

I wouldn't say my life is so bad that it needs an immediate change. But you know that feeling of being a fish out of water? Everything seems okay on the surface, but you can't take a deep, refreshing breath.

Lately, I've been finding myself yearning for something more, a feeling I can only describe as having my spirit filled with the energy and open spaces I crave. Fueled by this yearning and the conviction that a change was right for me; I sent my CV in response to Annikki's message. A few days later, to my delight, I received an invitation to my dream, my lovely sky. There was no question - I would fly!

***

Words can't describe how awful my night was: three connecting flights at night, and I couldn't sleep because my mind wouldn't stop questioning me: "Why am I feeling this? Why? Was I a little bit scared? Yes, I have to – New country, new people, new job - it's natural to feel apprehensive. No, please don't tell me such nonsense. You have been traveling around the world for the last 10 years, and it can't be something different: Same contract, same aircraft, same core responsibilities. Don't be silly! Embrace your new adventure and soak up as much knowledge and experience as possible from your future Indian colleagues and friends. And, please don't try to sing or dance; I know how miserable you are in this".

While I tried to maintain a positive and calm demeanor, the night wore on my nerves. Around eleven o'clock in the morning, I arrived in Mumbai and waited outside the airport building for a message from the HR manager about my following flight details. Believe it or not, Mumbai wasn't my final destination, nor was it the capital city. It turned out my final destination was a small, non-touristy city in the northern part of the country. And yes, I was stuck waiting outside the airport because of a rule unique to India: pax without a digital or printed copy of their tickets aren't allowed inside the terminal building. ("Pax" is just a shorthand term for "passengers"). This rule also applies to people accompanying passengers, relatives, and friends.

Honey, if you buy a ticket and forget to print it or save it on your phone or email, you won't be allowed inside the airport. That's right, you'll be stuck outside in the heat! At 54 degrees Celsius (129 degrees Fahrenheit), it's no fun waiting while you burn in damp, stuffy air and sweat, lose your cold mind, and try to find your airline booth to get a printed copy.

Here's another kicker: once you're inside the terminal, you can't go back out! Even for a quick smoke break or to grab a bag you left with a taxi driver, you'll need permission from the airline. It's definitely a surprising rule, and even though I've practically lived in airports for the past few years, I don't see the logic behind it, even for security reasons. Passengers and crew are different, of course, but this rule seems a bit much.

So, after baking in the scorching heat for an hour, I approached a company representative and requested them to check my booking for upcoming flights to my final destination city. Relief! I finally got my physical ticket, but there was still no word from the HR manager. Was I frustrated? Absolutely! Here I was, stranded outside the airport in a foreign country, with no answers and a ticket I shouldn't have needed in the first place. Yes, it was enough to make anyone question the situation. However, I tried to be rational and attributed her lack of response on WhatsApp to a busy day.

I touched down in my new home for the next six months. While I knew someone was supposed to meet me and take me to my accommodation, a sliver of doubt lingered. What if they'd changed their minds? Would I be left stranded at the airport? The thought sparked a nervous laugh. "Come on," I chided myself. "It's a huge, well-respected company with over ten thousand employees. They wouldn't fly you in and then abandon you."

Emerging from the cool, modern airport, I spotted him. A well-groomed Indian man, perhaps in his mid-forties, stood out in the crowd. Dressed in full white, a gold watch and ring gleamed on his wrist. This, I knew instinctively, was my driver.

-Mari Seahi?

-Mari Sea, S-e-a, good afternoon!

-Ma'am, please follow me. Do you have any other luggage?

-Nope, only one bag.

He looked like a doctor's assistant from one of those high-end medical clinics you see in blockbuster movies. You know, the ones about crazy genius doctors creating genetically modified people with superheroes' capabilities or doing some experiments that can change the universe's future. Oh, and that red dot between his eyes seemed to pulse with an otherworldly light, like a third eye awakened by the dawn of a new era in genetic manipulation.

I was so lost in my imagination that I didn't realize we were already in the car, driving to my new home. During the ride, he wasn't very talkative, so I simply observed the city.

"Indians, excuse me, why are so many cows living everywhere, even on the roads? This is fascinating to me. I didn't expect to see elephants and princesses singing around, but I also wasn't expecting a pandemic of cows that captured the city."

This isn't my first time in Asia, so I have a sense of what to expect. Coming from Europe, some Asian countries can be a shock with their post-apocalyptic infrastructure, unpaved roads, people walking barefoot, and the ubiquitous motorbikes zipping around like a swarm of rebellious wild bees. Dirt and disorder don't bother me. Unlike some people, I'm not easily put off by chaos. I see and feel something magnificent in that apocalypse stuff.

Maybe it's not for everyone—those who are easily scared or unwilling to try 'Asian street life' might not understand. That's precisely the point: experiencing the entire spectrum, from the heights of luxury to the depths of everyday life, allows you to appreciate the contrast and truly feel happy in both scenarios.

On a private jet, I serve crystal-clear water sourced from the finest natural springs, presented in a beautiful crystal highball or Collins glass from Bohemia or Cartier. One of the pax once told me: "Believe me, the experience of enjoying a drink from such exquisite glassware on a private jet is just as delightful as savoring one from a plastic cup at an Asian Street vendor in swelteringly stuffy dust weather after hours of walking." Can anyone really feel what he was talking about?

After a while, we turned off the main road onto a bumpy, unpaved village road. A strange feeling settled in my chest. Our accommodation, it seemed, was located in an utterly ungentrified area: no cafes, restaurants, shops, or even proper lighting. Despite the lack of amenities, it wasn't a disappointment; I'm adaptable. Still, I couldn't help but wonder why this was necessary.

We turned left off this desolate road, and within a minute, I spotted the first security post. Another one appeared shortly after. These posts, I later learned, weren't just for our safety.

The first person I saw after stopping near the office was a young man about 30-35 years old. He had a focused expression, deep black eyes, and a prominent nose that gave a vaguely Jewish appearance. This was Mr. Marbach, the estate manager, who was later demoted to a butler position.

Good afternoon, ma'am. Welcome to Pink Hell. I am Mr. Marbach, the estate manager.

-Hi! Thanks a lot, Mari!- pulling the hand towards him, he got confused and made a facial expression that clearly meant that they don't do it here.

- So?

- The housekeeping staff will be happy to show you to your room. Please don't hesitate to text me on WhatsApp if you need anything.

With a nod of acknowledgment, I followed the housekeeping staff. Exhausted from my wild journey with the Indian airline, I barely registered my surroundings.

The room itself was lovely - comfortable, with new furniture and a recently renovated bathroom. It had a simple, cozy vibe, perfect for unwinding. My initial impression? Cute green space, lovely bungalow... oh, AC! And a comfy bed...Perfect... Good night for me. So tired.

Despite the lingering headache and grogginess, I woke up with the urge to explore. The place looked like a small resort with eight wooden bungalows arranged in a double row - four facing each other on either side. A charming garden filled the center, adorned with colorful flowers, captivating shrubs, and two winding paths. Each bungalow offered two rooms on each floor, featuring spacious balconies with comfortable chairs. Behind this cozy accommodation, with a total of approx thirty-five rooms, stood an office building. The perfect option for office workers, perhaps not as ideal for crew. Anyway, the tour finished!

Despite not having eaten anything since yesterday evening, surprisingly, I don't feel hungry. That crazy flight must have wiped me out. I just want to get some more sleep.

The following day, I was woken up by a strange, high-pitched voice. It was difficult to tell if the girl was laughing or crying, but I was happy to hear it. It meant I could finally meet my colleagues and have a chat. Throwing on my jeans, I headed out of the room.

There, I saw a young woman with bright blue eyes and a ponytail that stuck out at an odd angle, almost resembling a transatlantic antenna for communicating directly with space aliens.

- Hi! How are you doing? Did you arrive yesterday? I saw you - you're the one in the white jeans.

-Hi, yes. It was my jeans.

-I am Helga. What is your designation?

-Mari, I am a flight attendant.

-Who?

-Ah, the personal assistant on a private jet.

-Aah, you mean, butler personal assistant

-Who?

-Yes. Your department title is Butler/Personal Assistant. The aircraft isn't here yet, but it should arrive soon, possibly in February.

-Oh, like this... I see...Okey.

"Hold on, February? It's November! What am I supposed to do until then?" Trying to make sense of it all inside my head, I figured maybe they brought me in early because of charter bookings. Ugh, never mind. Silly me getting stressed over nothing.

-Helga, do you know anyone from my "department"?

-Yes, you will meet them soon.

"Oh, dear reader, isn't life fascinating? The constant signs we encounter every day... Do you ever feel like our destinies are already written, that we're simply living out a script? Perhaps everything we experience is predetermined, something we deserve or are meant to endure. Or maybe these are signs, whispers from the universe urging us to pay attention. Listen closely, girl, to the rustling of the bushes around you."

***

The next few days were all about adjustment: the weather, the water, the air, the people, the smells, and yes, even the Indian vegetarian food. You'll never guess what my first encounter with their spicy food was like! The Indians assured me, "Oh, ma'am, it's medium spice, don't worry." Let's say it was a shameful experience I won't soon forget.

On that first day in the company office, I had to sign all the internal documents and get my laptop from HR. Lilith, a short, sturdy, barrel-shaped woman with kind eyes and typical Indian features, introduced herself. Unlike the Bollywood portrayals you might imagine, she wasn't adorned with elaborate gold jewelry or a flowing sari. Instead, her work uniform exuded a practical friendliness.

Lunchtime arrived, and I headed to the cafeteria with Lilith. Faced with a metallic tray instead of a plate, I felt a surge of confusion. "How does one eat from this?" I wondered. Sensing my predicament, Lilith kindly gathered a selection of dishes onto the tray, which she explained was called a "5 CP meal tray." With a gentle hand on my arm, she guided me to a small, private room off the main dining area.

-I will show you how to eat, don't worry, - Lilith assured me.

A wave of panic washed over me. "How to eat?" I thought. "Goodness, I don't even know what I'm supposed to be eating! This food looks completely unfamiliar; even after tasting it, I might not recognize what it is." I didn't want to seem scared or disgusted, worried people might think: "Look at that foreigner, making a scene over nothing!" "No, no, I'm happy to try new things. Just tell me what everything is, please.

-Lilith? - I whispered.

-Mhm?

-What is the name of this dish?

-Which one?

"Oh, come on! I blurted out, a touch of frustration creeping in. Just tell me something. I feel worse now than when I didn't know how to use the tray. I saw the looks I was getting, but honestly, knowing the names wouldn't change what I had to do - eat it. So please, girl, stop everyone from wondering if there's something wrong with the food. Just eat."

Taking a deep breath, I reached for the only utensil I saw - a teaspoon. I scooped up some vegetable sauce, feeling a flicker of self-consciousness as I looked at Lilith and the others. It was silly, really, like I was a spy waiting for a reaction from the enemy.

-Is this spicy? - I asked, with a little shaky voice. "Ugh, why did I have to sound so idiotic?" I thought to myself.

-It's middle spicy, mam. Don't worry, - a kind-looking Indian man seated across from me chuckled at my lyric question.

Taking a tentative bite, I braced myself. In the next instant, my mouth erupted in flames! It felt like a volcano had detonated inside me! A violent cough tore from my lungs, the sound of a screaming antelope giving birth echoing throughout the entire floor. The man who'd answered my question turned towards me, his face a comical mess of vegetable sauce and my expelled saliva. He confusedly opened his mouth to speak, but perhaps the dinosaur scream of my cough gave him a momentary scare.

Needless to say, the "medium spicy" was a bit more potent than I'd anticipated. Let's say everyone within a five-foot radius got an acknowledgment, with involuntary showers of flying saliva and food particles, that I don't like spicy.

So, You Want to be a Flight Attendant?

After this embarrassing week at the main office, I began my induction program at our smaller office near my accommodation, along with other new employee hires. That was the first day I met her: the "Goddess of Gold," a radiant 24-year-old Indian woman with captivating deep black sapphire eyes and a professional, beautiful smile. She possessed an uncanny ability to connect with everyone, radiating friendliness and openness that invited light conversation. I, on the other hand, am a completely different person, especially in the workplace. I tend to be laser-focused on my goals and keep all interactions formal. However, there's a reason why we bonded so quickly from the start. She exudes this positive energy, and guess what? She's also a flight attendant with a background in civil aviation!

You might think I'm crazy, but girls have an invisible connection. You know the feeling—you're talking to someone, and it feels like you've known them forever, even though you just met.

Civil Aviation training is intense. It hones your character in ways that stay with you long after you leave the profession. It's almost like military school in that way.

Imagine a fresh-faced 19-year-old named Lily, brimming with wide-eyed dreams of becoming a pretty stewardess. What a beautiful dream! All men are near your legs! She pictures herself soaring through the clouds, a vision in the crisp sky-blue uniform with its jaunty forage cap and gleaming snow-white gloves. The world unfurls beneath her, a tapestry of cultures, food, and landscapes waiting to be explored and posted on Instagram. Perhaps even a handsome, intelligent pilot catches her eye, the start of a whirlwind romance born beneath the airplane wing. Not wings, my dear reader; the plane has one wing, which is separated on the left hand and right hand.

But as Lily delves deeper into this seemingly glamorous profession, the rose-tinted glasses begin to show cracks. The initial excitement gives way to the relentless demands of the job. Grueling schedules become the norm, with long layovers disrupting sleep patterns and the constant hum of the engines a ruthless assault on her ears. The pressure to maintain a flawless appearance takes its toll, and the long hours spent standing in cramped cabins contribute to the achy throb of varicose veins. Lily finds herself battling insomnia, the exhaustion morphing into a low hum of depression.

The glamorous facade starts to crumble. The airline industry, while exciting, prioritizes staff efficiency, endurance, and schedule adherence. It's a demanding career, and "My darling," as the weary, experienced stewardess beside her might say, "you need the resilience of a warrior, both in mind and body, to navigate the challenges and find joy in the journey. Navigating challenges goes beyond dealing with unruly passengers. Lily is trained to handle medical emergencies onboard, such as heart attacks, fainting spells, severe nosebleeds, or choking incidents. These situations can be stressful, requiring quick thinking and calm action to ensure the passenger's safety till landing.

My point isn't to scare you but to highlight the gravity of the responsibility. While there are technical procedures for fire emergencies and serious breakdowns requiring an emergency landing, a flight attendant's role extends beyond that. Our young Lily is also responsible for passenger evacuation, which involves ensuring all exits are safe to use and guiding passengers to safety on the ground.

Here's a crucial aspect - during an evacuation, 19-year-old Lily needs to make quick decisions. She assesses the situation outside the aircraft before opening an exit. If there's a fire on the wing, for example, opening the wrong door could compromise the evacuation process and even more... While some might have heard a legend about aircraft burning in 90 seconds, actual evacuation times and procedures are more complex. But the "90 seconds rule" is burned in her mind as a survival priority for each pax.

Modern aircraft are designed for rapid evacuation, with enough emergency exits to deplane all passengers and crew within a certified timeframe, even using only half the exits. However, a critical decision for flight attendants is assessing the situation outside the aircraft before opening a door. Choosing the wrong exit in case of fire can undoubtedly hinder the evacuation process quality, but the focus is on ensuring passenger safety, not specific percentages. It's essential to understand the pressure Lily faces during emergencies and even every takeoff or landing. This is the most critical part of every flight, and during these 10 minutes, Lily has to think about her step-by-step actions in case of unexpected emergencies. She can't just enjoy the view of the disappearing city in amazing heaven clouds - she is preparing herself to be ready for your salvation. In my company, we had a "12 questions step" for a mental shake-up, and the last step was:" I am confident in my actions!"

So, how will a young 19-year-old Lily, fresh out of her teens, handle these challenges? Flight attendants don't have doctors or security guards on the flight. They need to be resourceful and capable of de-escalating situations with unruly passengers, whether it's someone who's had too much to drink or really gone mad.

The job requires a unique blend of skills. Beyond exceptional customer service, Lily needs to be strong and assertive all the time. She receives extensive training in conflict resolution and physical restraint techniques. But the pressure doesn't stop there. Imagine being the calming presence for over 200 passengers, each with their own needs and anxieties. Lily now is the face of the airline, a perfect-looking trained solider with good skin, make-up, and hairstyle responsible for ensuring a smooth, comfortable, and safe journey for everyone on board. It's not all about emergencies, though. The day-to-day routine can be demanding, requiring constant vigilance and mental preparedness. However, there's also a sense of cultural difference, and she should possess at least a basic knowledge of the cultural etiquette of different nations.

So, dear reader, what do you think is the motivation for a young Lily to endure these challenges and transform herself into a graceful figure in heels and a skirt, working in such demanding conditions? What compels her to wake up so early on weekends, holidays, even New Year's or Christmas evenings, to face such immense pressure and take responsibility for 200 passengers, some of whom might become disgruntled if she forgets to bring water or doesn't smile sincerely enough? Trust me; I'm sharing these experiences with my-address complaints. And where is the starting point of reborn herself?

The next time you see a flight attendant, consider this: "Did they ever dream, during their aviation training, about how they'd handle passengers, means you, in emergencies like a water landing or rapid decompression? Did they ever envision sacrificing themselves in their night dreams for you?"

That's the moment when a young Lily's perspective shifts dramatically. Her previous assumptions, ideals, and understanding of the world crumble away. She'll never be quite the same again.

If I told you there's something magical and almost addictive about the sky and airplanes, would you trust me? How deeply obsessed would you need to be to accept all the terrible downsides? Think about it this way: when you're in love with someone, do their flaws even matter? Love makes you blind just to experience that incredible, divine feeling again and again near it. That's why Lily accepts everything she does - for that feeling of magnificence.

Close your eyes for a moment. Imagine the endless expanse of the sky, a canvas painted with fiery sunrises and cotton-candy sunsets. Now, picture yourself soaring through it, nestled within the comforting embrace of a mighty iron bird. Can you feel the gentle hum of the engines lull you into a state of serene calm? Do you catch a glimpse of the world miniaturized below, a tapestry of bustling cities and serene landscapes? There's magic in the sky, wouldn't you agree? It's a feeling that becomes an addiction, a yearning that tugs at your soul. Just like falling hopelessly in love, the imperfections melt away when this celestial embrace envelops you. The long days, the demanding passengers, the constant pressure - they all fade into the background when you experience that moment of pure, unadulterated joy.

It's a feeling that transcends logic, a whisper of the divine sparking a fire in your heart. The sense of a soul connection is intoxicating. Once you experience it, you crave it like a drug. And that, my friend, is why she endures. That feeling of soaring above the clouds, a weightless spirit dancing with the endless sky - it's a love affair that only the heavens themselves can understand.

How many stories I have about those incredible adventures! Even 1,000 pages wouldn't be enough to capture all the amazing times and airport escapades. Do you ever get a real sense of the bustling energy and unique atmosphere of an airport? A strange mix of grandeur, peculiarity, and unexpected beauty. Each airport is strangely similar across every city on Earth. Places that have likely witnessed more heartfelt kisses and tearful hugs than any wedding venue. There's no day and night, no familiar social norms or rules. You can sip champagne at six in the morning or sprawl on the floor clutching your bag, wrapped in a scarf - no one cares.

Anyway, the book is not about this, but one embarrassing story I will tell you. You, my dear reader, already understand that I am "lucky":

"So, it was an international flight to a country I'd prefer to keep confidential. Let's call it Lalaland for now. From boarding time, I had a feeling it would be a crazy flight due to "specific" pax. I was working in a full business class cabin with 30 passengers alongside another new flight attendant, just starting her amazing career.

We'd already served two glasses of champagne to each passenger - that's 60 glasses in 10 minutes flat! And the biggest challenge? The plane door was still open, and I was already exhausted from this non-stop service. Just imagine: I realized I was alone with 30 passengers, and my colleague, new to the role in C class, wasn't yet experienced enough to handle such a demanding workload with personalized service. The flight is only two and a half hours long, but during this time, you'll need to serve two courses of dishes, along with a few drinks and dessert with tea or coffee. Serving during takeoff and landing can be tricky, so you'll effectively have only about an hour and a half. It's quite stressful to maintain individual services for 30 pax and stay on schedule.

By the end of the direct flight, I was mentally and physically drained. Honestly, I was close to breaking down and crying in the galley. As we began preparing the cabin for landing, we encountered some challenging passengers who feel necessary to ask about each and every step. One insisted:

-Why fasten my seatbelt? If we crash, it won't help anyway. We'll all die.

-Why can't I recline my seat? This is business class! The passenger behind me doesn't care. Get me another whiskey, please, - another argued.

-Mr. Cornel, we are preparing for landing; for your safety, we can't serve drinks right now. I'd be happy to bring you one after we land at Lalaland Airport.

-Honey, I've been handling myself for the past 45 years. Do you think I'll break your stupid glass?

-Mr. Cornel, I am warning about your safety. Thank you for your understanding.

I maintained my service smile, desperately trying not to lose my cool. Just three rows left, and then I could hand over to the purser that the R side of the cabin was ready for landing.

-Ms. Alison, - I said politely. - We're preparing for landing. Could you please fasten your seatbelt and your child's?

-He won't sit down! What am I supposed to do? Let him scream like a banshee for the next ten minutes.

-Mr. Alison, - I explained calmly, - it's a safety issue. Can I help you fasten your child's seatbelt? I can also bring some paper and crayons to keep him occupied during the landing

-My boy attends a prestigious preschool that costs hundreds of thousands of dollars a year, - she scoffed. - Your silly paper is beneath his highly developed intellectual abilities. Do you really think he'll play with that stupid paper? And what? He will draw you a plane??

-Perhaps we could challenge him with a problem to solve. I could write Collatz Conjecture formula on the paper – ten minutes should be plenty for him- a flush crept up my cheeks after my words, and I silently prayed this woman wouldn't lash out at me for my sarcasm, how even I dared to make jokes about her son!

Taking a deep breath, I reminded myself to stay professional: " What is going on with you? Shut up and do your job, girl! Calm down, please!"

-Yes, we can try. My boy will do it. Chickee, come here, my love! - This amazing woman was so interested in showing me her son in a deal that made him prove the hardest and most unsolved conjecture in the world.

I knew the formula because two days before this flight, I helped my friend in her university presentation about the genius Indian Mathematics Ramanujan and some general ideas of all conjectures. I am not cleverer than this woman because I dare to talk like this with a customer. But at least I accept the fact that I am stupid.

I'd just given him the paper and pen, feeling relieved that the situation was diffused, and reached for my jump seat. That's when I noticed an elderly gentleman in the first row who hadn't fastened his seatbelt. He'd been sleeping soundly the entire flight, and I hadn't even gotten his name.

-Sir, we are landing. Fasten your seat belt, please.

No reaction came from a deep-sleeping pax.

-Sir, would you like some water? We are landing in 10 minutes. - I asked louder.

No reaction again.

-Sir, fasten your seat belt. - I decided to shack his arm.

No reaction.

By the way, his companion, an elderly woman around his age, was seated awake nearby. She simply observed the situation with keen interest, curious about how I would handle it next.

-Ma'am, would you mind helping me, please, or fastening your companion's seat belt? – I asked.

She swung her hands and turned away, offering no assistance.

"Seriously?" I thought in exasperation. "Is it really too much trouble to lend a hand?" At the very least, she could have fastened the seatbelt herself without waking him.

Taking a deep breath, I began the process of waking the gentleman again. After several attempts to rouse him by gently touching his arm and politely requesting his attention, my frustration started to simmer.

I exploded inside and felt how my blood boiled, burning my venous system all over my body.

-Fasten your seat belt! - I squeaked, pushing hard on this old man's arm and ankle with the tip of my shoes.

Finally!!! He woke up with a deadpan face as if he had been pretending to sleep and playing a game with me the whole time. He made that open-eyed face because I had just broken this stupid game's rules.

-Sir, fasten your seat belt. – I met his gaze with a neutral expression. While his deadpan face did not show me any emotion, his black eyes were unmovable and directed in my face, but his hands complied with my request as he fastened the seatbelt.

A flicker of satisfaction crossed my features, and I offered a professional smile. In a slightly strained voice (to maintain the hint of frustration), I said, "Thank you, sir. For future reference, it's important to keep your seatbelt fastened throughout the flight for safety reasons. Have a soft landing!"

A wave of relief washed over me as he complied. Yes, I did an unprofessional act sweeping away anger and negativity on a man who is not to blame." But he is a man. He will handle it, and we will never meet again." That's how I calmed my conscience so that I could continue enjoying my win.

I sat at my jump seat and announced to the purser, "My section is ready for landing." He emerged from his laptop work and addressed me with a request.

-Mari, could you please make a "Passenger Survey" for the whole business class? I am drowning in the flight reports. Please ask random 4-5 passengers how their flight was and what their remarks or anything. You know what to do.

-Yes, sure.

-And ask passengers in the first row on your side for a more detailed response. They could share any remarks or suggestions they may have about their experience.

-Why the first row? Which one? - You should hear my voice that moment, like a problem child who understood that now his little dirty trick would be discovered.

-Oh, I forgot to tell you. Those old gentlemen and women are the Premier Minister of Lalalend and his wife. Be nice, please, with them.

Bingo, girl! You are a winner!!"

***

So, did aviation change something in Lily's character or mind? Definitely, it changed her life completely. Perhaps aviation wasn't just a career choice for her but a life-changing experience. There's a distinct difference between the "her" before the sky and the "her" after. It shaped her in ways she couldn't have anticipated.

Would she stop and help a stranger in need on the street now? Absolutely. The emergency procedures ingrained in her would kick in, and she wouldn't hesitate to take action until help arrived. The ability to react quickly and calmly in critical situations is a core skill honed through aviation training.

It's more than just following procedures; it's now about acting instinctively laid in the character foundation. There's so much more I could share about how the sky has influenced her, but that's a story for another time.

If you're curious about my embarrassing flight, don't worry! I hid in the galley area until all the passengers disembarked. It's a silly move, but a good lesson for exercising more restraint next time.

Theory of Hell

Let's come back to India and continue the story about the most complex and most complicated time in my life, which destroyed my mental condition and brought me to the ground without any instruction on how to get up and continue my life.

After two weeks of living in my new "home", a nagging question lingered in my mind: "Why am I here if the aircraft hasn't even arrived yet?" I hadn't spoken to any of the other flight attendants or anyone from my department. GofG (the girl I met in the office) and I, both recruits, were completely confused about what our specific roles would be now.

Based on my observations, our housing seems to be reserved for female staff only. I've noticed some girls hurrying in and out, running away without the opportunity to chat. The atmosphere reminds me a bit of a large rabbit hutch, with everyone scurrying in and out, seemingly afraid to be caught lingering in the open.

One crisp morning, as I sipped my coffee and enjoyed the view from my terrace, a flurry of movement caught my eye. Finally! A young woman hurried across the terrace opposite mine, her movements brisk and purposeful. She was of slender build, and her face, framed by dark hair, was a canvas of meticulously applied nonharmonic makeup, suggesting a formal destination rather than a casual stroll. The steps made it clear she was running behind schedule, likely on her way to work.

-Hey, how are you? Do you need any help?

-No, no! I am fine.

-Are you going on shift?

-My name is Jesabel. Please don't forget it next time.

"What was that? I didn't forget your name or call you with others. So weird and confused." I felt a pang of confusion.

-I apologize, - I replied. - I hadn't forgotten your name, nor did I call you by another. It must have been a misunderstanding!

Unfortunately, before I could explain further, she hurried off. I was already running to my Goodness of Gold's room to tell her what had happened. Jesus, she was so rude without any reason!

We both were confused about our mystic department; no one was trying to contact us or involved in any work routine, and now our "colleague" just kicked me away.

-Maybe she was in a hurry, and her mind was busy with work. GofG tried to find any respectable reason why this Jesabel said this.

- "Are you going on shift?" Do you hear something that can be interpreted in the wrong way?

-No, but she was in a hurry; maybe she heard something else.

-May be...

It was frustrating. Both of us are recruits, unsure of our roles, and we are still waiting for someone to reach out to integrate us into the team. Now, this seemingly out-of-the-blue interaction left me feeling unwelcome.

That day took an interesting turn when I finally got to speak with a new arrival! She'd only been here two days, and I saw housekeeping helping her with her two bags.

My age, snow-white skin, and captivating eyes that seemed to shift between blue, grey, and emerald green, she exuded a youthful grace. Her long, elegant fingers and well-groomed blonde hair completed the picture of a delicate flower, a young sunflower in human form. She was a stark contrast to both me and GofG. She was a static woman with aristocratic manners in everything. She exuded an air of quiet elegance. Every movement, from the way she carried herself to the hushed refinement of her voice, spoke volumes about her aristocratic upbringing. One couldn't help but picture her alongside a high-ranking official or perhaps even a titled English duke. It was almost as if nobility ran in her veins. Scientists might attribute good manners to genetics, but in Sunflower's case, it felt more like a carefully woven tapestry passed down through generations.

You might be surprised to learn that despite her seemingly reserved demeanor, a common thread - our shared background in civil aviation - quickly formed a bridge between us.

We are totally different: While I thrive on the adrenaline rush of off-road enduro riding, her idea of a perfect getaway involves a romance novel by a tranquil infinity pool. Our characters may be polar opposites, but that aviation connection forms an incredibly strong bond beyond our initial impressions. Even though we've only known each other for two months, I often find myself wondering how she's doing and where she is today. And guess what?

-You know, - she typed me back, - I was thinking about you the other day. How's your life going on, and where are you right now?

The speed of our connection is truly remarkable, considering we're not childhood friends or even five-year colleagues. Is it admirable?

From the moment I saw this new girl, I felt a pull towards her. Intuitively, I knew she spoke one of my languages, and I longed to connect. She turned out to be the first and only person I could truly confide in during this strange time.

One day, while going to lunch, I spotted a new girl and a friendly wellness girl. Why did I find her friendly? Because she was actually talking! Filled with excitement, I approached them in hopes of joining the conversation. So, this beautiful Spanish girl named Dina came over to me and introduced herself. She mistakenly assumed we were both from the same country.

-Nice to meet you, - I greeted them. -No, I don't think so. Where are you from?

-Ukraine, - she replied.

Ukraine. My heart sank a little. At that point, the country had been embroiled in a conflict with Russia for ten months. While I wasn't Russian myself, I spoke the language fluently, considering it a second tongue. However, I didn't feel comfortable initiating a conversation in Russian, even though her background might suggest she understands it due to the Soviet Union. I worried she might be sensitive to the language at the moment.

Dear reader, to understand the situation better, imagine Hindi as the unifying language in India, with each state having its own distinct language as well. In the former Soviet Union, Russia played a similar role. Both my parents and I went to schools where Russian was the primary language. Additionally, my curriculum included Romanian language and literature, English language and literature with economics, German language, and, of course, Russian language and literature. However, my native language, the one closest to my heart, is Bulgarian.

Can you imagine the linguistic melting pot I was navigating at 14 years old? Things have changed. Today, you'd be hard-pressed to find Russian schools in that city.

It sparked my curiosity. Since she spoke one of my languages, I felt a natural pull to connect. However, I was unsure how to initiate the conversation. Although I could likely understand Ukrainian as well, given the sensitive situation in Ukraine, I opted to wait for her to speak first.

-So, you speak Russian? - finally, she broke the ice.

-Yes, I understand Russian, - I replied. - I used to work there and have some relatives in the country.

The ongoing conflict in Ukraine was a heavyweight. I hesitated to express my own opinions, unsure of her perspective. Perhaps she held a different view, or maybe she simply didn't want to discuss it. It's a delicate situation - you never know if someone has lost loved ones, and you don't want to cause further pain by offering unsolicited condolences.

We steered clear of those topics, focusing instead on our experiences, previous jobs, and, yes, even some "girl stuff." Oh, and of course, the mystery surrounding our department, the "mystic crew butler personal assistant department." Even at that early stage, I had a hunch our duties wouldn't be limited to typical airplane work. So, we understood that we probably would go through some kind of induction process soon to learn more about this mysterious role and the "mystic jet" we were waiting for.

Guess what? The next evening, we received the training schedule for the following days. A jolt of unease ran through me as I received a peculiar email from the Head of the Regency. The contents triggered a wave of questions within me: "What on earth could this mean?" "Is this some kind of elaborate joke?" "Are we being restricted here?"

My unease quickly spread. My phone buzzed with messages from Sunflower and GofG, expressing similar shock. A collective sense of urgency arose - we needed to gather and discuss the implications of this email.

Doors open

-What is supposed to mean?

-I think it's for our safety... They just want to know if we are safe.

-Know what? It's not written that we have to tell our destination.

-It's really weird. I am not in prison to ask anyone's permission over the weekend.

But if I need to go out right now because I need some medicines from the pharmacy, and he is not answering, what? Will security not allow me to do it?

-No.

-What do you mean NO? I am a free person and can go anywhere when I want.

-Tell him, and answer his email.

-Ha-ha, so funny.

-I have a weird feeling that it's my fault.

-What?!

-What did you do?

-Nothing! Nothing bad, but I have a feeling that we are not allowed to make friends with anyone from the office.

-What do you mean?

- It's interesting to note that we seem to be the only department with an all-female staff, and conversely, there are no women in the other departments. Additionally, it's curious that we're restricted to this specific accommodation and recently prohibited from leaving the grounds. I wonder if there's an explanation for these unusual circumstances.

-Easy language, please! And we are allowed but with permission.

-Oh, come on, it's an arm of control.

-What did you do?? Tell us!!

-There is a guy from the office who offered to see the gym, which is 10 minutes away, and if I want, I can take an abonnement. You know, I was suffering without a gym, and it's nearby; I thought I could do it, but... And what?? What is the problem?

-He drove me and brought me back.

-And wha-a-a-at?!

-The day before this, he picked me up from a shopping mall, and security always observed us in a bad way.

-Do you think it's a lesson?

-I don't know but it's the only explanation for all this mess that is going on here. I already told you both.

-No, come on. I don't think they did it because you went to the gym once with your colleague.

-Now I can forget about gym... I don't want to write poems every week to go out and wait like a dog for a bone...

Let's see. Don't be so depressing.

Evidence Exhibit 20e Police Report.

"Dear ladies, good evening!

This is to inform/reinforce the following:

1)Exit from pink hell: if anyone wishes/needs to exit from pink hell, she needs written approval from the king head, ideally by mail. You would be asked by the security to show the mail (having approval from the king head, sir) during exit from pink hell. Hence, it would be handy to keep it ready before. The confirmation mail has to be provided at the security gate, put your signature before leaving and after returning.

2)No deliveries from outside: no one is entitled to order meals from a restaurant (either directly or through the app - zomato/swiggy). Everyone is expected to have meals from the staff cafeteria (either you can dine in or you can pack the food from the staff cafeteria and consume it in accommodation)

With best and regards

Mr. No-one."

Our living quarters house 35 residents, and residency to be restricted to females. This policy has sparked several questions and uncertainties for me. Why is it necessary to place educated women in such a perplexing situation? Surely, news of this restriction will spread throughout the office, potentially leading to speculation and jokes among male colleagues. All the office will know that we are now prisoners who have been given a shameful lesson.

There's always someone who breaks the mold, who will show the character and will go instead of rules. In this case, it was Suzi Nishi, a young Indian woman with extensive experience in the cosmetology cabinet. Strikingly beautiful, she captivated attention with her golden hair, flawless complexion that resembled a magazine cover, and a delicate, almost floral scent.

Suzi stood alone in what could barely be called a department. Her responsibilities overlapped with ours to some degree, but she worked from her own first-floor office and seemed to adhere to no typical schedule. She was the only woman in that office. She often put in short hours, which is likely why she simply packed her belongings and left to rent her place. What does it mean? Oh, year, she will be fired soon.

***

The next morning, I woke up with a throbbing headache and the same unsettling feeling lingering in my body. The thought of socializing or studying held no appeal. Reaching for my phone, I saw a message from Sunflower on WhatsApp:

-I have a weird feeling; something happened or is happening here.

-What do you mean?

-They are firing girls at the speed of light.

-Maybe they do it because girls don't keep confidential the movements of First Family or post on Instagram places which they are visiting.

-I think they fire Indians.

-Indians? But Suzi left yesterday, and there was no sound about her resignation.

-They don't need a lot of girls here, so if someone new comes, one of the old employees will be fired. Suzi, it's Suzi. She is not one of us.

-No way.

-Yes, I just saw an Indian with all her luggage waiting for the cab. She had been working here for 4 months.

-What did she say? Why she is fired?

-She did not tell me.

-Listen, maybe they took foreigners because we don't know anyone here and there is no information leakage…

-Yes, maybe you are right.

-Did you read the emails?

-No… it's too much for one morning.

-Open the mail with our training schedule…

Sunflower seemed as freaked out as I felt about all this. Maybe we're both getting a little carried away. Making drama like girls usually do.

-Did I understand right, we will have training next 5 weeks???

-I hope it will be shorted. We cannot study for so long; there is nothing that can be studied for 5 weeks.

-And this mail about the weight …

-Yes, we have always to be in that "middle".

-Listen, did you open the recipients?

-No.

-Check it. Check our department compound, girls' names, and their designation. Do you see something weird?

-We all have different designations…I am the manager, you are PA, and that girl Helga is a butler, but she told me she is a massage specialist.

-It's possible maybe we will have different responsibilities.

-I don't know, Mari. It's weird.

-Yes, I know why she has doubts; I have the same…

Hell Corporation Industries Induction

Let me explain what this induction is all about and why it's taken over a month! It's unbelievable how much we've had to learn in this time.

The office building near our accommodation houses various departments dedicated to serving the First Family. These include Housekeeping, Hospitality, Catering and Logistics, Food and Beverage, Finance, Preservation, Concierge, Male Butlers, Wellness, and Butler Personal Assistants. The last two departments don't have office cabinets at all. If we needed to do some work, we usually sat in the male butler's office or on the corridor sofa. But wait a minute; what job are you talking about?

Anyway, our induction aimed to give us a broad understanding of each department's responsibilities. The idea was that we could potentially fill in or assist them if needed. So, for the past month, we've been meeting with each department and learning about their roles.

Everyone we met was enough diligent and knowledgeable and sure cannot be replaced by one-month trained stewardess. There were no doubts these people served VIP customers. They were also incredibly helpful, patiently teaching us about their fascinating work. They functioned like a close-knit family, always supporting and sometimes even covering for each other (not us). The office environment was calm and "friendly". You should see the place during the holidays! They decorate every nook and cranny of the conference rooms and offices.

However, there's always a catch. Despite this outward appearance, I couldn't shake the feeling that something wasn't quite right. It seemed like these dedicated vitreous people were somehow involved in covering up a significant secret. No one seemed willing to reveal the truth…

Each week, we shadowed a different department for our induction. This week, it was housekeeping's turn. Most of our training took place inside a building that turned out to be the First Family's residence, located surprisingly close to the office building. The details of the house are best left undescribed for now.

Our supervisor for the day was a young man with large, expressive eyes and big lips that seemed to be created on a cosmetology appointment. He was well-educated and a professional in his field. Like a stoic Virgo, he remained composed and serious throughout the session, his gaze unwavering.

-Good morning, ladies, - he greeted us.- Today, we'll be practicing turndown service and bed-making.

He led us to a nearby bedroom where two of his colleagues awaited us with all the necessary equipment. One was a tall, imposing man with a bushy mustache, while the other was shorter and friendly-looking, with a youthful face and a faint mustache.

"I can only hope they both found better jobs after their time here; they seemed like good people who deserved a more normal work environment."

-My colleagues will demonstrate how to remove all the bed linens and then walk you through putting on fresh ones, - the supervisor explained. - Feel free to try it yourself afterward.

He was discussing the materials and brands they used when his two colleagues began the bed-changing demonstration. As someone who'd worked on private jets, I knew some aircraft have small double or single beds, and bed-making was part of the job. However, what they were doing here was different from how you make a bed at jet or home. This was a special hotel-style technique that guaranteed a flawlessly presented bed.

I was eager to give it a try, but I couldn't help but wonder why I needed to know how to make a bed when there was a perfectly capable and helpful housekeeping staff readily available.

-Why do we need to know bed-making?

-Mam, in the nighttime, if something happens and FF (First Family) asks you to change the bed, you have to do it.

-In the nighttime?

-Yes, you will make 2 shifts: day and night.

Internally, I grappled with the realization that this role extended far beyond what I had originally signed up for as a Flight Attendant and Personal Assistant. Do you share this sentiment? While I possess some fundamental knowledge of butler duties, I wasn't brought here to refine those skills. On the positive side, I consider myself a patient and courteous individual who can wait a considerable amount of time for clarification or answers, especially in a professional setting. I also have a strong work ethic and never repeat requests.

-What is required for the night shift?

-Oh, I don't know everything. You should ask your lead, Jesabel.

-I don't think this girl will talk with us one day or explain something. -Sorry?

-Nothing...

After observing the demonstration, we attempted the bedmaking procedure ourselves. Let's just say it was more challenging than we anticipated! Removing the old linens and putting on the new ones was quite a workout. It felt like a full 20-minute cardio session! Imagine the physical exertion required of the housekeeping staff who perform this task daily in hotels, sometimes single-handedly managing entire rooms, not just a single bed. Did you know some housekeepers can clean over 40 rooms in a day?

Here I was, exhausted after making just one bed while these dedicated individuals tackled 40 or more! This experience completely changed my perspective on the housekeeping staff. Traveling in the future, I won't hesitate to give housekeeping a break by requesting less frequent cleaning. I honestly feel a pang of shame and a newfound respect for this woman and man. Do you make your bed every day at home? No, I get it - this is a hotel, and you're paying for a certain level of comfort. But honestly, I bet your comfort wouldn't be significantly impacted by sleeping in the same linens for two nights. Speaking of comfort, any tips on tipping housekeeping? We rarely see them, but they play a crucial role in creating a comfortable hotel experience. They deserve our appreciation.

After that bed-making workout, we grabbed lunch and headed straight to laundry land! We learned all about washing clothes, the chemicals involved, and how to iron like a pro.

Let me tell you about another instructor who truly impressed us. A young, short man with kind, light-brown eyes and a welcoming smile, he radiated warmth and approachability. His lectures on various laundry chemicals, though not inherently exciting topics, became captivating due to his infectious enthusiasm. It was clear that he had found his calling in life, and his passion for his work was contagious. We often found ourselves lingering after his allotted time, eager to absorb more of his knowledge. It doesn't matter what he is telling us; it was always interesting to listen.

It's rare to meet someone who genuinely enjoys their work, and this laundry instructor definitely stood out. His enthusiasm was contagious, making even lectures about laundry chemicals interesting. It made me wonder what his secret was, what formula he had discovered to achieve such happiness in his work life.

So many people dread Mondays, waking up with the thought of the weekend ending and the workweek beginning. They dream of finding their dream job, one with a high salary and a generous benefits package. But for many, this remains a fantasy, a way to distract themselves from the monotony of their routine. They might not win the job lottery and achieve a dramatic life change.

This instructor, however, seemed to have found something far more valuable than a high salary. He had found a way to appreciate his work and live a fulfilling life. His positive attitude and passion for his craft were truly inspiring. This small Indian man caught a jackpot bigger than a typical manager in an average NY company whose salary is hundreds of times bigger. This man can teach you how to enjoy your workplace.

After each training session, we would gather in our room to debrief and discuss the day's learnings. We enjoyed close camaraderie as a trio, and sometimes, our intense discussions might have made us seem oblivious to our more reserved colleagues. Despite this, we were a dedicated and hardworking team. We were diligent in our note-taking and always eager to clarify any uncertainties by asking questions.

Our training covered a wide range of housekeeping topics, including brand recognition, proper cleaning procedures, and the selection of suitable fragrances based on room type and season. We even learned about the specific bath amenities required for each bathroom and the appropriate quantities to stock. Additionally, we created detailed charts outlining garment types and the corresponding laundry chemicals for optimal cleaning. We understood that this knowledge was an essential part of our job description, and we were prepared to apply it whenever necessary.

Rabbit Issues

"We're breeding rabbits faster than we can answer why they keep disappearing."

-Did you hear what happened that night?

-How and from where I just woke up, G…

-Let's wait for Sunflower, I will tell you.

-God, you like to make a person curious and keep him waiting.

I made a WhatsApp call for Sunflower at the same moment to come quickly, so my curiosity would be finally satisfied. How much does this girl like to make a little drama before telling the story? This is a typical Indian character; these amazing people like to place spicy everywhere. They cannot live this life peacefully without drama. Especially our GofG, she is absolutely in love with the super spicy staff. You have to see how she is searching for green chili in dhal and is always disappointed, asking for a chef or kitchen worker to bring something for her. I always wondered; looking at her eating that burning dish reminded my embarrassing situation in the main office cafeteria.

-Hi, girls!

-Finally, so tell us what's happened!

-So, I met this morning housekeeping guy, and he told me that something happened that night.

-What happened?

-I think one of the BPA….. a girl from our department will be fired today.

-Why?

-What? God, please tell us what's happened.

-There is a "Lipstick Incident" in son's bedroom bathroom.

-Lipstick Incident? What does it mean?

-There was a lipstick pomade in his bathroom's glass door

-What do you mean?

-Lips marks… someone kissed the glass door.

-Are you serious?

-It's a joke?

-No.

-Who found it …

-Jesabel.

-Why I am not surprised.

-She hates her, that's why she did it.

-You think Jesabel left these lipstick marks to frame her?

-I am sure. No one will play this stupid drama. We all are educated and adults.

-How do you know?

-But how do you know it's Jesabel?

-She is like this; people are talking about her. She can smile on your face but do some dirty things behind your back. You have to be careful with this girl.

-Who is telling you all this? Why no one is telling us?

-Because you are foreigners. They don't trust you.

-It makes sense…

"It's understandable to feel some initial hesitation from the locals towards foreigners. There can be a perception that foreigners won't be around long enough to form lasting connections. Unfortunately, this cultural barrier was a source of disappointment for me. I struggled to overcome it and often made the mistake of trusting people too readily."

It's hard to believe an educated woman like her would be involved in something like this. We haven't spoken much, but from our brief interactions, she always struck me as polished, focused, and dedicated. Hopefully, they'll get to the bottom of this situation and clear things up. All day, I've been preoccupied with this incident involving the girl and the lipstick. I can't help but wonder how I would react if I were in her shoes. Would my supervisor suspect me? It's unsettling to think she might be sleeping soundly right now, unaware that someone in the office is casting judgment. The thought of her waking up to the humiliation of being fired for something she didn't do is simply awful.

-Finished your lunch? Let's go to my room. We have 15 minutes before laundry training.

-Yeah, let's go.

-I want to have coffee; wait a second.

I felt that GofG wanted to tell us something again and there were too many people in the cafeteria. Our rooms are the safest place to discuss news so we went there.

-Tell us…

-So, you both have to pretend like you don't know what's happened today.

-We are not telling or discussing it with anyone. And I am sure no one will come to us and start this conversation.

-Yes, because we are new and you are foreigners.

-What did they decide to do with her?

-I don't know…

-They will fire her…

-I don't know…

-Girls, it's crazy if she will be fired for so silly reason.

-You don't know her, maybe she really did it.

-No.

-How do you know?

-How do YOU know that she did it?

-Girls, let's not guess. We will know by evening what the decision is.

***

After dinner in the staff café, like usual, we headed to the GofG room for a discussion of tomorrow's schedule. Our temporary cafeteria is located in the basement of another building, right next to the security checkpoint. It's a large, underground space with dull gray walls, and unfortunately, it feels rather stuffy. The overall impression is one of limited sanitation.

Upon entering, you'll find 5-6 tables on either side, along with a single, worn-out sofa without a coffee table. Seating options are limited, and those choosing the sofa must balance their meals on their laps. Two refrigerators and a coffee machine are situated near the entrance.

The buffet area, offering a "5cp meal tray" option, is positioned in the far-left corner. Surprisingly, you'll also find parked vehicles in the center of the space - yes, it doubles as parking for the First Family cars lot! After finishing your meal, used trays are placed in a designated container, while cutlery goes in a bucket of water located on the floor in the corner.

While the initial impression might be off-putting, this only lasts for the first week or so. Thankfully, the food itself is delicious and of good quality. The chefs deserve credit for their culinary skills, which manage to overshadow the cafeteria's many drawbacks.

We were informed that the cafeteria on the second floor of the office building would be ready next week, so this basement location is merely temporary. However, based on my experiences here so far, "temporary" in India might translate to a longer timeframe, perhaps months. This is yet another lesson I've learned during my time here.

As we made our way to GofG's room, we spotted the girl who might have left the lipstick mark earlier that morning. She stood near the office entrance, engrossed in a conversation with two other employees. Her appearance was striking - her face pale, her dark eyes wide with worry. At that moment, I became completely convinced of her innocence -Did you see her face?

-Shh!! They can hear us!

-Oh, come on! Everyone talks about it!

-We are not supposed to know it! Wait till the room.

-Yes, girls... she is completely confused and disorientated.

-Another one, please! Don't speak about it outside! Shh!!

-So, what do you think now? Had she really done it?

-Now, I have doubts also…

-Hello??!

-I think they fired her.

-Not yet. The fired girl leaves the accommodation immediately.

-What? Now you decided to speak, finally!

-Yes! So, listen if you want to know! So, the housekeeping guy told me… They give you 1 hour to collect all the clothes and relocate you to the hotel.

-And?

-And you finish all formalities in the main office.

-And?

-And that's all…

All these strange situations involving the girls have left me utterly confused. I can't grasp the motivations behind these actions - are they the instigators of these "dirty games" or simply caught in the middle? The girl with the lipstick incident wasn't the only one on the verge of leaving. There was also a girl from the wellness department who seemed likely to depart soon. They, like us, resided in the company housing and worked the same shifts. As for their department's responsibilities, the title "wellness" is quite self-explanatory.

Most of the time, these girls are more open to talking with us. Sometimes, in the evenings, they'd come to me or the GofG terrace like a big family to chat about things like skincare products and clothing brands. We'd get so loud, like a bunch of ducks on a lake, that even some BPA girls would peek out from their holes.

There was a woman from the wellness department who always impressed me. Dina. She is probably a lead for all wellness ducklings as the girls were always around her. She had a statuesque figure with long, dark chocolate hair that fell straight down her back. But what truly captivated me were her legs - incredibly toned, with a beautiful bronze sheen. Whenever we spoke, I couldn't help but notice them, and I marveled at the complete absence of cellulite. It was truly remarkable - here was a woman with three children and ten years my senior, yet her legs looked like they belonged in a razor commercial or on a Christian Louboutin model. It was almost baffling!

However, the most surprising thing was that even she wasn't entirely satisfied. Perhaps this speaks to the societal pressure women can sometimes face in the pursuit of an unattainable ideal of perfection. There's always something more to strive for, it seems.

One evening, she approached me and confided her doubts about her future here.

-I think I will leave.

-Why?

-My visa will expire soon, and I think they will not prolong it.

-How long are you here?

-6 months.

-Dina, why do you think they will not prolong it? Did you do something?

-No, I just know their behavior. They keep telling you that all is fine, nothing to worry and suddenly you are receiving a call with bad news....

-Ha?

-That you have 1 hour to pack your luggage.

-Why are they doing it? What's the problem with informing you in the right way, at least before 14 days? It's a law. You have to find a new job or send your luggage back to your hometown and prepare yourself psychologically that you are leaving. It's a big mental and physical stress.

-Not in this place. Listen to me Mari, don't trust anyone from this office. They all are liars. Be careful what you are doing and what you are talking about with people.

"Wow, that was unexpected to hear. Her words were a bombshell. Here was a foreigner with only six months of experience, seemingly privy to more information than I could have ever imagined. And now, she wasn't afraid to share it. It was clear Dina intended to leave soon anyway.

I was fixated on trying to understand why all these girls were leaving or being fired, seemingly without cause. Was I looking in the wrong place? Perhaps the problem wasn't with the girls themselves."

***

The next morning, I received a message from Sunflower on my WhatsApp.

-I saw Dina, she left this morning with her clothes.

-How are you doing it? Are you staying the whole day near the window and observing what is going on outside??

-No, I hear the suitcase wheels and quickly reach my window.

-You have super sensitive ears. I spoke with her last evening.

-With Dina?

-Yeah, she told me about her feelings.

-Which feeling?

-That she will leave soon…

-Soon? In the next 12 hours??

-I think she's also surprised by the suddenness of this weird office's decisions. Yesterday morning, they told her that there is nothing to worry her visa will be prolonged, but ….

-Why are they doing it? Just tell the truth; at least give some time for a girl to pack her luggage properly without hurrying.

-I asked her the same question. She said, "Don't trust anyone from this office. They are liars."

-Who is doing all this? Who's decision is to behave like this with girls? It's not right.

-I don't know. We should ask our Indian agent to make an investigation and talk with the housekeeping guys. They know everything …

-Ha-ha! Do you mean GofG?

-Yes, who else I can mean?

-Where is she?

-Still sleeping, like usual. Time to wake her up.

Our lovely GofG possessed an enviable talent – the ability to sleep soundly through anything. She could easily slumber until the afternoon, or even for an entire day, completely undisturbed. Are phone calls buzzing for an hour straight? Unfazed. Her alarm clock could shriek every thirty minutes, and she wouldn't even stir. Sometimes, I marveled at this superpower of hers, but other times, it proved quite frustrating, especially when we needed to get in touch with her urgently. Waking her up was no easy feat.

Clapping

-Finally! Good morning, darling!

-What's the time?

-Time to wake up!

-Dina left this morning, and Sunflower saw her.

-What? Again, a girl?

-Yes...

-There is a new one, she came 4 days ago.

-Where??

-Which girl?

-She joined the wellness department and already started to work. I think that's why Dina left...

-Did you see her?

-Yes, she is staying in my bungalow on 2nd floor.

-Indian?

-No, foreigner.

-God... that's why they kicked Dina so fast. But still, I cannot understand why they cannot tell you the list before 24 hours it's so bad.

-I don't know...

-I think they will leave soon—all wellness departments.

-You think or have you heard?

-I heard.

-Mari, do you have her number?

-Whom?

-Dina, can you text her on WhatsApp and ask what is going on? Because she told me yesterday that her visa expired today.

-What?? How does the visa department accept such a huge mistake? She can be deported...

-Maybe they wanted it.

-Oh god, let's go to F&B training and stop this drama. For everything, there is a reason or answer.

I thought so; I wanted to stop this because I hate it, especially in the workplace. That's why I found it frustrating in a work setting. At the office, I need to be focused to be productive, and workplace drama is a major distraction.

Looking back, I realize I was naive. Blinded by my desire for a perfect career in India, exciting experiences with a new culture, and a different way of thinking, I was unwilling to see any imperfections. I was completely absorbed in my idealized vision of an "Indian dream".

This week, our training took us to the Food and Beverage Department, and to my surprise, they have a staff of butlers! It was puzzling why some of our cleaning responsibilities overlapped with their duties, especially considering their team of at least 30 highly experienced butlers. It truly seemed like a mystery to have so many dedicated staff catering to just two people who, as I understand it, don't even serve the food themselves, as it is our responsibility.

The head of the department was the most serene and stress-free person I've ever met. He meticulously trained us in service basics, including the specific preferences of the "FF". We learned the exact beverages, their ideal temperatures, preferred food types, and any special requests. The training went into incredible detail, covering everything from the appropriate food and beverage presentation based on the situation, seating area, time of day, and even the supposed mood of the FF. We learned the precise way to present fresh cutlery and wet towels, from which side to approach, and in which hand to place them. In essence, we were trained to serve the First Family so flawlessly that even if our faces were hidden, they would never suspect we were new staff. We anticipated their every habit, potential reaction, and question before ever meeting them in person.

That week also happened to be the last week before New Year's, and I was curious about how Indians celebrate it. Their culture seems to have an incredible number of holidays and festivals - just browsing the list of public holidays is impressive, and that doesn't even include all the regional and religious celebrations!

It was also a week marked by strange occurrences. As you recall, the girl from the lipstick incident left without us ever discovering the truth. Then, to our surprise, another girl packed her bags and departed alone in the night. This sudden double departure was a shock to us, and for the first time, a sense of unease settled in - something wasn't right.

-Maybe she is like this.

-Like what? So proud and irresponsible to leave without informing anyone at nighttime? Do you understand what's happened?

-Yes, I got it.

-I don't think so.

I have a feeling the answers we seek won't be easy to come by. This has led me to re-evaluate all the confusing situations I've encountered so far. For instance, what would prompt me to leave suddenly in the middle of the night?

Several questions remain unanswered: "I'm still not registered in the country, and I haven't received any information about my salary. I understand they were supposed to open a bank account for me, but that seems impossible without the registration documents. What's causing the delay? Why haven't they addressed this? Additionally, the lack of communication with our colleagues is puzzling. Why are they so reluctant to interact with us?"

Thankfully, I'm not alone in experiencing these uncertainties. Having two wonderful girls by my side provides a sense of comfort and security. The sight of more than 15 girls vanishing unexpectedly or in strange circumstances since I arrived here fueled unsettling doubts. Initially, I tried to ignore them, but…

Naye Saal Ki Shubhkamnayein

Just before New Year's Eve, the housekeeping department took charge of decorating the office building. One evening, as everyone was heading out,

they brought in a festive array of Christmas tree ornaments, decorations, little figurines (Santos, I believe?), and reindeer figures. The sight ignited a spark of joy in GofG's eyes, and I felt the same. It undeniably stirs the inner child in all of us, bringing back warm and fuzzy childhood memories.

We couldn't resist getting closer to the boxes overflowing with decorations, examining them with childlike wonder. The housekeeping staff member busied himself assembling the small artificial Christmas tree, carefully fluffing out the branches. Seized by a wave of nostalgia, I reached out to place the first ornament.

-No, no! No, Ma'am!

He spoke briefly to GofG in Hindi. From what I gathered, it seemed they weren't interested in our help decorating.

Do you know any historical cases when you said a woman "No" and she really stopped doing it? No, my darling, never! Despite their initial refusal, I decided to help out anyway. I selected a variety of ornaments and decorations, placing them within reach of the housekeeping staff member. He seemed appreciative as he chose items and continued decorating. At least we were able to contribute in some small way. After 1 hour, I saw my lovely GofG decorating a small lighter in the office corridor. It's a big step!

Why they don't trust a woman to do her job, I could not understand. The cultural differences regarding trust in women's work possibilities were quite surprising. In my home country, women are traditionally seen as the ones who create a warm and inviting atmosphere in the home. Decorating and beautifying spaces is a skill I possess, and I am eager to contribute my vision. Unfortunately, it seemed our offer to help decorate wasn't met with enthusiasm.

After three hours of what felt like constant supervision and corrections, any hope I had of adding my creative touch dwindled. It was like a little piece of my childhood joy chipped away - the freedom of imagination and expression restricted. The initial excitement faded, replaced by the reality of the situation. This wasn't a magical, whimsical task anymore; it was a task to be completed according to specific guidelines set by the head of the department…

GofG, a few housekeeping staff members, and I headed to the first floor. Our supply of decorations wasn't extensive, but I decided to take charge. With a handful of ornaments in tow, GofG and I approached the last door on the floor and began decorating without waiting for further instructions.

The act felt almost clandestine, like mischievous children up to something they shouldn't be. However, I was confident that the finished product would be well-received. We fashioned a charming Christmas tree using string and ornaments, and the result was delightful - warm and inviting. I felt such a sense of ownership over our creation that I would have readily defended it against anyone who dared take it down.

-It's so cute! Can you believe it? -I exclaimed to GofG.

-Yes, Mari, it looks nice, - she agreed.

As I turned around, I saw the lead housekeeping staff member, the one overseeing the entire office decoration project, standing behind me. He observed our handiwork with a look of quiet interest. In that moment, I felt like a master artist receiving critical acclaim, perhaps even a Nobel laureate! The elation was overwhelming - a small decorative tree, accepted by a single person, sparked a joyous explosion of emotions within me. My heart pounded with a surge of pride, and I eagerly awaited further praise or recognition. Even his mere curiosity brought me immense satisfaction.

-Good.

"Good", seriously?! Are you serious?! That's the best and cutest thing in the entire office, and you are telling me "Good"?! I know, I know, I'm probably being a little childish, but it's hard to suppress that part of me sometimes. A little praise would have been nice. Oh, please, come down from the clouds, girl. It's only a decorative tree in a small "village" office building, not a NY park Christmas tree.

Despite the festive atmosphere, I wasn't particularly in the mood to celebrate New Year's for a few reasons. Firstly, my job contract prioritizes work commitments, regardless of holidays or personal celebrations like birthdays. My focus is on my professional responsibilities, which is something I readily accepted in my contract. While some might find this dedication weird, it's simply my personality. When I'm working towards a goal, I thrive by channeling all my time and energy into it, minimizing distractions.

Secondly, the absence of the traditional wintery elements associated with New Year's celebrations in my home country slightly dampened my spirits. Experiencing Christmas and New Year's during winter truly amplifies the magic of the holidays. Without that familiar seasonal backdrop, the 31st of December felt like an ordinary day devoid of any special excitement.

As evening arrived, we traded our work clothes for something more comfortable and headed to the office building for the much-anticipated New Year's Eve celebration. The festivities were meticulously planned by an event manager from one department. The guy who later, after a few months, was bulling me to pack my luggage and leave the country. His dedication to creating a perfect and enjoyable evening for everyone was truly commendable. Live performers, a DJ, and an energetic host kept the energy high throughout the night, and the event manager ensured everything ran smoothly. The highlight of the evening was undoubtedly the magnificent buffet table overflowing with a delectable array of Indian dishes and desserts, all prepared by our talented chefs.

The relaxed atmosphere was a welcome change, and the casual attire made it almost unrecognizable as our usual office environment. For a blissful moment, surrounded by colleagues and the festive cheer, it felt as though we were transported to a completely different world, a world far removed from the eastern part of India.

-I can't eat anymore!

-What do you mean? We didn't try half of the buffer table.

-Yes, I want to taste lasagna, but I don't have a place in my stomach...

-Let's walk a little bit and come back.

-Let's go and play pool!

-No, please, not now.

-I am sure the table is busy now; we can just go to have a look at it.

There's something I almost forgot to mention - we have a pool table on the first floor in what's supposed to be the future cafeteria, although it hasn't actually opened yet. This triggered a wave of nostalgia, reminding me of playing pool with my brothers after school or on weekends. Back then, we frequented a rather dubious local tavern - a place with a rough atmosphere full of cigarette smoke and questionable characters. Looking back, I can only imagine our parents' reaction if they knew we spent our evenings there, surrounded by such an environment. But of course, as kids, we were oblivious to all that. Our focus was entirely on the magic of that pool table. The moment the green felt beneath the table lit up; it was like stepping into an incredible adventure, a portal to our own personal Narnia. For hours on end, nothing else mattered -school, meals, homework, friends, even our phones. We were completely engrossed in the game, strategizing complex shots, banking balls off the rails, and gradually increasing the difficulty with each turn. Time seemed to melt away in that space, an hour vanishing like a blink of an eye. Have you ever seen those movies where the protagonist enters a peculiar club, drinks a mysterious concoction, and loses track of time, emerging days or even weeks later? Well, for us, the pool table wasn't fueled by drinks but by the sheer captivation of the game itself.

As you can imagine, having a pool table here rekindled some wonderful childhood memories for me, especially of playing with my brothers. My girls, however, weren't as familiar with the game. GofG, in particular, wasn't initially interested in trying it out, preferring to watch from the sidelines. But one quiet evening, when the cafeteria was empty, she decided to give it a shot. To my delight, she ended up thoroughly enjoying it! From then on, she became a regular player, spending hours each evening after work honing her skills. It was clear that the game sparked a similar sense of magic and enjoyment in her that I had experienced as a child. While a part of me might have felt a twinge of envy – knowing I wouldn't recapture that initial innocent joy – the dominant emotion was happiness. Seeing her enthusiasm was truly infectious.

-He is calling everyone to come downstairs. There are no people there, and the host event is a little bit confused about what to do.

-We should go, girls

-Yes. He was preparing it for all of us, and we should respect it.

Stepping outside, I encountered a group of male housekeeping staff or perhaps from other departments. It wasn't easy to tell since they weren't wearing uniforms. A wave of unease washed over me as I realized the gender imbalance. There were significantly more men (perhaps around 30) compared to only the three of us women. For some reason, this unexpected ratio made me feel awkward and out of place. For a few minutes, my mind raced, searching for an excuse to retreat to the cafeteria or even my accommodation.

I glanced at Sunflower, and her expression mirrored my discomfort. GofG, however, seemed completely absorbed in the music, enthusiastically beckoning us to join her on the dance floor. Dancing in public was completely out of my comfort zone. The most I would ever do is dance privately with my girlfriends in our room, but this was entirely different! Loud bars and clubs were my idea of a nightmare. My ideal setting is a tranquil, intimate space surrounded by nature where I can relax, converse with friends, and enjoy soothing music in the background. That was enough excitement for me.

-Let's go and dance!

-No!

-Please!! I want to dance

-You can do it. Don't look at us. We are old women.

-Yes. Need to take rest after food.

-Please! Come with me. I cannot go alone!!

While GofG's enthusiasm for dancing was infectious, it wasn't quite my cup of tea. The idea of dancing in the open with such a large group of unfamiliar men, likely around 15, from what I could tell, made me feel incredibly self-conscious. I wanted to decline politely without dampening her joyful spirit. It was clear the music held special meaning for her, perhaps evoking happy memories from her past. Seeing her so genuinely happy made me willing to step outside my comfort zone a little. After all, it wasn't every day I witnessed such festive cheer in her. In a way, it was heartwarming to see her embrace the spirit of the occasion.

-Honey, go and dance, please. Don't look at us or anyone else. You know everyone here, don't think too much just enjoy it!

-Okay, I will go. – sunflower said. It was surprising to hear it from her, but thanks to her a lot, she saved my ass from a big shame.

-Let's go with us, stand up!

-No, please. Just go! Girls go! I will enjoy you from my chair.

There was a genuine delight in watching the two young women dance with such uninhibited joy as if it were their last chance ever. Their enthusiasm was truly infectious, and I couldn't help but be swept up in their merriment. At that moment, an unexpected feeling bloomed within me - a newfound appreciation for the spirit of New Year's celebrations. It was as if familiar traditions were taking on a new and personal significance.

This wasn't a negative feeling, nor was it necessarily positive; it was simply different. It reminded me of the bittersweet realization that Santa Claus isn't real. While our parents might have created a magical atmosphere during our childhood, the love and effort behind it remain. We mature, our perspective changes and our love for our parents deepens, albeit in a different way. We grow up, my dear. Discovering that Santa isn't real, that Mom was the one leaving cookies and presents, shatters the illusion for a moment. The sparkly, rose-colored glasses we wear as children fall away, and the world takes on a more realistic hue - ordinary, yet still logical. Childhood innocence fades.

While my experience wasn't quite as emotionally charged, it did prompt a reevaluation of my perspective. Perhaps the metaphorical rose-colored glasses represent the various filters we use to navigate life, seeking comfort and warmth. Did you Think back to cherished childhood experiences - playing with friends, exploring abandoned places, the comfort of a homecooked meal, a mother's gentle kiss on your forehead, checking your fever when you were sick, and the excitement of finding a sweet treat in a grocery bag which she just brought. I trust you can relate.

Again, I went deep inside of thinking something not regarding the main theme. When I came back from my childhood memories trip, the host of the event started a game and asked me to participate.

-Oh, please! Let me sit on the chair. GofG will take my place with a great place!

I had a feeling the host would pick me to participate in the game, and I tried my best to ignore the host's curious body language, which I interpreted as slightly pushy. While I knew Sunflower would relish the game, I wasn't particularly enthusiastic myself. However, after a few rounds, Sunflower decided to join in the fun. Her participation became a highlight of the evening. As she sang, her voice - gentle and delicate - filled the room, first with Ukrainian melodies, then transitioning to a few Hindi phrases. The enchanting melody sent shivers down everyone's spine, a captivating vibration that resonated deeply. At that moment, she resembled a captivating siren from the depths of the ocean. I was filled with excitement and admiration for her grace and beauty. It was hard to imagine the impact she must have had on the men present.

And then, midnight struck. Happy New Year.

Rabbit in a Stuck

Looking back, the three of us truly had a remarkable time working and learning together. The power of collaboration is undeniable - three minds working in unison can generate such creativity and innovation. Countless times, we convened in the conference room, fostering a collaborative atmosphere that undoubtedly boosted our productivity.

One Sunday morning, I woke up with a clear vision: to create a comprehensive manual for the BPA department. This resource would streamline responsibilities and provide a user-friendly format for both existing team members and newcomers, ensuring a smooth onboarding experience. I knew instantly that my girls would embrace this idea and help refine it into something truly exceptional.

It's incredibly rewarding to be surrounded by girls who not only share a similar work ethic but also forge genuine friendships. This camaraderie fosters a sense of unity, fueling our energy and confidence.

So, we decided to meet again together in a conference room in an empty office and properly discuss everything.

-How we can create a proper manual, we had never worked.

-Honey, we have enough information from all departments on the list to place a foundation for our future book. When we start to work - we just will add the missing details.

-Yeah, it sounds like a good plan.

-Girls, let's work!

-And we will play pool!

-Oh, yes. G, please! But after…

That particular Sunday is a day I vividly recall, not necessarily for the after-work pool session (although that was enjoyable too). The entire eight hours were incredibly productive. Despite being a Sunday spent within the confines of the office, the time flew by. We were completely engrossed in our discussions and debates, finding genuine pleasure in the intellectual exchange.

Following this productive stretch, we unwound for a few hours with a game of pool. The soundtrack for the evening was a lovely Indian song called "Na Na Sha" (if you haven't heard it, I highly recommend it!). The music looped throughout the night, blending harmoniously with our laughter, enthusiastic shouts, and impromptu dance moves around the pool table.

A warmth and tenderness bloomed within me, leaving me with a constant smile and an inexplicable urge to laugh. We reveled in a sense of childlike silliness, drawing pure joy from our camaraderie. The happiness I felt that day was truly profound.

-Girls, let's go to my room.

-Continue after the party!

-I am too old to dance like this. I can't move anymore… - Ooooh, come on, please, you are only 27.

-No, no, no, no… You mean you are already 27. Survive till my age, firstly, kid.

-I will not say anything …

-You are 2 years older them me. Shut up, please, and you.

-Oh, girls, let's go; I want to lie on the bed.

Stepping outside the building, a wave of cold air washed over us. It wasn't freezing, but there was a noticeable chill that nipped at exposed skin, particularly our noses and hands. The cool air served as a welcome contrast to the warmth of our previous activity.

-Do you hear it?

-Yes, peacock, I guess…

-No, it's sound different.

-Sounds like someone is trying to identify itself.

-Let's go inside the room. It's cold.

-We have to check what this is.

-How we can't go there, it's dark and outside of our territory.

-Let's ask security to check…

-Yes, girls, it's not a normal sound from a peacock's daily routine song, and it's midnight. I never heard them be so loud in such a time.

GofG, concerned about the source of the noise, approached a security guard and spoke to him in Hindi, inquiring about the commotion coming from beyond the perimeter. We, the three of us, ventured over to the concrete fence lined with barbed wire - for clarification, our territory was secured with a barbed wire fence. In an attempt to see what was happening, I stepped on a nearby stone and activated my phone's flashlight, but the darkness remained impenetrable. The sound, however, grew steadily louder.

As I turned around, I saw the three security guards intently scanning the area, trying to pinpoint the origin of the noise. Witnessing the fear in my girls' eyes, a knot of unease tightened in my chest - a sense of dread.

-They have to go and check what is going on there.

-Yes, GofG, ask them to go, please…

-I can't sleep with these sounds.

-Me too.

The security guards, armed with a firearm and long poles, proceeded towards the source of the sound through the back exit. We, on the other hand, decided to relocate to the first floor of the nearest bungalow, opting for the vantage point of the balcony. A complex mix of emotions roiled within me - a childlike curiosity intertwined with a sense of dread. Glancing at my girls' faces, I saw a reflection of my anxieties mirrored in their expressions.

Huddled together on the edge of the balcony, we strained to see over the railing, wordlessly waiting. For the next twenty minutes, all we could perceive were the ongoing "calls" and the approaching footsteps of the security guards. The darkness was absolute; the faint beam from a single flashlight sputtered ineffectually, failing to penetrate the thick cloak of night or illuminate even the immediate path ahead of the security personnel. Despite our desperate efforts to pierce the darkness, we were left with nothing but sightless observation and a growing sense of helplessness, and each passing minute stretched into an eternity, surpassing even the most tedious Friday afternoon class back in school. The silence, punctuated only by the sound of our ragged breaths, felt suffocating. An urge to break the oppressive quiet, to utter anything simply to disrupt the gnawing anticipation, welled up within me.

-Do you hear?

-Yes, it stops to noise…

-They are returning.

-It's done?

-What was exactly done? Any idea?

-I will ask them, girls. Wait…

I intently observed GofG's face, hands, body language, and overall demeanor during their conversation. Despite my eagerness to understand the situation as quickly as possible, my attempts to glean any answers from GofG's nonverbal cues were unsuccessful. She maintained a neutral expression, revealing no emotional response.

-Why they are talking so much…

-Mari, please, it's just a few minutes. Don't also panic.

-It's getting cold and chilly; I just want to come inside…and that's all, Sunny. Her silent response was accompanied by a specific look and facial expression that seemed to convey, "Come on, girl. I know you well enough." This prompted a wave of self-doubt within me. "Am I truly that transparent? Do my emotions wear so blatantly on my sleeve?" The logical part of me knew this couldn't be entirely true. After all, I spend most of my life consciously concealing my emotions, feelings, and thoughts. Perhaps, however, I'm not as adept at masking them as I believe.

-Girls, let's go…

GofG abruptly approached us, and without a word, we followed her like children trailing their mother, a sense of impending reprimand and the prospect of returning home hanging heavy in the air. We entered her room and sat on the bed, silently observing her. Just five minutes prior, I had been consumed by a desperate need to know the details of the situation. Now, however, an unsettling silence had descended within me, a suspension of my internal monologue.

Have you ever experienced that intense, almost primal desire for an object - a new dress, the latest phone release, anything that sparks an immediate craving? It's a feeling of "I must have it, regardless of the cost," followed by days of scheming and planning to acquire it. But then, once you finally possess it, a sense of disillusionment sets in. You question your initial motivation - "Why did I want this so badly? It doesn't bring the satisfaction or joy I anticipated."

That's precisely the sensation that began to creep into my mind - a premonition of dissatisfaction before I even knew the outcome.

-So?

-So..

-And?

-And..

-Say it.

-So, it's a baby cow there …

-Crying because couldn't find mommy?

-No…. oh, shut up and listen.

-So???

-The baby cow gets caught in a barded net …. wire …..and damaged …ahm… cut itself. They probably, I mean the pack of coyotes or dogs, I don't know,…. They were forcing cows….

-Did they help this baby cow to get out from the net stuck? I mean the security guards.

-No, when they reached that baby cow, it was a lot of coyotes already eating his stomach…internal organs. The intestines were chewed and thrown out of the body. They drove away that animal, so that's why it stopped to scream. I mean, the baby cow stopped screaming.

A heavy silence descended upon our cramped, dimly lit room. The whirring of the ceiling fan faded into the background as if someone had muted the world around me. We avoided eye contact, each one of us lost in our mental replay of the past hour, piecing together the harrowing sequence of events. The echoing scream replayed in our minds, the horrifying realization that a helpless creature had been devoured alive, trapped, and unable to escape.

For that young animal, innocent and incapable of comprehending the excruciating pain it endured, a swift demise became the only merciful outcome.

The horrifying scream of the calf echoed relentlessly in my mind, a relentless loop of terror. My heart pounded, and I could feel my blood pressure skyrocketing. A throbbing sensation intensified in my flushed face and neck as if my veins were on the verge of bursting. Panic threatened to consume me, and I frantically darted my eyes around the room, searching for an escape from the mental torment. A wave of nausea rose from my stomach, threatening to erupt. Desperately, I tried to maintain a composed exterior, willing myself to regain control. "Get a grip," I silently commanded myself.

-Did they kill the baby?

-Nope, they can't. It's a law….

-So, it passed away by itself.

-Yeah, I think…

-So, the unbearable torment finished…

Raising my gaze, I met the sight of my girls' pale and drawn faces. Their posture spoke volumes, conveying their shared pain, horror, and sorrow. In that moment, the shared experience offered a strange comfort, a solace akin to a calming cup of sedation.

-Let's go to sleep. This day has to be ended as soon as possible.

-Yes, I am also tired

-Have you noticed that one of the wellness girls left today?

-Which one?

-I don't know her name. She just came, and even not 2 weeks, she is fired.

-I have no comments... And the most frightening thing is that for me, it's something usual.

-Yes, for me also. We are like a wild animal, and if we are not strong enough, we will be eaten like this pure cow.

-Oh, come on, please, I just forgot about it. Stop it -But it's true!

-And what? I want to sleep peacefully this night without nightmares.

It was a comforting thought but a cruel fantasy for this night. Not tonight, my dear. Not tonight...

The final words hung heavy in the air, punctuated only by the chilling echo of my voice. Then, in an instant, a wave of prickly itching erupted across my entire body. Terror, sharp and sudden, pierced my heart, so profound that it took several seconds to catch my breath and grasp the horrifying reality. The scream returned, closer this time, sending a fresh wave of terror crashing over me.

-It's alive....

-Hah?...No....

-It was alive all this time, and dogs started to eat it again.

We attempted to engage in conversation on anything else, anything to distract ourselves from the horrifying reality. However, the effort proved futile. Each time that wretched cow let out its bloodcurdling scream, a wave of terror and a prickling, crawling sensation would engulf me. It was as if hundreds of knives were being plunged into my heart and stomach simultaneously. This unrelenting assault on my senses was agonizing, draining the life out of me with each passing second.

-Girls, I am going to sleep. I want to put the headphones on to stop it.

-Why they can't kill him?? This is inhumane!

-They can't! It's a law; they can be arrested.

-Who will know??

-How will they kill him? With a gun? If police investigate it and find the bullet numbers?

-Knife?

-Knife? Seriously?

-Yes, God! We are not in the jungle! We can't just sit and do nothing.

-You have to.

-Okay, enough.

-Time to sleep.

-You mean "try" to sleep.

While girls engaged in a spirited discussion, my mind fixated on a single desire: escape. The thought of venturing outside terrified me. The horrifying screams of the calf would undoubtedly be amplified in the open air, shattering any hope of sleep.

-Mari, let's go.

-Yeah…

Desperate to shut out the harrowing sounds, I squeezed my eyes shut and tried to distract myself as I made my way back to my room. The specifics of bidding goodnight to Sunflower, opening the door, and entering my room have faded from my memory. Only one objective consumed my thoughts: to locate those infernal headphones and blast music so loud it would drown out the world.

The agonizing pricking sensation intensified a relentless assault that seemed to quicken with each passing moment. It felt as if a malevolent force within my head understood my impending escape and was determined to inflict maximum psychological damage in these final seconds. The entire ordeal was pure torture.

The time it took to open the headphone case and finally press them onto my ears stretched into an eternity. Taking a series of deep, measured breaths, I fought to quell the raging fire within my body and mind. The pounding music filled my ears, an ache that somehow offered a strange sense of solace, a necessary counterpoint to the raw emotional distress.

I desperately tried to focus on the mundane details of my room – the color of the wardrobe, the clothes hanging inside, the clutter on my table and chair. But every ten to fifteen seconds, a horrifying image flickered through my mind: a small calf, splayed on the cold ground, entangled in a net. Its stomach hung open, blood staining its fur. Large, frightened eyes seemed to plead with me from the darkness.

With squeezed eyes, prayer spilled from my lips in a desperate torrent. A hundred times, I repeat the plea, begging God to end the baby's torment. More than an hour and a half pass before I finally reach for my phone, my fingers trembling as I lower the volume. Silence descends, thick and heavy. It's five in the morning. The only sound is the ragged echo of my breathing. The baby is gone.

The night exacted its toll, leaving behind a crushing weight of emotions – the sickening feeling of complicity in a collective act of murder, a crime reaped through inaction. But for now, the details would remain buried. The horrors of that night were more than enough.

Rabbit in a Cage

Wrath a Sullenness.

The very concept of hunting is abhorrent to many people, myself included. The violence and cruelty associated with it are undeniable. Here, vegetarianism is a prevalent dietary choice, and the reasons behind it extend far beyond religious beliefs. There's a strong argument to be made for respecting cows and abstaining from consuming their meat, even in situations where the animal is suffering, and euthanasia might be considered an act of mercy.

However, the fear of divine retribution often clouds judgment in such cases. Now, let's shift the focus from animals to humans, specifically employees in the workplace. How do our feelings change when we consider the concept of "hunting" in this context? Does it become any less objectionable if we're talking about mental or psychological manipulation instead of physical harm?

The scenario you describe - a leader using intimidation or pressure tactics to motivate employees - does indeed raise ethical concerns. While it wouldn't necessarily be classified as physical violence, it's a harsh approach.

Without more context, it's difficult to say definitively whether this constitutes "hunting." More information is needed to make a clear judgment.

However, the core question remains: is there a meaningful distinction between these two forms of "hunting"? Why do we hesitate to apply the term to the psychological variety? Perhaps because, in the latter case, the target remains physically unharmed. But the emotional and mental toll can be just as devastating.

The past two weeks have been a whirlwind of presentations, completely absorbing my attention and leaving little space for contemplation. In a way, I welcomed the relentless workload; it was a refuge from the disturbing memories of that horrific night, the lingering images, and the persistent nausea.

I thrived on diving into new research, crafting compelling presentations, and tackling any task thrown my way. From sunrise to sunset, my focus was laser-sharp, meticulously evaluating the perfect linen brand for bedrooms or researching the ideal cutlery design for brunch service.

The allure of the fashion world, particularly the coveted brands like Dior, Baccarat, and Lalique, is undeniable for many women. Whether indulging in a personal shopping spree or selecting a gift for someone special, the ritual remains the same: admire, select, acquire, and revel in the possession. Often, however, the initial thrill of discovering a stunning cocktail dress in a boutique leads to an impulsive purchase, followed by the garment languishing unworn in the closet. Why? A multitude of reasons can contribute, but the core truth lies in the satisfaction of acquisition itself. The desire has been fulfilled.

Perhaps a glimpse into my typical routine for the next month will provide a window into my world. Imagine, if you will, the following: Monday through Saturday, a consistent wake-up call at 9:00 am, followed by the daily ritual of dressing in skirts and applying makeup with meticulous care.

The workday unfolds within the confines of their office, where I delve into brand research, meticulously analyzing color palettes and cushion designs for various family estates. Lunchtime brings a welcome respite, shared with my wonderful girls. After a brief break of thirty to forty minutes, we return to the familiar grind - researching, compiling brand databases, crafting presentations showcasing the most suitable collections, and the like.

However, one particular morning shattered this predictable routine...

-Can you get ready faster? We are again late!

-I am coming, don't be in so rush, it's just a coffee training...

-And what? After, it will be just a shift, or it's just a flight. We can be late, and later, you will say: "This is a private jet. They will wait for us." Honey, we are at work, not them. We have to be more responsible. Come fast!

Our mornings with GofG began with an unchanging routine. I cherish the memories of watching her prepare for the day, perched on the edge of her bed as she meticulously applied makeup and styled her hair. She always looked stunning, and yet, she'd invariably seek my opinion: "Does this look alright? Should I change something? Would a different lipstick be better?"

Fortunately, such decisions were never a source of contention. Perhaps due to the local custom of embracing a more relaxed approach to time management, we never encountered any difficulties. On that particular day, our destination was a guest house where we were scheduled to attend a training session on various coffee machines and culinary techniques.

-Sunflower, are you in stockings?

-Yes, I know it's not allowed, but inside his house. We are in the guest house. Look at the guys. They are wearing socks. So why they can but I can't.

-Hmm, you are right. And it's cold here... good idea.

-Let's go! What are you both chilling here.?

-Oh, excuse me, "miss sleeping till afternoon", almost on our way.

-Who is there?

-Is it Jesabel? And that girl. I forgot her name...

-Yes, but why are they here? It's only for new joiners... Have no idea... let's see what she is doing here.

I already describe our lead as a small, tinny girl with 1 kilo of foundation and amazing lipstick color. That day, she was especially interesting. I couldn't see anyone else in that room; she was almost everywhere. Her infectious laughter seemed to fill the entire room, and she buzzed around with the boundless enthusiasm of a puppy unleashed after a long period of confinement. By lunchtime, I must admit, her boundless energy and constant voice had left me feeling quite drained—finally, a chance to rest and savor some delicious Chinese cuisine.

-Let's go for a rest in our rooms.

-I feel the same.

-Amazing idea. Both of you come to my room.

So, I was lying on GofG's bed when we got an interesting email that started the Cold War.

-What the hell is this??

-What again, please don't tell me we have new rules: "Share your location during a day off in the city. "hehe.

-No, open it and read.

An email was sent to all departments regarding a violation of grooming policy guidelines by Jesabel, the lead of our department, specifically targeting myself, GofG, and Sunflower.

The email took particular offense to the fact that as a "Lead," she chose to look into the infraction as she cannot accept such behavior! We were issued a stern and final warning. Guess the transgressions! In my case, a lack of lipstick and eyeliner. GofG was cited for neglecting eyeshadow, and Sunflower dared to attend the training session entirely makeup-free, even daring to wear stockings! The horror! Looking back, the incident is almost comical and silly. However, at the time, we were understandably furious. Our daily tasks involve interacting with various departments, unlike Jesabel, who seemingly spent her days cloistered in her room. When the First Family was absent, the female staff's departments essentially shut down in their room - there were simply no duties to be performed in the empty house. Only now can I truly understand why.

From that moment we went in a long competition which finished when Jesabel was fired. And trust me, I was disappointed in that. I was left alone in the house.

-I will call her now.

-Leave it, S, stop yourself…

-No. She can't play such games …

-That's what she wanted; don't give her any reaction.

-No. I will text on chat everything that I think about it.

-S! Stop it, give me the phone. Don't do it!

But it was too late…

The email incident struck a particular chord with me. It transcended a mere question of makeup and attire; it highlighted a deeper issue within our workplace. The expectation of steadfast adherence to arbitrary rules, coupled with a complete lack of support from our leader, was a source of immense frustration. Making mistakes, even minor ones, was tantamount to failure in her eyes. There was no guidance, no opportunity to learn and grow - only the threat of punishment. Was this a healthy work environment? Hardly.

The constant state of flux - girls leaving every week, new faces replacing them - only amplified the underlying tension. The feeling of being expendable, of walking on eggshells for fear of making a single misstep, was pervasive. While termination might not have been the immediate consequence of the makeup fiasco, it certainly felt like a looming possibility at that moment.

-Talk with him.

-Explain everything

-He knows her, don't worry. He didn't pay attention to this email. Relax.

-Are you sure?

-Yeah, just in case he will ask, both of you sent me your pictures.

-Can you explain to him that it's ridiculous to make such vulgar make-up in a workplace?

-Okay, I will talk with him.

"With whom? "

As you may be aware, our "village" office operates within a hierarchical structure. At the helm is a head of departments, who acts as the key decision-maker for all matters concerning the First Family. This individual oversees every aspect of their lives, from the selection of breakfast items to the color and style of cutlery used during meals. Furthermore, all service procedures, events, travel arrangements, and movements require his explicit approval. No changes, however minor, such as removing a type of cookie from the snack table - can be implemented without his authorization.

My first encounter with him came in August during a Zoom conference. He was grilling me with questions about my future role. One particular query stands out in my mind for its sheer oddity: "Do you understand the proper way to prepare a bed for our clients?"

The question struck me as peculiar for several reasons. Firstly, within the context of private jet service, bed-making wouldn't necessarily rank as the most critical skill. Undoubtedly, the bedding must meet the highest hotel standards, but that's just one facet of exceptional service. Every interaction, every word uttered, must adhere to a set of protocols. A poorly made bed pales in comparison to offering a beverage in the wrong glassware, presenting it directly to a VIP passenger, or providing an overly hot oshibori towel. Improperly ironed table linens and dishes resembling fast-food fare are equally unacceptable. The art of food presentation and service is akin to a painter's canvas - each dish is a masterpiece designed to tantalize the taste buds and satisfy the aesthetic senses. When it comes to private jet cuisine, one must cultivate a genuine culinary spirit not just to serve food but to create an experience.

Now, let's turn our attention to the enigmatic leader who oversees this vast department of over 300 employees. I'll refrain from offering any descriptions for the time being; his introduction will come at a more opportune moment.

GofG was the only one of us who had direct communication with our Head. How and why, I don't remember. Till that day, I saw him only a couple of times in the office building, and we didn't even greet each other. Still, she already had some personal meetings and direct communication via apps, so maybe that's why she had his number, and thank god we could explain our 'mistakes'.

-Girls, did you see the new email from the Head?

-Which one?

-Where? Wait! I will check.

-What?? Is he serious??

-Did you ask him to do it for us?

-No… I think he realized that it would be better for all departments to work in health conditions.

-But new girls.. when new girls will come, can they choose where to go?

-I don't know I have to ask him!

-I don't think anyone will want to be with Jesabel.

-Oh, leave it, don't think now about her anymore. She is not your headache.

-But how will we work if we can't…

-Stop, please. I will get all the information from him and let you both know…

"Dear regency

From today, I will separate Butler's Personal Department into two divisions. Jesabel will lead the first one, and GofG will lead the second.

No communication and crossroads between divisions; both leads will report directly to me.

Do not hesitate to ask me any questions.

Best and Regards

Head of Pink Hell Regency."

This petty competition among the girls effectively pushed all thoughts of the unsettling staff departures and the strange occurrences within the First Family's residence to the back of my mind. Consumed by this internal rivalry, I was completely unprepared for the blindsiding blow that awaited me.

At that time, our living quarters were sparsely populated - just six of us in the BPA department and three from Wellness. The silence was almost deafening.

***

On a Sunday afternoon, I received a message from GofG inquiring about my availability for a conversation. She had flown back to her hometown the previous day to attend to an urgent matter. Her sudden departure, shrouded in secrecy, had caused me some concern. It was the first time in months that we hadn't seen each other for more than two days.

Phone Call

-Tell me! - I pleaded.

-Mari... - GofG's voice trembled.

-What? - my heart pounded in my chest.

-She's fired.

-Who? Jesabel? - I blurted out.

-No...

Grief and regret colored her voice as she searched for solace, for any crumb of comfort. I felt a pang of sympathy - I could almost see her before me, her large, black pearl eyes rimmed red and overflowing with tears, pleading for a word of reassurance, anything to alleviate the agony etched on her hunched form.

It took a moment too long for the truth to sink in. When it did, I slumped onto the corner of the bed, speechless.

-They made the call already, - GofG stammered. - She's probably packing her things.

-What? Today? Now? - my voice rose in disbelief.

-Did you forget? - she choked out. - That's the rule here in the Pink Hell - anyone who's fired leaves immediately! You have to return your uniform and...

-Wait, - I interrupted. - Are you saying you're fired, too? Is that why you left?

-No, no, - she replied hastily.

-But Mari, I feel awful... terrible.

-I know, - I offered weakly.

-No, you don't understand, - she insisted.

-What is it? - I pressed.

-He asked me... my opinion was the last one that mattered. I chose you. - her voice dropped to a whisper.

Have you ever witnessed a mirror shattering into a million pieces right before your eyes? Imagine the sound, the visceral reaction - a gasp of horror, a torrent of bewilderment, a crushing sense of despair, and then... numbness. Now, add to that a searing pain in your gut, a heart that feels like it's been stabbed, and the chilling realization that you're standing in the middle of a battlefield, and your closest comrade has just been sacrificed to save your life. What do you say? What do you do?

-Why us? Why not from 5 other girls?

-He said to choose from 2 of them...

-He knows we are the greatest team here, supportive and productive! Why?? Just why? These girls were just lying on the bad hole day and doing nothing!

-I don't know Mari! Stop it! They both know how to work firstly, the new girl just came, it's not even 2 weeks. Who else? I am the lead of this team. You both came at the same time. So, who else?

-Why anyone has to leave now?? She didn't even start to work, only a stupid presentation that didn't show her professionalism like a flight attendant. It is not fare! It is stupid; she hasn't done anything wrong or made a mistake!

-Someone has to leave. He decided it had to be someone from you both.

-It is cruel and oppressive to ask you about it. He knows we are like sisters here, always together and working, creating something new. In 2 months, we had more than a hundred meetings with all departments and typed a manual for all BPA departments, composed and approved a checklist for the day/night shift. What had been done by other girls in the last 6 months?? Nothing!!

-Mari! Please! Look … I can't discuss it now. You have to go to her room. She needs you…..

-I will update you.

-Okay.

My mind reeled, caught in a suffocating fog of confusion, fear, and a sickening sense of betrayal. The truth GofG had revealed was simply too outlandish to comprehend. Denial, a powerful defense mechanism, kicked in. It couldn't be true.

Driven by a desperate need for answers, I bolted from the room. My gaze darted towards her windows, searching for any sign of movement, any indication of what was transpiring within. I knew I had to act.

-Are you there? -I entered the room.

-Yes, come in, - she replied.

-They only gave me forty minutes, - she announced breathlessly. -The car is waiting by the gate already.

-How can anyone pack in just forty minutes? - I exclaimed, the injustice of it all simmering within me.

-I don't know, - she admitted with a shrug. - But perhaps this is for the best. I'm finally free from this gilded cage.

A hint of defiance flickered in her emerald green eyes, momentarily eclipsing the tears glistening there.

-I can go anywhere: the mall, a cafe, anywhere at all! Freedom! - she repeated, her voice gaining strength.

I watched silently as she moved around the room with practiced efficiency, shoving clothes into a small red suitcase. Despite the obvious frustration and humiliation of the situation, her bare arms, normally the color of creamy silk, were marred by angry red welts. Yet, her face remained a mask of cool indifference. Even in this demoralizing situation, she maintained her composure, determined to leave with a semblance of dignity.

"Oh, Sunflower," my inside voice woke up, unable to hold back any longer," No one here deserves your tears or your loyalty after casting you out like this in a foreign country, no less. You are young, beautiful, and highly educated. A woman who raised herself by her bootstraps. Never forget who you are."

A knock on the door interrupted my thoughts. Two housekeeping guys were waiting to escort her to the exit. She picked up the suitcase and made a straight look at me.

-They said to hand over the uniform to you.

-Leave it here. Don't think about it.

-I am free, Mari. My prison is over. Good luck to you, hope to see you again…

"Prison." The word hung heavy in the air, a stark contrast to the illusion surroundings. It reminds me of our evening walks from her room to the security post. There was nowhere else to walk properly. As we reached the security post, we'd feel their watchful eyes on us, like they were making sure we wouldn't run or cross some invisible border. It felt like a prison walk, those 200 meters being the only exercise we got each evening. Why did it resonate so deeply within me? An unsettling truth, perhaps? Sunflower's choice of words felt eerily apt, a perfect encapsulation of the stifling reality beneath the gilded surface. Here we were, ostensibly living a normal life, and yet, a gnawing sense of confinement pervaded our existence.

Heresy

The following morning, GofG returned from her brief vacation. We proceeded with our usual routine lunch and office work - a futile attempt to maintain a facade of normalcy. The elephant in the room, however, was impossible to ignore. Every curious glance, every whispered inquiry about the absent Sunflower, "Isn't she feeling well?" felt like a thinly veiled attempt to pry into the matter. Their poorly concealed astonishment, the way their eyes darted around like inquisitive fish, only served to heighten my anger. It was abundantly clear that their concern wasn't genuine; they simply craved gossip to fuel their conversations in the staff cafeteria. Perhaps they had grown accustomed to the revolving door of new faces - girls arriving with wide-eyed hope, only to be discarded just as quickly. I doubted they even remembered Sunflower's name. Cynically, I wondered if they placed wagers - a morbid pool predicting how long each newcomer would last.

In the afternoon, we retreated to GofG's room, seeking solace in a brief respite. I knew a conversation was inevitable. I craved answers and explanations to alleviate the gnawing pain and emptiness that had taken root within me.

-Do you know why?

-Why what?

-You know what. Did he, a big, super smart boss, explain to you why?

-I don't know for certain, - she admitted -He claimed there were visa issues - a problem with her visa apparently, that it couldn't be processed.

-Indian visa?

-No, Europe visa.

-So, what? - I scoffed -If that were the case, wouldn't they have given her a proper 30-day notice instead of throwing her out on the street in 40 minutes? Are you serious?

-I don't know, Mari!! Please don't ask me! Did you forget where you are?

A sharp pang of guilt pierced me. Yes, I had forgotten. Blinded by my comfortable routine, I had conveniently ignored the strange occurrences, the inconsistencies that had plagued this place. I'd chosen blissful ignorance. How foolish, how naive I had been. Sunflower wasn't an anomaly; she was just another casualty in this revolving door of expendable girls. There was no justification for their actions.

-She is still in the town. I want to request "him" permission to go out to meet her. Are you in?

-Make sure no one knows that you are meeting her.

-Wtf are you talking about?!

-She is not a part of the company anymore.

-Are you serious right now? What happened with you, G?

-Nothing Mari, just follow the rules and don't pretend over smart.

Deep down, I knew she was right. Anger and indignation clouded my judgment. It's a common pattern, isn't it? Employees blame their superiors for everything. In the face of hardship, it's always easier to point fingers - the government, the taxman, the boss - everyone becomes a target for our misfortunes. But a nagging suspicion lingered. The legalities of it all just didn't add up. There was something undeniably fishy about the situation. Perhaps waiting for my execution wasn't the wisest course of action.

Should I leave? But where would I go? I'd severed ties with my previous life, and there was nowhere to return to.

This evening, I drafted an email to the King Head requesting a three-hour leave pass for tomorrow. Having delivered a well-received report today, I felt I could justify a brief respite from the confines of Pink Hell. Oh, yeah from now I will call him King Head because only a king can pass judgment without proper investigation and required following procedures. The day when I will get to know him closer will fulfill your picture. Just give me more time.

The following morning, I donned my sports attire and proceeded directly to the security checkpoint. The obligatory sign-out procedure, while shameful, was a hurdle to overcome. My taxi awaited me at the second security post, a convenience I now cherished after the unsettling encounter with the stray dogs. Speaking of which, they had completely slipped my mind. Lost in thought, I spent the entire journey to Sunflower dwelling on the events of that fateful evening:

"One day, while returning to my accommodation on my day off, my driver dropped me off at an intersection, insisting in his broken English that this was the designated location. The language barrier made explanation futile, so I decided to walk the short distance - no more than 100 meters - to the gate, familiar with the route. Halfway there, I spotted two redheaded dogs sprawled out on the road. Curious about their reaction, I stopped.

An unsettling feeling prickled in my chest. The dogs stared intently at me, completely silent. Taking two cautious steps back, I watched as one of them rose and circled behind me without a sound. Convinced it was leaving, I was caught off guard when the dog lunged toward me, sinking its teeth into my leg like a piece of flesh.

Terror surged through me, paralyzing me with fear. My mind, usually adept at formulating escape plans in emergencies, went eerily blank. Frozen in place, I didn't even consider evasive action. Time seemed to stand still. What had happened? Why was I immobilized? Was this some kind of defense mechanism, a malfunction that prevented me from protecting myself? Highly trained for emergencies, this reaction defied logic. I had to unravel the reason behind my inexplicable paralysis.

The horrifying realization that I could sustain serious injury jolted me back to reality - a phone ringing, a blaring alarm. I scrambled to answer the call, my gaze darting around frantically. Spotting a small, open fence leading to a yard, I bolted towards it. Just as I began to slam it shut, the dogs erupted in a frenzy of furious yelps, snapping at my heels. The caller was Sunflower - a text message flashed on the screen - promising to arrive at the accommodation in five minutes. A fervent prayer escaped my lips - a desperate plea for her to be my rescue.

- Where are you? Hello?? Do you hear me? Wait, don't drive fast!

-On my way, what's happened??

-I am stuck in someone's garden next to our gate. Can you pick me up from here? Are you in the cab, right?

-We just turned left to that off-road. Wait…What are you doing there??

-It's some dogs here; I am scared to go; I don't know how they will react. So don't forget me, please!

-Wait, I am reaching. Do you see a white car?

-Not really, just some light. Oh yeah! God…I see you!! See!!

A fervent prayer for rescue…and then, Sunflower's call. Was it a divine intervention, a beacon of hope sent to pull me from the jaws of this horrifying ordeal? My demeanor shifted dramatically. Gone was the usual guarded expression, replaced by a genuine smile and a lighthearted joke about my shopping bags. It wasn't denial - I hadn't forgotten the terrifying encounter. But for a fleeting moment, in the presence of my friend, the terror receded, replaced by a wave of relief

-Why were you in that garden, Mari?

-The driver dropped me in the wrong location, so I decided to walk… but these dogs, damn, I decided not to risk

-Were they aggressive or yelping? What happened?

-No, not at all…- My voice trailed off, laced with a hint of deception. I decided to downplay the incident to avoid causing unnecessary alarm. But a seed of doubt had been planted. Had I lied to Sunflower? Shame washed over me - a cocktail of embarrassment about the encounter and a fear of appearing weak or vulnerable. Why this sudden need to maintain a facade of strength?

A searing pain pulsed in my leg, a constant reminder of the attack. Every step felt like walking on burning embers, yet I forced a smile, masking the grimace that threatened to contort my face. A desperate yearning to reach the sanctuary of my room consumed me. With exaggerated cheer, I bade Sunflower goodnight, the lingering pain a dull throb in the background. Ignoring the throbbing, ignoring the incident itself, I retreated to my room and willed myself to sleep to forget the terror that had unfolded.

Throughout the following week, I played a charade. Makeup became a shield, expertly concealing the telltale marks of the bite. Any questions regarding the source of the injury were met with a dismissive, "I don't know." Why the charade? Why shroud the truth in a cloak of secrecy? Was admitting vulnerability truly so difficult? A silent scream echoed within me - a plea for self-understanding. I wasn't assigning blame; I simply craved clarity, a reason for my illogical actions. Why lie to myself and everyone around me?

I paused in front of a store window, my reflection staring back at me. Uncertainty gnawed at me. Should I confide in her and finally reveal the truth about that terrifying encounter? The memory sent a shiver down my spine. Could I bring myself to tell her everything?

-How are you, darling?

-Hey! Good, did you receive all your documents and salary?

-Yes for documents, but no for salary. I will be out of India when they will send it.

-Do you trust them? Because I don't. I didn't get my salary for all these months, and now you are fired, and I have doubts that I will be less lucky than you soon.

-No, they will not fire you. You are doing a great job. Everyone knows that you typed that manual for the BPA Department and the Checklist for the girls' shift, but we just added some information, so relax.

-I can't relax after you leave. Nothing is stable here; I can't work in such stressful conditions. I will start to check the job here.

-You didn't start to work, relax, and don't look at me. They fired me because of the visa issues.

-Do you believe in this bullshit?

-No.

***

The impending separation from Sunflower loomed large, a source of undeniable grief. Yet, I clung to the belief that a renewed focus on work would be a balm to my anxieties. Everything had shifted after that fateful encounter. One of my rose-colored glasses, a symbol of my previous naivete, tumbled from my grasp, shattering into a million pieces. A newfound wariness replaced my trusting nature. These constant upheavals, this relentless barrage of news and changes, offered no respite. Now, it seemed, GofG was to follow the same path.

A few weeks later, I awoke to a message flashing on my phone, shattering the morning tranquility. "Someone hacked my email. Come to my room," it read in GofG's frantic voice.

"What the hell is happening again?" I muttered, frustration lacing my tone. Was a single day of normalcy too much to ask for? With a sigh, I threw on clothes, my mind refusing to speculate on the nature of the crisis.

Door open

-Can we have at least one morning in peace?

-This is crazy... I received a message on my phone that someone logged in to my mail account and an email from support that someone logged in from this location; look, I made a screenshot...

-Where is the email? Show it to the IT department.

-It's gone.. the person who logged in deleted it...

-What?? Oh no I just realized what is going on. But why? Who the hell needs your work emails?

-I think... I doubt... because of him...

-Whom?? King Head?

-Don't call him like that. He is a nice guy.

-Holy Jesus Christ, are you in love with your boss????

-I don't know... -You? What?

-We discussed in an email about the next people.. who will be fired, so I think it can be Jesabel.

-What? Why would she do it? Anyway, I think she is the only one who can do it.... but for a different reason.

-Which one?

-I heard some rumors that she was in love with King Head and once I saw him coming inside her room. She was late for the shift or flight, and he just came directly to her room.... I told you about it. Did you forget? Or have you completely lost your mind?

-No, they are not! I know they are not. She tried, but he rejected..

-Did you speak about it with him?? So, you want to say that a young guy who works 24/7 and never gets out to meet friends or have fun in a club and whatever rejected the girl's feelings? Right?

-Yes. He works a lot... never sleep properly...

-Do you hear me?

-Yes, I think it was her. She knows how much we talk in corporate chat... whenever he is online, I am also, so I think she is watching us. She also asked him about me .....

-Are you serious??

-I am a lead now and we had discussed something regarding my job in emails. -What kind of?

-I can't tell you...

-Are you kidding now?

-It's confidential. This is the rule! We were preparing the schedule, which is also confidential.

-Are you joking? I do not know when I will start to work and on which days!?

-No… this is the rule.

When did she change? GofG's transformation was undeniable. The once easygoing friend had morphed into this guarded stranger, her personality seemingly warped by her new position and her interactions with the elusive "King Head." This cloak of secrecy surrounding the most mundane details was maddening. Why couldn't they simply work without this constant shroud of drama?

Over the next few days, I sought refuge in work, a necessary balm to soothe the prickling unease that had taken root. Ignoring the unsettling conversation with GofG and the email fiasco, I poured myself into my tasks. I had nothing to hide no secret conversations, no classified information littering my inbox. Yet, the nagging question lingered: "Who had hacked GofG's account, and for what purpose?"

While I knew the IT department would eventually unearth the culprit, a deeper concern gnawed at me. Would GofG even share the truth once they did? The woman I once confided in seemed to have vanished, replaced by this reserved, almost suspicious version of my friend. We still spent time together, but a subtle distance had emerged, a chilling undercurrent to our interactions.

Was I worried that GofG was getting romantically involved with the boss? Perhaps, but how did that affect me? This wasn't my concern. Professionalism, girls! Stay clear of entanglements. Less information meant less stress. He'd be here soon, anyway.

The ominous reminder jolted me back to reality. How had I forgotten? The First Family's arrival was tomorrow! Maybe then,

I'd finally get some answers and finally start working. But where? Who was I in all of this?

Days bled into one another, a monotonous blur. The routine had settled in so insidiously that I couldn't pinpoint its origins. One minute, I was oblivious; the next, the entire estate - managers, housekeepers, and even most of the office staff were in a frenzy, jolted from their slumber by the news: the First Family was arriving tomorrow! My workaholic slumber had been shattered.

-Are you nervous?

-Why?

-Your love will come tomorrow.

-Don't call him like this!

-How should I address to your boyfriend?

-Please stop!

-I am joking; come on. Why are you so nervous if it's not true?

-I don't know

-Will he investigate the hacked email?

-Yes, I think…There is also one accused. I mean, who it can be?

-Oh, and who?

-Do you remember that guy from the office who was the head of one department? Who showed you the gym?

-Oh, yeah. Are you joking…Of course, I remember him…

-So, he was demoted… and maybe he was trying to find the reason for….

-How does it explain why he hacked your email account?

-Because he knows that we talk a lot.

-From where the hell?

-They are friends with Jesabel.

-Oh, my God... Do you remember that day when I went to the gym?

-Yes, so?

-So, he told me that Jesabel and one more girl she was fired that month, a small one who looked like 15 years old.

-Ha, ha, yes, so?

-They were in his house and had some party or whatever.

-Yes, you told me it already. That's why I think they were working together to get in my emails. She has her goal, also.

-Let's not guess. We will know soon. Time to plan your B-day.

-Yes, I think we just will order some food and chill in my room. I will invite the new BPA girl and Suzi from the office.

After arrival, King Head had spent the entire day holed up in his office, a flurry of meetings keeping him occupied. We hadn't anticipated such a swift response.

The evening found us gathered in GofG's room for a small B-party. A recruit mingled with us, along with the ever-rebellious Suzi - the sole rulebreaker who dared to have her own rented accommodation. The night unfolded in a typical girly fashion - mountains of delicious food and a lively conversation centered on the elusive male mind and how it works.

Following this delightful evening, I retreated to my room for some well-deserved rest. A knock on the door shattered the silence. Who could it be at this hour?

-Yes, come in.

-Mari, we received the answer. – GofG had just knocked down the door and flew into my room. -What answer?

-I know who hacked my email…

-Say it, stop making drama

-You will be shocked…

-Are you kidding me?? Say it for God, please!

-It's a girl, not Jesabel

-Than who?

-Look at the email response.

-OMG!

-Yes.

-No way!!

-Oh, yes.

-That can't be true!!

-It is!!!

-Suzi? No way… No way!!

-Yes, and just a few hours ago, she gave her comments that a crazy person hacked my email. Ha-ha, can you believe it?

-No!!

-He texted her to come for a meeting, and he asked why the hell she did it.

-Will you come? She is aware?!

-I think she understood…

-Where is she now? In the office?

-No... she disappeared... and not answering the phone

-I am so shocked... we should call Sunflower and tell her everything.

I craved normalcy, a life devoid of drama. This whole situation left a bad taste in my mouth. But little bit I know, it was merely the prologue, the creaking door on the threshold of a personal hell. Soon, I'd be thrust into the heart of its torment.

The following days were shrouded in an unsettling quiet. Suzi, the lone dissenter, was predictably dismissed. We attempted to resume our daily routines, but an unsettling feeling lingered. The gears of some unseen machinery continued to churn, and an oppressive premonition hung heavy in the air - someone was destined to suffer. This place, it seemed, thrived on misfortune.

A few days later, when I just woke up, and again a new message from GofG, which consisted that new shit happened and I should come to her room for fresh updates. I was wondering what again... what? I collected my body from the bed, took a coffee for both, and went to her room, almost sleeping:

-Something happened this morning.

-Good morning for you. Did you have breakfast?

-It's serious...

-Oh, serious... is it?

-Listen, I had a meeting with the head of department...

-You just woke up, girl.

-Yes, it was morning time at 7 am

-So? What did he say? We are guinea pigs in an alien project.

-I am serious...

-Me also, trust me …. Okay, tell me.

-So, we were sitting in the conference room and discussing… and someone knocked on the door … and I saw Jesabel.

-Oh, gosh.. what was she doing there?

-She asked him to go out for a talk.. but the doors were transparent, I could see everything.

-So?

-So, she started to shout at him so loud, so loud! "I hate you! How dare you do it with me!! Why are you doing it with me? I will destroy this company!" -Holy….

-And she slapped him…

-Holy….no.

-Yes, on his face.

-They had relationships.

-No

-Why not?

-He told me.

-And you trust him? So why did she do it, then? Why did an employer, a woman, walk into her boss's office and slap him when he was with another woman?

-It is not like this. I trust him. And also, the housekeeping guy saw it.

-Ha? What?

-I said the housekeeping guy saw it and recorded it.

-He recorded "the slap"??

-Yes… don't tell anyone!

-Oh god… what a mess…

We talked for hours that morning, but my logical arguments fell on deaf ears. Love, it seemed, had a way of muting reason, of painting everything in shades of rose-colored denial. Her mind conjured a fantasy, a perfect narrative where she ignored the glaring red flags, the obvious manipulation. I knew, with a heavy heart, that she wouldn't remember a word of our conversation, the warnings I desperately tried to convey. One thing was becoming increasingly clear - this "King Head" was playing a dangerous game, and we were all his pawns.

The drama wasn't over. As the First Family prepared for their departure, a collective sigh of relief swept through the staff. Sleep-deprived office workers logged in overtime, some even resorting to sleeping in their chairs just to be readily available. "Why not institute a proper schedule?" I thought wryly. "Wouldn't that ensure everyone is well-rested and, consequently, more productive?" But logic seemed to have taken a vacation in this place. Apparently, chaos was the preferred management style, and who was I to question it? Just another lowly employee, my degree in human resources is worthless in this bizarre place.

***

Someone knocked on my door and interrupted my morning high reflection:

-We need to talk. Are you awake?

-Come in, - I sighed, responding to GofG's frantic knock.

-I'm leaving, - she blurted, barely giving me time to step aside.

-Leaving? G, what's going on now? - Alarm bells clanged in my head.

-I'm going with them to Europe, - she stammered, her voice laced with a mixture of fear and exhilaration.

-So, you'll finally start working then? - I said, trying to mask my surprise with a casual tone.

-Yeah... I'm scared, Mari. I don't know what to do - she nodded, a flicker of uncertainty clouding her eyes.

-Hey, you have the manual, right? Just spend some time familiarizing yourself with it. You'll be fine, - I reassured her, offering a smile that I hoped was convincing.

-I need to pack, - she muttered, her gaze darting around the room. Her movements mirrored the turmoil within - a flurry of frantic activity, a chaotic symphony of misplaced items and nervous energy. Her hands shook as she picked things up, only to abandon them moments later. Her legs seemed to propel her in random directions, her mind struggling to keep pace. Fear and confusion danced in her eyes, a reflection of the whirlwind of emotions swirling inside her.

Two months of waiting, punctuated by a constant undercurrent of anticipation, had finally culminated in this unexpected development. It was a situation that could trigger anxiety in anyone. After all, routine offered a sense of comfort, a predictable rhythm to life. Any change, be it a new workplace or a shift in responsibilities, necessitated a period of adjustment, a fresh wave of stress. While my nomadic lifestyle had equipped me to handle such transitions with more ease, I empathized with GofG's plight. She had left, a whirlwind of nervous energy that had briefly invaded and then vacated my space. Now, I was alone, and the specter of my looming adaptation loomed large. Perhaps, I thought with a hint of trepidation, no one could ever truly be prepared for what awaited them.

Entrance

"Lasciate ogni speranza, voi ch'entrate" Dante Alghieri.

The week of solitude passed in an unexpectedly serene and balanced state. Gone was the constant drama, a welcome respite. But you, dear reader, know me well enough to understand that my life rarely embraces prolonged periods of tranquility. Drama, it seems, is an unwelcome yet persistent companion. The key, I've learned, is acceptance, an acceptance that borders on emotional detachment. I rarely reveal my true feelings in the face of adversity, a self-preservation tactic honed over time.

One tranquil morning, a message from GofG shattered the peace. "You will start work tomorrow," it read, curt and devoid of details. A manager, the message promised, would be in touch regarding my schedule. Undeterred, I met the news with steely calm. After all, I was confident in my abilities and prepared to handle the demands of serving Ultra High Net Worth Individuals.

WhatsApp Chat, GofG:

-Sleeping?

-No, but I will go now.

-Are you doing night shifts?

-Yes, but Head King is with me all night… and we are talking and talking.

-What about his father?

-Nothing interesting.

-What are you exactly doing?

-Nothing, just bring water when he asks, and that's all.

-Bed preparation?

-No.

-Opening the door or ..

-No, there are butlers there for this. Relax.

-What am I supposed to do?

-Just be at the gate near the car, open the door seat in front, and accompany him. If he will need something, he will ask you.

-Hm…

-Mammon will update you.

Who is this guy…I don't recall.

Determined to avoid any missteps, I meticulously reviewed each step of my new assignment. Reaching out to Mammon's contact, I retrieved his photo and recognized him. A young, impeccably groomed man with a sharp jawline and piercing black eyes. His blue suit seemed molded to his form, and his expression was as unreadable as a polished mirror. He exuded an unsettling air of detachment like a robot inhabiting a human shell.

-Anything else I need to check besides my travel kit? - I typed, hoping to glean more information.

-Nothing. That's your only responsibility. - came the terse reply.

-Okay. - I replied, a knot of unease tightening in my stomach.

-Come to the office after a while, - the message continued. We'll discuss the details.

The cryptic message and Mammon's enigmatic persona fueled my apprehension. What exactly was I getting myself into?

Naturally, after completing my assigned task, I couldn't simply sit idle. Curiosity, a cornerstone of my character, propelled me to the garage. There, I familiarized myself with the vehicle, ensuring everything was in order. I even took the initiative to check the radio settings. Back in the office, I turned my attention to the staff, observing their interactions and workflows. This practical application of the knowledge gleaned during those two intensive months solidified my understanding and boosted my confidence.

Finally, Mammon freed himself, and we delved into a detailed discussion about the travel itinerary, meticulously outlining each step of the journey.

-So, I have to accompany him every step and carry the mini-fridge. Right?

-Yes. Don't worry; the butler will be with you.

-Any over responsibilities?

-No, just always open the door and be available for any services.

-Okay. I checked the car. It was some issues with the pen drive, but now it's ready to use.

-Okay. Be ready tomorrow at 9 AM near the gate.

-Noted, Sir.

"Noted what? What the hell did you note, stupid girl?!": The question echoed in the vast emptiness of hindsight. "Why was I so blind, so eager to believe their reassurances? They were paving the way for my descent, making it all seem so effortless, so innocuous. A year later, it was all too easy to blame myself, to judge my naivete. But hindsight, as they say, is always 20/20."

Day 1

Sleep eluded me that night. My mind ping-ponged between anxieties, tossing and turning until dawn. The uncomfortable bed, with its unforgiving gap, didn't help matters, leaving me with a dull ache in my lower back.

By eight o'clock, I was dressed and ready. For the first time, I ventured into the staff cafeteria-garage for breakfast. My intention was simple - to meet the staff I'd be collaborating with and establish my readiness. An unsettling calm had settled over me, a cold indifference to the impending events.

Thirty minutes later, I stole a glance at my watch, silently inquiring of the manager if it was time to proceed. The seasoned veteran, probably the most experienced worker in the office, likely scoffed internally. "What does this newbie want?" he must have thought. "Teaching ME how to do MY job on her first day?"

A sardonic smile played on my lips.

-Let's go, - he finally grunted. - The driver will bring the car around to the main entrance shortly.

-Okay, let's go, - I echoed, the single sentence a testament to the chilling disconnect that had taken root within me.

We walked in hushed silence towards the main entrance. Donning the white gloves - a mandatory part of a BPA's uniform whenever the First Family was around - I couldn't help but scoff internally. Hands needed to be pristine, but legs? Apparently, those were exempt from the sartorial code. The unforgiving sun beat down, a relentless inferno. I winced, a thousand needles pricking at my forehead. Like an idiot, I'd forgotten sunscreen, adding another layer of irritation to the already simmering pot of emotions. Peering through the glass doors, I searched for any sign of movement inside. He'd emerge soon; I knew it. The moment Jesabel appeared to unlock the door, that's when he'd make his exit. Calm, I assured myself. Absolutely calm. No amount of searing sun or irritating distractions could break my focus.

Then, after what felt like an eternity under the relentless sun, a figure materialized inside - Jesabel. My heart hammered in my chest, but not for the reason I expected. She stared at me, a look of utter bewilderment etched on her face, as if I were some sort of exploded atomic bomb. What on earth was she doing? Did she think I'd abandon my post before even starting? Or perhaps, just perhaps, did she know something I didn't?

The main door creaked open a moment later, revealing him at last – the WS. An elderly figure with wispy gray hair, he clutched a newspaper in his wrinkled hands. His small, dark brown eyes, magnified by thick spectacles, seemed like those of a curious rat peering out at the world. As he drew closer, his gaze fell upon me, and a flicker of surprise crossed his features. He studied me with an intensity that made me feel like a museum specimen under scrutiny.

Before the awkward exchange could escalate further, the seasoned manager materialized beside him, launching into a flurry of morning greetings. Seizing the opportunity, I opened the car door, offering a polite excuse as I took my place in the front seat. Protocol dictated my every move. Turning on the radio after a few minutes of silence felt less like a choice and more like a well-rehearsed act. Radio wasn't selected on a whim, dear reader. There was a precise time and place for everything unless, of course, the WS himself expressed a preference. His desires reigned supreme.

-What is your name?

-Mari

-Ah, okay, you are…?

-Flight attendant, sir.

-Who?

-Butler Personal Assistant

-Hah, Hah, ok.

Oh, can you keep thinking before answering, girl? He is not interested in your complaints, that you were brought here to work on an aircraft that still has not been received, and now you have worked like a BPA for some time because "mess" is the main tagline in this company. Just don't do it, at least on the first day.

The moment we touched down at the airport, I practically leaped out of the car, grabbing my ticket from Mammon's bewildered grasp. The WS was a blur of movement, a wisp of gray hair darting towards the boarding gate at an alarming speed. Never in my life had I witnessed such haste from someone his age. By the time I scrambled through security, he was already ensconced in the car, no doubt fuming over my delay.

It was unacceptable. Here I was, a highly trained professional, and on my very first day, I'd fumbled. The weight of expectation, the knowledge that even the most meticulously planned operation could unravel due to a minor misstep, pressed down on me like a suffocating fog. Yes, you might think it's an overreaction, but for someone who received enough instruction to do the job with flawless execution, this imperfection was a glaring blemish.

We went inside the airplane, and I saw the butler Behemoth, who was kind of helpful during the pre-travel preparation. I knew that he would help me and explain what I should do and where I could sit if it was allowed. The flight attendant made all the necessary preflight services, and I understood that she would do all the job during the flight, maybe because I would be needed later during the meetings.

I was feeling weird due to the useless and unnecessary being on an airplane. The flight attendant was a European woman with a big experience, which I could observe from her wrinkles and doll-like smile. The only one think confused me was that she was in stockiness. Yes, she is not part of the company, but she works with UHWI, and his preferences are not jet company standards. The arbitrary grooming rules, a glaring reminder of the invisible lines that separated us, only amplified my sense of alienation. Behemoth remained a silent sentinel near the WS, who himself seemed content to retreat into a world of solitary card games.

As for me, I was relegated to the role of a decorative lamp, an ornament positioned awkwardly in the back cabin. The landing brought little relief. Behemoth informed me that I would be following the WS to a construction area, where, wait for it, another butler awaited my arrival! This whole operation felt like a labyrinth of unnecessary steps and redundant personnel.

This time, I was faster and followed him in a proper doggy way. Good job, girl, 25 diplomas and 2 graduates was this truly the culmination of my academic endeavors? A sarcastic laugh bubbled up within me.

The construction site was a sprawling expanse of scorched earth and sand. Portable cabins, ubiquitous symbols of temporary habitation for the workforce, dotted the landscape. Dust devils danced in the distance, a swirling testament to the harshness of the environment. None of it fazed me except for the incongruity of my attire - a short skirt and heels, utterly impractical for this terrain. Standing beside the newly introduced butler, I scanned the area, waiting for the WS's next move. Then, a flicker of recognition. This wasn't just any butler; it was Mr. Marbach, the estate manager, who had greeted me on my arrival day. A sliver of reassurance eased the knot of tension in my stomach.

"Umbrella?" Mr. Marbach's voice startled me. Confused, I blinked. "Umbrella? Did he ask for an umbrella? Where would we even get one here?" The absurdity of it all washed over me. "What was the point of having multiple personnel here when one would suffice? Was this a deliberate display of wealth, a way to flaunt the extravagance of having staff cater to his every whim? It wasn't my place to question, but a dull resentment simmered beneath the surface. None my business, just do what you were asked, girl, please".

For the next four excruciating hours, we circled the dusty field, a silent procession trailing several meters behind the "meeting" group. The relentless sun beat down, turning my face and legs into what felt like sizzling slabs of meat. My presence felt utterly pointless, a superfluous ornament amidst the testosterone-fueled discussions. The sole female in a sea of men, inappropriately dressed and demonstrably useless, I couldn't shake the feeling of being a living doll on display. Shame burned in my throat - shame at my inadequacy, shame at being a part of this gilded cage.

-Ma'am.?

-Yes? - I turned around to one of the securities.

-Your legs ...

-What? – I took a look at my leg's backside and was shocked. Full red and burned, and it started to itching.

-It's red, Madam.

-Oh, yeah. It's okay, just gentle skin.

-You should wear pants next time.

-Yes, thank you for the advice…..I should wear my brain next time, that's for sure.

-Sorry?

-No, nothing.

Two things dominated my thoughts during those interminable hours: escape and the pathetic state of the umbrella. It billowed precariously in every gust of wind, appearing more out of place than even I. Here was this powerful man, the owner of this vast construction site, reduced to fumbling with a broken contraption amid a crucial meeting, all while three butlers stood by passively. The sheer absurdity of it all left me num.

-Let's go

-Yes, I am trying. It's kind of difficult in these heels.

-Hurry

Finally, we retreated to the relative comfort of the worker containers. I gulped down some water, collapsing gratefully into a chair. My first order of business was discarding the now-grimy white gloves, a tangible reminder of the demeaning walkabout. Resuming my position near the car, I cast a questioning glance at Mr. Marbach.

-No need to stay here; you can go and sit inside. Take some rest.

-Rest from what? And if he will come …

-I will call you. Don't worry.

I am not worried; just confused about you and my work, guys. I experienced a lot of businessmen, but this is a kind of King Service, and Kings would never go for such meetings. It's a mess of 2 different types of high individuals. Anyways, who am I to judge? Not my life and not my money.

The return trip to the airport was fraught with tension. The car, a luxury vehicle ill-suited for the rough terrain, shuddered with every bump and dip in the road. The driver, a young man whose knuckles shone white on the steering wheel, exuded nervousness. The car cannot shake; it doesn't matter what is happening outside. Yes, that is the rule.

-You shouldn't bring such an expensive car here,- the WS rumbled, his voice heavy with displeasure. - Next time, send something more suitable.

-Yes, sir, - the driver stammered. - It will be done.

-This isn't the first time I've mentioned it,- the WS pressed. Who is your boss, anyway?

A surge of initiative, unexpected and unwelcome, flared within me. Raising my voice for the first time, trying to be helpful at least here, I interjected:

-I'll handle it, sir. I'll make sure the head of the department is informed.

-Oh, okey.

This, it seemed, was the crux of the problem. No matter where in India the WS traveled, his vehicle had to accompany him for city commutes, airport transfers, factory visits, and the whole gamut. This meant the driver often had to arrive a day or two in advance, making grueling journeys to ensure the car was readily available. For trips exceeding twelve hours, a two-driver system was employed to guarantee the fastest possible arrival. The driver currently at the wheel had likely spent the entire night navigating treacherous roads to meet their arrival time and would repeat the feat upon their departure by aircraft. What about that?

Finally, the comforting familiarity of the airplane interior greeted us. Spotting Behemoth in the galley area, I practically skipped over, relief washing over me. Slipping off my shoes with a sigh, I was about to head towards my designated area at the back when a hand clamped onto my arm. It was the WS.

He leaned in close, his voice a low murmur, and whispered something that sent a jolt of terror through me. He ordered me to bend over and whispered. The rest of the sentence hung in the air, unfinished.

"Don't be so shy," the WS murmured, his voice a husky whisper against my ear.

Confusion washed over me. "Sorry?" I stammered.

"Did you understand me?" he pressed his gaze intent.

"Yes..." I breathed, the single word heavy with uncertainty. Yes? Was that truly the only response I could muster? Frustration bubbled within me, laced with a growing sense of unease. What exactly did he expect of me?

Seeking refuge, I retreated to the back of the aircraft, the WS's cryptic words echoing in my mind. "I should text her. What the hell does it mean? Was I overthinking things? Yeah?! Again??" Perhaps fatigue had dulled my judgment. All I craved was the comfort of my bed, a sanctuary away from the absurdity that had become my reality.

For the rest of the flight, I remained glued near the table, a silent observer. The WS, an enigma shrouded in shadow, continued his solitary game of cards, his every move calculated and precise. A strange sense of foreboding settled over me, a premonition of things to come.

The moment the aircraft touched down, the WS practically bolted from his seat, his form disappearing through the airplane door with an urgency that bordered on desperation. My "interesting" day had finally reached its end. Mammon, waiting for us near the aircraft like a weary soldier returning from a grueling campaign, offered a tight smile that failed to reach his eyes. Something was amiss, a discordant note in the carefully orchestrated performance. The question was, what?

-Will I accompany him?

-He is probably reaching pink hell in the next 10 minutes. So, my answer is no.

-Oh.. god, okay.

-But you will travel again tomorrow.

-Again?

-Same timing. To the factory.

-Oh, okay. No issues.. – "No issues? Are you mad, girl?"

-All the same, so don't worry. Behemoth will be with you. Let's take some tea before reaching the Pink Hell. Are you ok with it?

-Yes, sure.

Mammon and Behemoth's friendly demeanor offered a welcome balm to my frayed nerves. Finally, nestled in a cozy Indian cafe, the aroma of spiced milk tea filling the air, I found myself engaged in a pleasant conversation. Despite the lingering fatigue, a sense of normalcy washed over me - the simple act of venturing out freely, of being amongst regular people, felt like a forgotten luxury. How much I missed it, going out without control and not alone.

Day 2

"Wake up, girl, just wake up; I know it's hard, and you want to sleep till the afternoon, but you have to wake up. Check your WhatsApp messages. It always helps you."

Memories From Whatsapp Chat GofG 7 Am: Evidence Exhibit 20b Police Report.

"-Hi, how are you? How was it yesterday?

-Weird, G..

-Why?

-He asked not to be shy. What am I supposed to do? Dance??

-Who asked? Where is your flight to Pink Hell 2? And will you be there in a helicopter?

-Mine? What? No idea, no one told me.

-Okay, I am not sure. Pack your bags you'll be going to Pink Hell 2. At 10 AM departure. Car, then aircraft, then helicopter.

-Honey, I will be home at 12 in the night .. tell it to me later."

My body jolted awake, a rude awakening fueled by the events of yesterday. Escaping the confines of the bed, I found myself drawn towards the bathroom. A touch of concealer was a feeble attempt to mask the dark circles under my eyes, a testament to the sleep that had eluded me. My mind, already bracing for the onslaught of the day, mirrored the relentless gear shifting within my body. Coffee. Coffee was the only thing that stood between me and utter collapse.

By eight o'clock, I had locked the door behind me, the silence broken only by the determined clink of my heels against the floor. My first order of business - a potent cup of coffee, the lifeblood of survival.

The morning air here was reminiscent of early summer back home - crisp and invigorating, sending a pleasant jolt through my system. The weak winter sun peeked through the clouds, offering a fleeting promise of warmth.

The next few hours unfolded with a nightmarish sense of deja vu. The same meeting point, the same car door opening with the manager holding my ticket, the same retinue of butlers, and the ever-present flight attendant gracing the aircraft. Seeking refuge, I retreated to the back, collapsing thankfully into a seat near the dining table. Takeoff. A precious three minutes of respite as the cityscape below dissolved into a tapestry of morning clouds. But even as I gazed out the window, a knot of apprehension tightened in my gut. What new trials awaited me today? And how long would I be able to maintain this façade of normalcy?

The two-plus-hour flight felt like an eternity, my mind churning with anxieties about the day's "adventures." Internal unease and the sheer number of employees surrounding the WS made any direct communication a conscious effort to avoid.

Last night, sleep had remained a distant dream. Instead, I had poured my energy into a comprehensive report detailing my observations on the VIP services. Strengths, weaknesses, everything was meticulously documented. The ridiculous umbrella debacle, the car troubles, even the subtle but offensive issue of the flight attendant's "stockiness" - all masquerading as concerns about "grooming discrepancies." Yes, I knew I could be a thorn in the side at times, a relentless stickler for perfection. I could only imagine the silent grumbling my presence incited. The theoretical annoyance of the office had now been translated into a very real, practical experience for them. But changing my nature was simply not an option. Precision, it seemed, was the only currency I truly valued. I can't change myself – perfectionism is a priority. You can hate me also, I don't mind.

Upon landing, I braced myself for the familiar sprint behind the WS, a personal marathon I was determined to win.

Thankfully, the day itself proved less taxing than yesterday. Confined within a nondescript building near the factory, we simply awaited the conclusion of the WS's meeting, lunch, and then, the inevitable return to the Pink Hell.

-Hey, you should eat something.

-No, I am fine, I think.

- Sandwich at list. It is a long day; don't challenge your health.

-Mhm…

- Take it and head to the back kitchen area. Get some rest.

Rest? From what? Still, the break was welcome. We had a brief respite, a rare moment free from the constant shadowing. I sank into a creaky chair, wincing as my skirt brushed against the dusty surface.

The peace was shattered all too soon.

-Are you done? Come here, hurry! - the urgency in Behemoth's voice sent a jolt of apprehension through me.

-What? Now? - I stammered.

-Hurry! - he barked. - The WS wants to show you something.

My heart hammered against my ribs. "Oh God, now?" I bolted to his side, finding the WS standing near the building's main entrance. He stared straight ahead, yet I could feel his gaze burning into me. We began to walk, me trailing silently behind him. Reaching a corner, he grasped the hefty wooden handle of a door.

-This is my bedroom, - he announced, his voice devoid of warmth, - In case I need to rest after meetings.

-Noted, sir, - I managed, my voice barely above a whisper.

-Listen, - he continued, gesturing towards a wardrobe and bathroom. - I have some clothes here. They need to be checked next time.

-Yes, sir, - I mumbled, the meaning of his words sinking in.

A curt nod, and he disappeared into the bathroom. Knowing my cue, I started to move towards the doorway, intending to give him some privacy. But before I could take a single step, a disgruntled voice boomed from behind the closed door.

-Why did you leave?

-Sir, I thought you were finished, - I stammered.

-You should always be near me. Did you understand or not? Let's go.

-Yes, sir, - I choked out.

-If you want to work as my assistant, - he leaned in, his voice a low growl, -you have to know everything about me.

He slowed his steps, his presence looming large behind me. My face, burning with a mixture of confusion and fear, remained stubbornly downcast. A hand clamped onto my back, sending a fresh wave of shivers down my spine.

-We should not have any barriers, - he whispered, his voice husky and laced with something dark. - Did you understand me?

-A-um…- my voice caught in my throat.

-Do you understand what I'm telling you? - His voice brooked no argument.

-Yes… yes, - I stammered, my voice barely audible.

-Repeat it, - he commanded.

-That we should not have any barriers, - I mumbled, the words tasting like ash in my mouth.

-Correct. Let's go. - He released me, and I retreated to the main entrance, frozen near it. My gaze fixed on a point beyond the area. The echo of his words hung heavy in the air, their true meaning sending a tremor of confusion through me.

-Mari, let's go. We are leaving back to the aircraft

-Yes, coming… yeah

-Are you okay?

-Sure. Let's go. Let's go nowhere …

The return flight to the Pink Hell was a tempestuous journey, a battle raging within me that mirrored the turbulence outside. Exhaustion, confusion, and a gnawing sense of unease gnawed at my insides. Following takeoff, I took up my usual position near the sofa, a silent sentinel awaiting his every whim. How utterly pathetic it felt. Behemoth and Mr. Marbach stood behind me, their presence adding to the cramped quarters of the small aircraft.

-Perhaps one of us could sit down? -I ventured, my voice barely above a whisper.

A curt "No" cut me off before I could finish.

-But…- I stammered, frustration prickling at my skin.

-No, ma'am, - butler countered, his voice leaving no room for argument.

Defeated, I turned back, only to be met with a new sight. A man, old and vulgar with eyes like predatory rats, leered at the flight attendant, his wrinkled hand hovering inappropriately low on her back. A whispered conversation, a head bowed in submission, and then the inevitable - the cabin door shutting with a finality that mirrored the closing of a cage. Heavy curtains descended, shrouding the scene in unsettling darkness.

I spun around, my face burning with indignation, desperate for answers. But the two butlers, educated and seemingly decent men, stared resolutely at the floor like chastised children. Not a single one dared to meet my gaze, to offer a shred of explanation or even a flicker of silent support. The message was clear - I wasn't a colleague but rather another pawn in the WS's twisted game, a doll awaiting his cruel amusement. Were they afraid to acknowledge my awareness of the situation? Or perhaps ashamed, complicit even, in the blatant degradation unfolding just beyond the curtained threshold?

For the next two hours, we remained frozen in a tableau of silent tension. They, waiting for the uncomfortable charade to end, a charade they could then pretend never happened. I should desperately start formulating an escape plan, a strategy to extricate myself from this gilded cage.

The door finally creaked open, the "king" swaggering past, his dismissive glance sending us scrambling out of his path. With that, I concluded my silent conversation with my so-called colleagues, the weight of the situation pressing down on me.

This entire scene was an outrage. Why hadn't someone spoken up for the flight attendant? Why hadn't someone told her she didn't have to comply with such demeaning requests? You, the strong, capable woman you are, deserved so much better. There was no justification for this blatant disregard for reducing a human being to a mere object. Don't let anyone tell you otherwise - no one enjoys having their value diminished or their work belittled. Think of your mother, and your wife - how they react when their efforts go unappreciated. This was far worse, a deliberate assault on her dignity, her very sense of self.

The bathroom door clicked shut, followed by the sound of movement. Curiosity, laced with a hint of apprehension, spurred me to turn around. The WS emerged, his hand clamped tightly on Mr. Marbach's shoulder. The butler's entire body seemed to shrink under his predatory gaze, his large frame hunched over in a posture of abject submission. Fear, naked and raw, radiated from him, his eyes wide with terror. It was a chilling display of dominance, a master tightening his grip on a cowering pawn. And for the first time, a new question gnawed at me – what monstrous power did the WS possess that could instill such abject fear in a grown man? "All good, Mr. Marbach?" the WS inquired, his voice dripping with a false sense of concern.

"Yes, sir," Mr. Marbach stammered, his voice barely audible.

A curt nod and the WS retreated to his seat, a smug smile playing on his lips. The entire display had the unsettling air of a cruel joke, a performance meant to intimidate and subjugate.

My blood ran cold. What exactly was that? A veiled threat? A chilling reminder of his absolute power? No, I realized with a jolt it wasn't meant for me. I was, as always, the oblivious doll, the silent witness to his twisted games. Mr. Marbach, however, was a different story. Fear, raw and unconcealed, clung to him like a shroud.

This only strengthened my resolve. I had to speak with G as soon as possible. She needed to know what was transpiring within these gilded walls, the darkness that festered beneath the surface of wealth and power.

Memories From Whatsapp Chat GofG 11 Pm: Evidence Exhibit 20b Police Report.

"-I will be fired... Soon.

-Why? Don't say that. Your bag for tomorrow's flight to Pink Hell 2 is placed in your room.

-Yes, I will be. I will die this week. He already told me. His plans for me. Call me.

-Tell me. I am in the car. Is it okay if I text?...

-He gonna fuck me

-I'll call you after landing then... Why?? What happened??

-I need to sleep. Will talk tomorrow.

No, tell me what happened.

He showed me his bedroom near the factory and said that we should not have any barriers and that if I wanted to work like his PA, I had to know everything about him and touched my back.

-Are you sure you didn't understand it wrong?

I cannot make the night shift...

Are you sure you didn't understand it wrong?

"We should not have any barriers."- Explain it in another way...

He already told me...

Who?? What plans did he tell you?

-The WS...I told you.

I cannot make the night shift.

But he sleeps; I was doing the night shift, too...

-Oh, year, with his son. Please.

-Okey, maybe work-related

-It means only one...He fucked the stewardess. Come on...

-Okey, don't think about it. I think it was only with the stewardess...

I don't think he will do anything to you. Don't think that much... There are butlers also; He won't do anything to you in front of them...And the night shift he will be sleeping.

-Oh, come on... He did it with the stewardess in front of us...

-But she is not a part of the company. You are, don't get scared.

-Just upset. That final is near.

-Why is it near? You're going to leave?

-I have no choice.."

Day 3

<u>Memories From Whatsapp GofG 6 Am: Evidence Exhibit 20b Police Report.</u>

"-Behemoth called me

Asked if I wrote smth about stewardess.

-I didn't get... What? Wrote where?

-He asked not to tell anyone about the stewardess.

-Oh, okey. Don't tell anyone that you already told me. Don't worry. Because he doesn't want anyone to know about all that."

Does a rabbit understand when someone is hunting them? Do they always check and observe for dangers and predators? A rabbit was born as a victim and is constantly on high alert; their senses are tuned to detect any potential threat. Every rustle in the leaves, every snap of a twig, sends a surge of adrenaline through their system, a primal urge for survival.

But what happens when the predator is not a mindless beast but a cunning human? Humans, unlike animals, possess the ability to deceive, manipulate, to lull their prey into a false sense of security. The rabbit, in its naivety, might not realize the danger until it's too late, until the cage door slams shut.

However, you are not a rabbit. You are a human endowed with reason and foresight. You can analyze situations, predict strategies, and take steps to avoid becoming trapped. Unlike the rabbit, entirely dependent on instinct, you have the power to fight back, to outsmart your pursuer, don't you?

Knock in the door

"Ma'am," the voice started, "the car with catering and provisions is leaving for the airport in the next twenty minutes. Do you have any bags to send?"

"Yes, one minute," I managed, a flurry of activity erupting within me.

"Sure, take your time," the voice replied with practiced courtesy.

Moments later, I emerged, clutching my bag. "Here," I said, handing it over.

"Thank you," he replied, disappearing. "Please be ready for travel in one hour," he called back over his shoulder.

"Noted," I muttered, the weight of the upcoming trip settling on my shoulders.

The rule was clear: no personal belongings when accompanying the First Family. Phones became invisible companions, tucked away and silenced. For extended trips, belongings were entrusted to colleagues who would arrive at the aircraft beforehand, ensuring a smooth and seamless transition.

Today, however, a new kind of awareness bloomed within me as I stood by the car, waiting for the WS. The seemingly mundane actions around me took on a new significance.

The driver meticulously polished the car's mirrors, the manager leaping to open the door for a butler carrying a minifridge -

all of it seemed imbued with a sinister undercurrent. A new color suffused my world, a shade of crimson, a stark warning sign.

The change extended to the aircraft as well. The sight of the familiar flight attendant sent a fresh wave of pain through me. There she was, fluttering around the WS, offering a welcoming drink, a silent expectation hanging heavy in the air. Disgust churned in my stomach.

I retreated to the back, my sanctuary near the dining table. A pointed silence greeted me, the butlers already present. Their lack of acknowledgment from yesterday still rankled, their dismissive behavior a fresh wound.

The takeoff was a sensory assault. Exhaustion from the limited rest, coupled with the jarring shift in my perception of reality, left my stomach churning. A wave of nausea washed over me, forcing me to squeeze my eyes shut and focus on deep, controlled breaths. How I loathed this feeling of helplessness, this surrender to my body's involuntary reactions.

Just as I began to regain some semblance of composure, Behemoth materialized beside me, his voice laced with a new urgency.

-He wants you to serve breakfast.

-What?! - The word exploded from my lips, a mixture of disbelief and indignation.

-Is it ready to serve? Have you heated everything? - I pressed.

-She did it, - he mumbled, gesturing towards the flight attendant, - The flight attendant.

-Okay, let's start, - she barked, leaving no room for argument.

My hands trembled slightly as I lifted the first dish onto the tray. Moving on autopilot, I reached the dining area, where the table had been transformed - adorned with crisp white linen, gleaming cutlery, and a dazzling array of china. Silently, I placed the prepared dishes on the table, my face a mask of silent protest.

-Where is the sauce?

-Sorry?

-Whe-re is the sau-ce?

-I will be back in a minute, Sir.

I went back to the kitchen and, with a cold voice, asked to request subjects from butlers and the FA.

-Guys, where is the souse?

-Oh, shit. I didn't heat it.

-So do it now.

-Wait, just wait …

-No, I have to inform him. He can't just wait.

-I am giving it; just wait, please!

I took that big plate full of weird red souse and went back to the dining area. With the same facial expression, I placed it on the table, waiting for his reaction or permission to get the hell out of there.

-You see, just one small mistake, and my breakfast mood is spoiled.

-I am sorry.

-No, understand. Look here, these buns are already cold now and if I ask you to go and reheat it, my sous will be cold also. Do you understand me?

-Yes, sir.

-This is not your fault. I just teach you not to make the same mistake.

-Sure, sir.

-Is it so hard to do it properly from the beginning?

-No, sir.

-Call Behemoth. I don't like the taste.

-Sure, sir.

-Did you understand what I said?

-Yes.

-Am I asking something impossible?

-No, Sir.

A dismissive wave of his hand sent a fresh wave of anger coursing through me. "Get out," it seemed to say, "I am done with you."

I retreated to the back, finding the butler. "Your turn for a serving slap, it seems," I announced, a touch of sardonic humor lacing my voice. Despite my frustration, I couldn't help but empathize with him. Three grown butlers to serve one measly breakfast - a task so simple, so utterly pointless.

Behemoth stormed back into the kitchen, the dishes clattering precariously in his hands. His mood was predictably foul. There was nothing I could do to offer comfort or a solution, and frankly, I didn't care. My concerns were far more pressing - the metaphorical cage had a loose bar, and escape, however unlikely, seemed a possibility. I am a rabbit who has to find a way from unlocked stuck as soon as possible.

Finally, after what felt like an eternity, we reached a small airport. Our mode of transportation was about to shift - a helicopter would whisk us closer to the Pink Hell 2, a luxurious estate nestled amidst the lush embrace of the mountains. Apparently, a five-hour drive was deemed an unacceptable delay for the First Family. That's why we were relocating to drive peacefully for only 20 minutes.

The helicopter beckoned, a gleaming metal dragonfly promising a swift journey. I clutched the mini-fridge tightly, following close behind the WS and Behemoth. Another butler would handle the five-hour trek by car, transporting the rest of the catering and luggage. A pang of envy, a desperate yearning for freedom, shot through me. If only I could be the one driving away with him.

-Behemoth, who is going by car? – WS addressed the butler curiously.

-Mr. Marbach, Sir

-Will he be alone?

-Yes, Sir

-But won't he be bored all the way there? - the WS inquired.

-No, sir, - Behemoth assured him. - He'll be fine.

The concern for Mr. Marbach's entertainment during the car trip was puzzling, to say the least.

Reaching the helicopter, Behemoth offered me a hand to assist me in boarding. Protocol dictated that the BPA sit opposite or near the WS. However, I took a seat in the back row, a subtle act of defiance.

Behemoth, clearly unhappy, shook his head and gestured for me to move. "Sit properly!" he hissed.

The WS entered the cabin with the agility of a rock climber, taking the seat closest to me. He turned to Behemoth.

-Are you sure he won't be bored on the drive?

-Sir, he'll be fine, - Behemoth repeated.

-Maybe you should go with him? - the WS mused.

Behemoth's glance at me at that moment was a revelation. The helicopter's passenger cabin was completely isolated from the pilots, shrouded in white canvas. We couldn't see them, and they couldn't see us. If Behemoth agreed to switch, I would be trapped alone with the WS for the next forty minutes in the deafening roar of the engine. My eyes burned with a mix of anger and fear, and my expression radiated a silent threat - dare to discuss me like this in my presence and face the consequences. My eyes were covered with blood, and my facial expression showed readiness to kill both of them.

Behemoth hesitated. "Sir, as you wish. If you want me to go, I will."

-No, I'm asking you, Behemoth.

-Sir, as you wish...

-Alright, alright, leave it. Let's go. - The WS turned away, sulking like a child denied a toy or a clueless boyfriend unable to read his girlfriend's mind. I yearned to connect with Behemoth but knew it was a lost cause. He'd avert his gaze, pretending the exchange hadn't happened. Every man for himself, that was the unspoken rule.

During the next forty minutes, I stared out the window, battling nausea brought on by an empty stomach and the sheer repugnance of my situation. Every five minutes, I'd close my eyes, willing the flight to end, yearning for a moment of respite.

Finally, we started to land in the middle of nowhere. I was trying to find the helipad or the proper pad for us, but can you imagine, instead, we touched down on a dusty, uneven school football field! A gaggle of village children, clad in pristine white shirts and shorts, spilled out onto balconies, their eyes wide with wonder. This, no doubt, would be a highlight of their childhood - a real, live helicopter hovering within ten meters, the wealthy elite disembarking. Their cheers and excited shouts filled the air.

The entire thing looked like a badly prepared spectacle. As the two drivers clumsily unfurled a red carpet - landing squarely in a puddle - I was overwhelmed with shame. We were playing royalty, indulging in a grotesque charade before a backdrop of poverty, in front of a bunch of poor barefoot kids from the small province.

We exited the helicopter and piled into a waiting white car, my apprehension escalating with each passing moment. The journey stretched before me, a winding road disappearing into a dense jungle. Small houses became increasingly scarce, replaced by thick foliage and treacherous serpentines. Finally, we crested a hill, and a vista unfolded before me a tea estate. My first stop in this personal hell.

The car screeched to a halt before the grand entrance. The WS bolted from the vehicle, disappearing into the house like a disgruntled mole. His sudden exit was a welcome reprieve, allowing me a moment to compose myself. The last thing I wanted was to draw any further attention.

-Come this way, - a voice beckoned, leading me towards the kitchen area.

-Where is my room?

-In the house.

-What?

-It's near the Wellness Room. I will show you…. you can keep your staff there.

-No, I don't want to come inside the house.

-But..

-No, please. I said I don't want to.

-What do you mean?…. Listen, we have to serve lunch. Will talk later…

"Will talk later"??? Are you joking right now with me? There are no talks that I will stay inside the house during the night.

Why am I feeling so bad?? Why it's happening, and everyone pretending that it is normal?

I started to text GofG, pushing with questions and explanations of what I should do. I don't want to be part of all this and pretend like others that it is normal.

-Mari, King Head wants to talk on the phone.

-Behemoth? I thought you were serving lunch.

-Please, take my phone, he is waiting

-Give it…

Phone talk

-What's happened in the helicopter?

-Nothing.

-He is screaming at me now! Explain what is happening. Why he is pissed off at Behemoth?

-He didn't do anything wrong! Your father wanted to stay alone with me in the helicopter. That's why he is pissed off now.

-Okey, okey. Give the phone to Behemoth.

I was staring at Behemoth's face, which was full of consternation and terror. His eyes darted around the corridor, his grip tightening on the phone he held. Sweat beaded on his brow, and his voice trembled as he stammered, "I… I assure you, sir, I haven't done anything".

I sank onto a dusty bench near the main kitchen, my stomach churning after a long shift under brutal conditions. Like an orphan, alone and exhausted, I desperately tried to quell the rising nausea. One thought hammered in my mind: "I cannot continue like this." This is what I would say if they dared to ask me to come inside the house.

The weight of doubt presses down on me, suffocating. Why am I drowning in this sea of anxieties? Did some past mistake unleash this storm, or am I simply caught in a whirlwind of my overthinking? My body simmers with unease, a counterpoint to the chilling dread that freezes my thoughts. But a flicker of hope ignites. Perhaps this is just a figment of my fear, a shadow cast by my imagination. Yet, the whispers of "what if" cling to me like cobwebs, threatening to pull me back into the darkness. What if it's a real threat? What if this storm is real?

-Mari..

"Again, you? What the hell do you want now? What did happen after 20 minutes?" -Mari, do you hear me?

-Ha? What? Sorry, what did you say?

-You have to go inside the house.

-For what?

-For your shift.

-Which shift?! We just came.

-The WS told everyone to get one out and he will pass the request from you. No one has to be inside the house.

-No.

-You have to go.

-I said no. I will not go there after what happened in the helicopter.

-Nothing happened. Don't worry, you will be fine. We are all here.

The reason why I couldn't argue with him is simple: I am a weak person when the matter of question is considering to work task. I can't say no because I was embarrassed to tell him the reason.

With silent and no comments, inexplicable aversion coiled in my gut as I approached the house's door. It's silenced a stark contrast to the storm raging inside me. Stepping over the threshold, I entered what could only be described as entering the Hell. I was greeted with a long, dimly lit corridor stretched before me, lined with doors that promised untold secrets. The first one was a bedroom and how I realized for "wellness sessions," which sent a shiver down my spine. Next was my designated "Girls room," a grim prospect considering the man I was forced to share this house with - a man whose "no one is allowed inside" rule hung heavy in the air, laced with unspoken implications.

On the left is the dining area connecting with the living room, and the last is the main bedroom. The interior was simple, with traditional elements and furniture. Opaque curtains shrouded the windows, casting rooms in an unsettling perpetual twilight. The silence was deafening, broken only by the rhythmic thud of my own heart.

-Who is there?

-It's me, Sir

-Come here

-How can I assist you?

The old man, who created a fuss about me being here, sat hunched over his phone; his gaze was glued to the screen. He was oblivious to my arrival until I cleared my throat, drawing his attention with a faint "Ahem." He looked up then, his eyes glazed with disinterest, and mumbled my instructions through pursed lips without a shred of enthusiasm:

-Check my wardrobe and remove all old oversized pants.

-Should I throw it?

-I don't know, maybe give it to workers from the tea plantation.

-Okey, I will hand over it for donation.

I started to do the requested task: In the opened wardrobe, randomly moving the hangers with different pants, trying to concentrate and understand which were old or too big, not presentable; I was arguing with my mind. Does it mean that I am overthinking? Or maybe my comments on the phone talk with the Head of Hell Departments bear fruits worthy of repentance.

Despite the churning fear in my gut, I found myself completing the mundane task. The silence was deafening, a stark contrast to the storm brewing within me. Was this a sick joke, a cruel lull before the real torment began? Or something more insidious, a deceptive calm designed to lull me into a false sense of security before the inevitable storm? However, "what" brought me to the routine work without an explanation would reveal the truth soon or later.

During the day, I stayed 20 meters behind the king and followed his movements. If he stays in the living room, reading something, for example, I have to be near the entrance door, visible and at the same time inconspicuous, so as not to annoy him with my present there.

The main actor, the WS, was out of his body, concentrating on work on his laptop and phone all day, requesting some obvious tasks for water or tea didn't match with my main questions inside my mind:" Why did he drive all servants from the house and keeps only me?"

My curiosity didn't calm down and still, I was pretending in front of everyone that I was fine. But my body was sending me signals that something was wrong; I felt like the prey of a redactor; I couldn't eat or drink and think about it or any over physical needs.

-Come.

-How can I assist you?

-Come closer... -he pulled me up, trying to hug me as if I were his old friend.

-Sir? – I moved a step back, staring at him, shocked and confused

-Hug me, come. I need a proper hug and kiss.

-Can you stop, please?

-Why?

-Why?!

-Okey, go - he waved his hand offendedly.

"What just happened?! How am I supposed to react?! How!!"

At that moment, I remained blissfully unaware that this was just the beginning. I entered the girl's room and sat down on the bed. My ordeal wouldn't start for another hour, but I was so lost in thought that I didn't realize it. I was already stuck.

***

After sunset, the dinner starts and it means that butlers who serve the food are allowed to come inside for handling. I went with big relief to the kitchen area with a face of bewilderment and hoped that I would leave this place after dinner with over workers.

-Take some food; you didn't eat anything during the day.

-I am not hungry, Behemoth...

-Eat, please; we made it for you.

He presented me with a big plastic white plate with yellow, cheesy curry cavatappi and a large soup spoon. Cavatappi is a type of pasta my mom always cooked for me with milk and sugar when I was a child. After I left home and started taking care of myself, I'd cook this simple, warm, and comforting dish whenever I felt sad or depressed. It would probably make any Italian cringe, but it always brought me a sense of home.

I took a bite but couldn't taste anything. Though I could recognize the ingredients based on my memories, the flavor was absent. I felt like a robot who could only send signals from the mouth receptors to the brain.

What's wrong with me?! Panicked, I began shoveling spoonsful of pasta into my mouth, one by one. How to stop it?! My mind couldn't accept these new sensory feelings and the altered behavior of my receptors. This unexpected change filled me with fear and pain. I found myself hating both the food and myself. No, I don't hate the food. I hate my actions and attitude to it. I hate it!

<u>Memories From Whatsapp GofG 10:13 Pm: Evidence Exhibit 20b Police Report</u>.

GofG:

"-He wanna talk with me when everyone leaves. That means you will come tomorrow and I will leave. I cannot sleep with him.

-What is going on?

When everyone leaves, mean? There is going to be someone, no??? Or only you??

-Only me

-No butlers??? Who said?

-No one. They are not allowed to come inside.

Who said?

He said

It's disgusting 2 hours ago.... He was in the washroom....And asked me to come....He was sitting on the toilet....Doing his things

And said, can you please check the night suit, like it is normal.

He wanted me to look how he shit.

-What...

-Yes.

-I don't believe this is happening for real. How creepy.

-You don't know him when he is without his son. I don't know what to do. I just wanna pack and run."

Steps behind me

-Mari, the wellness session is also finished. Help Erela to clean the room, please. Go..

-Clean the room?

-Just go into the house.

I went inside the house and turned to the first room. A young, beautiful woman dressed in a black uniform was collecting nervously white sheets and towels from the massage table. I knew her; I'd met her before. She's a truly noble, self-made woman who knows her goals and pursues them relentlessly. She exudes the strong energy of a real businesswoman. Her crystal blue eyes, always full of power and unwavering confidence, seemed dimmed this evening.

-Do you need any help?

-Oh, hi Mari.. No, it's fine. Thank you.

-Are you okey?

-Ahm.. yes, I think.. but not really. He is pushing me... I don't know if I can handle it.

-Pushing for what?

-He was trying to kiss me aggressively during the massage treatment.

-Are you serious?

-Yes…and they were asking me to stay here in the house. I don't want to. I need rest. I have to stay in my room, alone and out of work. This is ridiculous.

-They told me I will stay here.

-No, you can ask the manager to send you to the hotel. You don't need to stay here.

-There is no BPA here; I am the only one who can do the shift.

-But there are a lot of male butlers. They can do the night shift or whatever is required.

-The boss wants a woman in the house.

-You don't need to stay here if you don't want to.

-I think so, too.

-Get my number and text me if something happens.

-Take rest.…

We entered the girl's room, and she gathered her bag, visibly relieved to be finally leaving this place. I sat down on the bed, unsure of what to do next.

-Text me if something happens. We are here; you are not alone.

-Okey … thank you…

-Buy, love

-Good night.

The door had closed, and a deathly silence enveloped the room. I could hear some commotion in the kitchen, but the rest of the house was quiet. I must close my door and try to get some sleep. But what am I supposed to do if he asks for something? Will I hear his request from the further room? Can I pretend that I didn't? Can I stay here till the morning stuff will come? Is anybody in the kitchen during the night? If he will ask me for food or masala tea? I know how to do it, but still. Is there anybody? Anyone?

"Everyone go home! What are you doing here?! Go sleep! I don't want anyone here. Go home!"

The back door slammed shut, and hurried footsteps echoed through the house. I heard metallic clanging but couldn't understand what it was. So, I decided to get out of my safe space and check what it was.

The WS stood by the terrace exit, securing the metal lockers on the door. He then proceeded to close all the interior doors within the house. It's 3 doors. Feeling confused, I wondered why the doors needed to be closed if the area was secure and there were no animals around. Am I overthinking it again???

-They left home, - a voice came behind my back when I was staring at the kitchen door.

-Sir?

-They left home, come to my room I need to talk with you.

-But..

-What?

-But..

-What? I don't hear you, - he said and came closer. He grabbed my arm and moved his face close to my mouth, pretending to understand what I was asking.

-Sir, I left my charger with Erela. Can I get and take it?

-They left already.

-No, she texted me she is here, - don't say it! If she is not there, you will come without a charger. He will catch you on the liar.

-Okey, go and come back.

He opened the back door, and I almost flew out of the house. I put on some pink slippers; thanks for the rule "no stockings." It was easy, and I started to run around the back area. It was dark no one was around, they could not leave so fast!

I went deeper inside the staff area and heard someone laugh. Finally! I saw Erela around butlers and came directly to her.

-I can't stay there. Something is wrong, - I whispered to her.

-What happened? Come with me to the hotel.

-I am scared…

-Don't worry, nothing will happen to you. Go back, Mari, - Behemoth addressed me with a tired and confused smile.

The guy who was today fucked and thrown from the house because he went inside the helicopter with us, the guy who told me, "Don't write anything about stewardess in your report," now he is so confident and almost making excuses for my worries. How am I supposed to react to that?

-Mari, go. You will be fine, - he convinced me again louder.

How do the hell he can be so sure?! I am looking now stupid in front of everyone and not professional. There is nothing professional inside the house. They have to understand me, have to!

Feeling utterly lost, I observed the others seated in the cab and clinging to my fading possibility of altering fate. However, paralyzed by fear and the potential humiliation of appearing foolish and hysterical, I remained silent and immobile. I didn't want to go back; I was ready to sleep outside on the boxes near the kitchen area. I meticulously prepared my speech, filled with professional reasons and explanations for why I would not go to his room for a talk. If he had questions, he could ask me here. My mind raced, my hands shook, and I paced from left to right, rehearsing the ill-fated speech and feeling a surge of disgust.

The quieter I entered the house, the less likely I was to be caught. I brushed my hands off and quietly lowered the doorknob. However, as I took my first step, the motion sensor light switched on, exposing my movements. I sprinted to the "girl's room" door and, with a sigh of relief, began to open it. Even if he came, I wouldn't answer or open the door.

-You are back, finally... You forgot to close the back door lockers.

-Sorry, Sir

-Go close the door properly, remove your uniform and makeup... and come to my room. We have to talk.

This surge of realization crushed any lingering hope that I was overthinking the situation. "How stupid you are, girl...how stupid..." My brain felt numb, a void of emotion or thought, as I stared blankly at the door. I was paralyzed, wishing I could simply disappear. It was a shot that I couldn't handle.

Moments later, I saw his back as he walked towards the door to lock it. Locked! Wake up, girl! He then disappeared into the house, probably going to his bedroom, saying something, but I could only hear indistinct noises in my head.

Instinctively, I entered the girl's room, grabbed my phone from the bed, and headed straight to the bathroom. Locking the door behind me, I collapsed onto the floor. Panic surged through me as I opened Google Maps, desperately trying to locate myself and the nearest city or airport. Airport! I needed to get to the airport. Six hours drive? How could you forget?! There weren't even any towns nearby. With shaking hands, I opened the Uber app and frantically started calling for a cab, willing it to take me anywhere, just not here. But the reality was bleak. Walking wasn't an option. I was stranded in the middle of nowhere, surrounded by forest or plantations. No towns for miles, a six-hour drive to the airport, and no cabs available. What is in my head?

I am a foreign girl; I don't know where I am or anyone who can help me. I am trapped with a psycho in his house, a house guarded by his unapproachable security who wouldn't help me, and even worse. Maybe they will finish what he will start to do with me. Why remove makeup? For what? No evidence on the pillow or bed linen? Should I call someone? Whom? Police? Oh, yeah, and what you will say? There is a rich guy and I am in his house, and what? What next? No, I will not go out of this bathroom. What is this? What is wrong with you?? Can you calm down?

Overthinking? Again? Does it look like overthinking for you?! Control yourself, idiot. Control and think. Text Erela, text her. And what will she do? The way locals react to our behavior and fears means they know and would not help. I remember the butler's face on the airplane that day. Back then, their averted gaze seemed like mere fear. Now, however, it would signify something far deeper and more unsettling.

<u>Memories From Whatsapp Erela: Evidence Exhibit 20b Police Report</u>.

"*-Fuck*

He told me to remove my makeup and come to his room.

This is not funny. 12:20 AM

-Are you okey? 12:36 AM"

"*LUISA:*

-I don't know what to do

-Did he call you?

-Yes, No one is here

-Omg..

-He said to remove makeup??

-Just see what he wants.

Remove makeup. What the fuck??

This guy, he is insane?

But did you ask him: Please, Sir, advise me what you will require.

Just play stupid.

-He said I will talk with you, come on…

-Ok, just listen to what he wants to tell you. You can go to talk, then if he does something weird you leave the room with an excuse.

-Why? It's crazy.

-I know, babe, it's weird. Fucking bastard.

-I cannot come again. I am scared.

-Don't be, keep the phone always with you in the pocket. Don't leave your room. 12:28 AM

-All good? I am worried about you. 2:22 AM"

<u>**Memories From Whatsapp GofG: Evidence Exhibit 20b Police Report*</u>.

-Can you act sick? Like you are not feeling well and cannot be there at night today. Like very sick. So that they remove you and keep sneezing and coughing.

-Who? No one is here!! He asked them to leave; he was crazy. I am sitting in my room, and I am scared.... Really... What time are you arriving tomorrow?

Missed voice call at 12:44 AM

-Sorry, I was in the car. I will be afternoon by the time we come."

***

"This part was incredibly difficult for me to write. For more than 2 months, I struggled to force myself to sit down and focus. Was it harder to dredge up all these abominable memories I hate so much, or was it the overwhelming feelings they bring back? Or maybe embarrassing to open the closed wardrobe. I know I have to face them and finally let go. But even after more than 1 year of therapy and treatment, I still burn inside from vomit shit and hellish pain remembering these days. Sometimes, I think these embarrassing struggles will always be inside till the end of my life. Accepting it happened is still impossible for me. I just want to be normal again, not shattered.

One of my therapists suggested that I write it all down on paper. Imagine all of those thoughts and feelings confined to the pages, no longer swirling around in your head. Now I feel stuck, perhaps even afraid of reliving the memories from that month."

Struggling to articulate what happened with my mind and body that night in the bathroom of the girl's room. Words fail me to describe the chaotic mess of shame, pain, mud, and utter disgust. Perhaps my mind was in self-preservation mode, desperately seeking explanations. Why? Because it's easier and more comfortable to craft a secure illusion and adapt to a new reality. I am an unbearably weak-willed person with a spineless, suspicious, feeble, overly sensitive character. I'd constructed a persona of a confident, experienced, and strong woman – a carefully crafted mask, I believed.

This situation has simply destroyed the illusion. I haven't had the chance to confront it before. I felt treated and danger first time in my life being completely alone in a foreign country. Always traveling alone, enjoying this beautiful world, meeting amazing nationalities, and experiencing their cultures was the stupidest shit I've ever done for myself.

"Look at you, hiding in a bathroom from your boss. You came to this company, you traveled to these jungles, and you came inside the house. You had a chance to avoid all this mess. Your mind sends you hundreds of signals that something is wrong from the beginning. Why were you so blind?? Busy to enjoy your life? Get it? Enjoy it! Do you deserve it for your past actions? Probably… unresponsible movements around the world alone, maybe that married guy 8 years ago, maybe that stolen dress when I was 16, maybe my previous life? Was I a bad person in my past life? Have I done some heinous act and now I am getting justice? Maybe I was the same as him, hunting and raping girls. And now I get this weak character and another role in the play. But even if it was, I don't remember it. I don't!! Why do I have to struggle today? What has been done wrong? "

Sitting on the cold floor with my arms wrapped around my legs and my claws digging into my skin, I was swaying from side to side. The questions were increasing in my mind; I felt how they would explode soon from my mouth in a terrible scream. My breathing quickened, and the feeling of anxiety steadily intensified. No matter what I tried, nothing seemed to help. Panicking, I didn't know what to do. I lurched to my knees, clutching my stomach. I am sick, it's sick, I want to vomit. I crawled to the toilet and vomited up the cheesy pasta I'd eaten earlier. My vomit was continuing next 20 minutes as my stomach probably thought to find more food there; it was a vomiting reflex that was constantly repeating and didn't give me a chance to breathe. My head spun so unbearably that I was sure I'd faint any second.

"Did I close the door? If I faint, I don't want him to find me; I can't faint. No! Please get up, don't do it with me right now."

Shivering uncontrollably, I whispered a desperate plea to myself, "Calm down, calm down. All symptoms worsened significantly. A wave of nausea hit me, and I vomited a yellow, bitter liquid with intensified pain in the stomach and burning under the left rib. It was the bile. I sat on the floor, feeling a wave of relief wash over me after that hellish ordeal. Tears welled up in my eyes, and the intense pain radiating from my stomach forced me to lie down. Curling into a fetal position, I clutched my knees and sobbed hysterically.

I was tired of thinking of this place, of my messy worries, the pressure around me. And it's only been three days since my shifts started. My last free days. I don't want to put myself through it anymore.

I knew I should get up from the cold floor and do something, but my body felt like it was stuck. I tried to move my hand, but it wouldn't respond. My brain was sending signals to my muscles, but they weren't firing. Even breathing felt like an enormous effort, and the thought of any further movement seemed impossible and unnecessary. Look at you; you gave up when the fight didn't even start. How weak-willed and amoebic. Hey, did you hear it? Someone knocking on the door, wake up! Peace of shit hopelessness!

Slavish Humility

I bolted upright, grabbed a towel, and rushed out of the bathroom after wetting it. I was hoping that my pathetic snot-puke face would help me to get out of it. I had no smart plan or professional explanation, I even didn't know what was waiting for me behind this door. I just wanted it to finish and get out of this place as soon as possible.

-Are you sleeping? – he opened the door.

-I don't want to work here.

-Are you crying?

-Can I just go?

-Don't be silly. Take rest now and don't worry, no one will come inside the house till 10 AM - I stared at him, confusion etched on my face. I don't remember his facial expression, only the laughing intonation in the sentence. He turned and added, - Come in the morning when you wake up. Good night, silly.

The moment he left, I felt like I was frozen in time. Then, it dawned on me: he had opened the door I had just closed. This meant the door wouldn't stay shut. Furthermore, his reaction led me to understand he was prepared for my behavior, he wasn't surprised. He plays with me.

That night transformed something within me. It wasn't until six months later, searching for a starting point, that I understood. Every time people asked why I didn't leave that night, I delved deep within myself, seeking answers. It's easy to judge or dispense useless advice from the outside. None of these people truly know how they would react or behave in a similar situation. I don't blame them; I was the same.

"According to research in the journal Jackson Health System:" Every 98 seconds women are sexually assaulted and it takes weeks, years to tell someone about it: friends, family, police."

So, what happened to me? Researching the psychological conditions of sexual assault victims provided many answers explaining my actions, thoughts, and behaviors, but not a complete picture. Age, social status, childhood experiences, religion, and education can all influence how someone reacts, but many survivors also share common experiences.

My sole reason for typing my experience is to find answers and reclaim my happiness and my normal life. Right now, I feel numb, merely existing rather than truly living, and I hope sharing my story and thoughts can help potential victims avoid similar mistakes...

***

So, returning to that night, I remember my mind felt utterly drained, and my brain was useless. My instincts took over, the primal urge of an herbivore mammal: survival. I stumbled into the bathroom, seeking my reflection in the mirror. My face was swollen, and I turned on the cold water, splashing it on my face with raw force. I brushed my teeth and attempted to apply makeup and style my hair, but my bloodshot eyes betrayed the truth of my health and emotional state.

At that moment, my thoughts were consumed by the next steps. On autopilot, I retrieved a fresh black uniform from my luggage, carefully removing the old one before putting it on. Finally, I donned the white gloves and stood near the door inside the room.

Propped against the small table beside the door, I waited. I waited for his arrival to question my absence from the morning "talk," the arrival of the kitchen staff and butler to begin their shifts, and Erela for the morning wellness session. It was approximately 3 am when I caught that table, and till 9 am, I didn't make any movements.

For some time, I kept falling asleep and woke up from a feeling of fear that someone was near me. My brain was my biggest enemy that night; my mind seemed to work against me. I suspect it waited for me to fall into a deep sleep before sending horrifying dreams of real-life dangers. Jolting awake, I'd scan the room for any sign of someone near me. Whispers behind the door sometimes added to my terror, blurring the line between dream and reality. Occasionally, the dreams felt so vivid that I was convinced they were real, only to realize with a jolt that I was still asleep, exhausted, and unable to wake myself truly.

I was used to sleeping in uncomfortable positions in my past in civil aviation. I remember those nightmarish return flights. Direct flights are always a breeze, but when you're returning home at 5 or 6 am – prime sleep time- and you are restricted from sitting in the pax area, you get creative. I'd head to the galley (kitchen) area, perch near the kettles, and pretend to be writing something. In reality, I was catching sleep. The first time is the hardest because your body naturally wants to collapse. It takes three or four deep falling asleep to adjust, straighten your posture, and finally fall asleep standing.

In the morning time, memories from the past surfaced, allowing me to fall asleep for a few hours. Around 8 AM, I woke up with a knot of worry in my stomach. I finally was able to get in touch with reality, so I took my phone and texted to girls. I wasn't ready to discuss what happened with me, and I even regret mentioning the embarrassing shit from yesterday.

Erela WhatsApp messages:

-Hey, good morning. This is my first and last night with him. The house door will be closed till your arrival.

-I will arrive a 9 AM.

-Okey.

So, I need to wait only one hour, and I am saved. I will not be alone, and he will not dare to do anything with me. The question of my leaving is staying open till I will not understand how I can do it safely for me.

I remember a weird situation that also happened yesterday in pink hell. I received a message from the housekeeping department that they needed to come inside my room and do some pest control or cleaning. Also, I received a message from Luisa, the BPA who left there, telling me that a lot of people were inside my room, so that means they already allowed themselves to get inside and just did a protocol procedure by texting me. I requested Luisa to get my wallet and documents from the room just in case someone decided to touch my luggage.

Now, the question is pending in my mind: Was it deliberate? I can't help but wonder why only my room was under pest control. Did they plan for me not to return, to disappear, or something else entirely? Did they take out my stuff? If something really happens to me, Luisa has my documents and defiantly she will understand that I cannot leave without them. Will she do something? Will she try to find me or report it to the police? I don't know that girl a lot, but the way how girls are disappearing from this Pink Hell can give her doubts that something happened to me. Girls typically come and go every week and it means no one will pay attention to my missing.

Voice behind the door

-Hello??

He was awake, and in the next second, he opened my door without even knocking I stood from the table and made a few steps back.

-Oh, you are awake!

-Erela is here; she is waiting to start the wellness session.

-Okey, okey. Hug me - he started to come close, and I made one more step back.

-Sir, she is waiting …

-Okay, just hug me. What is wrong with you? - he came aggressively closer and started to grab me. He pushed me twice, teaching me like a stupid kid how a hug has to be done when he asks.

-You see? This is a proper hug! – he proudly declared.

-She is waiting…

-Oh, okey, go. I will come in a minute. – as an offended child, he disappeared from my room, leaving me feeling confused and deeply affected again.

Leaving my room, I hurried to the back door, opening the lockers of my prison, desperately hoping to find at least someone. Relief washed over me as I heard the clatter of dishes coming from the kitchen.

I marched straight to the kitchen, intent on voicing my concerns. I entered the kitchen and scanned the faces around me, hoping to get everyone's attention. Probably, I was looking like an angry child, scared to show his emotion. I yearned for any acknowledgment so I could voice the pain and suffering I was experiencing. Finally, someone made eye contact, and a wave of numbness washed over me. I felt an unexpected surge of embarrassment, silencing the words I'd planned to say. I can't do it; this place is not going to help me. Don't make stupid decisions, you don't know who is aware, and cover all this shit inside the house.

-Where is Erela?

-Good morning, Ma'am. She is on the way… will be soon here. Can you place the breakfast menu in the dining area? And the newspapers?

-I don't know where it has to be placed. Please go inside and do it by yourself.

-I can't go …

-Why?

-Because..

-Because what? Go and place it, please. I don't know the locations.

-Let's go together when the wellness session starts.

-Got it. Ok.

Leaving the kitchen, disbelief washed over me. Here I was, unable to express my concerns or voice my discomfort. I acknowledge that I tend to be gentle and avoid voicing complaints, whether in restaurants or at home, often fearing I might hurt someone's feelings. However, this situation is different. Pushing it down and moving on isn't an option, girl. Ha! Easy to advise yourself after almost one year. It would be a game-changer to have my future self as an advisor.

Keeping in mind that the wellness session probably will take more than 1 hour, the next breakfast will start, and after, my GofG will arrive, and I will not be alone.

-Hey, what's happened yesterday? You didn't answer I get scared for you.

-Ahm… Erela… I got sick.

-Sick? Did you go to his room?

-No.

-OK, let's talk after the session. I have to go now…

-Sure, I will wait for you.

As I watched her enter the house, I came to terms with the fact that I wouldn't be able to share my worries, fears, and experiences with her. I can't.

During the wellness session, we went inside the house with one of the butlers to place whatever was required. I was doing all this stupid, unnecessary task, playing the role of butler personal assistant in front of male staff. Why? This is a big resonance for me. Men, whom I once saw as a symbol of protection and support, had become my biggest adversary. I watched that young butler checking the table set up and asking myself: should I tell him? Should I confide in him now?

Would he offer genuine help, or would he dismiss my concerns like Behemoth, deeming them trivial and passing them on to the White Shirt? His smile is a mask that doesn't hide his true nature; He's likely aware of his boss's preferences, as evidenced by his quick exit. The boss seems particular about his staff adhering to "them".

Everyone knows the girl is the only one holding off until her "designated" time arrives. They were all just playing with you in stupid induction and training, so the day you start work, you'll feel stuck. Do you know why? Fear cripples even the most capable mind when we're stuck, making it difficult to figure out what to do. A Fear? Is it a fear that I am feeling right now?

-Can you bring me water? – a short voice from the WS interrupted my reflections, and I found myself frozen near the table in the dining area where the butler was checking the table set up recently 1 hour ago.

-Yes..?

-What yes?

-Yes, Sir. – answering him, I hurried out of the dining room and paused near the back door to catch my breath. And heard Erela still making noises in the wellness room:

-Hey, how it was?

-Awfully

-What happened?

-He kissed me, old bastard.

-What??

-I have nothing to say, and he did it so aggressively. He also said that he needs someone like me in all his traveling.

-What does it mean?

-I have no idea. And I don't want to know. Be careful.

-I will. I totally forgot he asked me for water, I have to go. Will catch you later…

I wasn't prepared to talk to her about it and learn the disturbing shit. I had already begun to focus on protecting myself and avoiding the harsh realities, as difficulty believing in what had happened was my starting point. With GofG's imminent arrival, I clung to the hope that this nightmare would finally dissipate: my relief point.

I ventured into the kitchen and requested a glass of water from the same butler. As I repeated my mantra of hope and relief point within my mind, I returned to the dining area. I found the White Shirt waiting in the same spot. With a hand gesture, he invited me to follow him to the living room. I trailed behind him, holding the tray with his glass of water as a shield. He settled into a comfortable spot, finished his drink, and placed the empty glass back on the tray. Then, he requested that I place everything on the nearby table. I obeyed his request, but as I did, I noticed his long, aged hands reaching out for a hug. Instinctively, I recoiled, my gaze drawn to his vacant eyes. A flicker seemed to pass through them, the emptiness replaced by a sudden, burning intensity. His voice boomed, "What is your problem?! Hug me! Come here!" He lunged forward, his embrace suffocating in its aggression. Stuck in the memory of the morning's events, I was paralyzed, unable to react for a terrifying moment.

-I have to go; Erela is waiting for me.

-Wait, Wait, - he was briefing harder as he was exiting from this vomit procedure. I broke free from his embrace, snatched the tray, and vanished from the room.

Gasping for air from the fresh wave of shock and disgust, I retreated to the kitchen, struggling to hold back tears, put on the tray, and went to the girl's room.

***

The arrival of King Head, son of the White Shirt and head of all Pink Hell departments, brought a flurry of outdoor activity. Today they are supposed to have some teatime in a fresh area and probably a short walk. King Head, apparently responsible for his father's daily itinerary, flights, meals, events, vacations, and service protocols, would naturally be aware of his father's preferences. But I have to complain and try to get out of here without any damage.

The next few hours were a lull. I managed to calm myself and simply waited. The White Shirt remained in his bedroom upon King Head and GofG's arrival. Two butlers stood near the front door with a tray of welcoming drinks and wet towels. I lingered behind them, hoping to catch a glimpse of who emerged from the car. I just wanted to see her and felt relief. A small, anorexic, scraggly young guy with black hair and dark eyes like two polished stones went out from the car and hunched over straight to the entrance door carrying a tablet in his small, thin, matched arms. I'd seen him before, but today, he seemed different. Returning my eyes to the car's door, I saw her coming out, confused about where she should go. The manager waved her hand to indicate she needed to go to the back. Driven by a need to see her, I hurried towards the back door.

-Finally, you are here…

-Yes, where is our room?

-Inside. Come. I will show you.

-Inside?

-Come, - I opened the girl's room door, and we seat on the bed to take a short talk.

-Can you lock it? -, she was staring at the door

-No, it cannot be locked -But if I need to dress?

-It's your problem.

-Ha? What's happened here? Are you okey?

-No, I am not. It is a big joke and a lie.

-What?

-Everything here… We are just a peace of joke for pleasure and nothing more.

-I can't believe it's truth… We have to go out soon. And we have to schedule our shifts… -What shift? I will not sleep with him.

-Talk with King Head.

-I will text him that I want to talk.

-Evening time than.

-Be ready today. Don't stay with him alone and do not follow him if he will ask you. He can try to hug or kiss you or touch you.

-Omg... I can't believe it's true. King will not let me be alone.

-I hope so ...

Her eyes reflected fear and shock during our conversation. At least now, she seems prepared to avoid such confusing situations. Did I feel relief? Honestly, no. But a sense of solidarity emerged. Knowing someone else shares this ordeal makes this hell seem a little less unbearable.

She explained the plan: I'd handle the day shift while she takes nights. This way, he'll know someone's in the house throughout the day, including his son. They'll be off to Europe in a week, and then it's Pink Hell for us. Despite her plan, I wasn't ready to accept it. I needed to speak with King directly and make him understand the injustice of this situation.

With the house hushed by their outdoor activities, I seized the opportunity to prepare for the evening conversation. To keep myself occupied, I even helped the butlers pack for the picnic, pretending that I was interested to know the packing procedure. The day slipped away unnoticed. They are back.

The kitchen staff buzzed with frenetic activity, preparing a feast fit for a hundred rather than just two. Butlers scurried about, clearing picnic remnants and setting the scene for dinner. The controlled chaos mirrored the frenzy of a bustling Sunday night in a top restaurant. Amidst the whirlwind, I found a strange sense of normalcy, pushing away the unsettling memories of the past few days.

Dinner started! It commenced an elaborate display that resembled a Feast in the Time of Plague. I sat outside by the kitchen, observing the flurry of activity. Butlers weaved in and out, bearing freshly prepared dishes towards the house. A designated butler stationed near the dining area vigilantly monitored the state of the table. When a course neared completion, he'd discreetly signal his counterpart by the kitchen, prompting them to prepare the next round. I was silent and calm, waiting for this event to finish. I went inside the girl's room to ask GofG about today's activities. Also keeping my mind busy with stupid things.

-I am scared now to make the night shift.

-Why? Son is always in the house. He will not dare to do something to you.

-Yes, but he can ask him to leave for a while…

-And so, what? Your boyfriend will leave you alone?

-Stop it! He is not my BF!

-Oh, come on…

-No, really, I am thinking all day, what to do… You know that I had an incident when I was a teenager…

-Yes, I remember it…

-And I was stuck…. I couldn't do anything. I am just waiting for when it will finish.

-I know, but now it is different. You are an adult and…

-And what?

-Don't think so much. Nothing will happen to you. Avoid his requests if they feel weird.

- He is ready to talk with you. Outside, near the kitchen.

-Going.

I stole a glance at her before escaping the house. The weight of our conversation pressed heavily on my mind. What a travesty: two educated young women strategizing how to avoid harassment.

Reaching the confirmed place, I found King Head hunched over his tablet, working intently as always. Yet, his demeanor seemed strangely helpless and aloof. A wave of doubt washed over me: how could this kid help me? When would I break free from self-deception and accept reality?

-Yes.

-Hi.

-You wanted to speak?

-Yes.

-So, what is the issue?

-First of all. You should explain in an interview the specific details of working here. Your father is a monster. Do you know it?

-Yes, I know… It's hard to work with him

-Hard?? No, it's not about hard! He is a pervert. He asked everyone to leave yesterday. So, he can stay with me alone all this time. He is trying to touch you and kiss you always. Do you know that he kissed the wellness girl today? This is not normal at all.

-I know …

-Can you imagine GofG will be in the same position next time? Do you think she will handle it?

-No, she will not.

-So what?

-I will put butlers to work at night also, and they will always be near you. -He is a psychopath -Yes, I know.

-Do you know that he can throw you a pan or a book when he is pissed?

-I know… He has a difficult character. That's why we keep such a salary.

-It's not a high salary at all. Can you just hire prostitutes and not touch educated girls? What is the problem?

-No.. they can't do such a job. It has to be a professional who knows the rules and etiquette.

-This is ridiculous…

-And GofG needs support. I am scared for her.

"My God…. He is just a kid; what are you expecting from him? What? He is scared." – the thought which started to bleed in my mind.

-Listen, I can't do it. I will leave. Find something for you, GofG, a different position or kind of protection because I will not be near her all the time. She will get in trouble.

-I know, but what can I do?? I will take her with me to Europe and always keep someone on shift.

- I have no idea, but it has to be stopped.

-You can't do anything. He can destroy you.

-No one can do it.

-No, you are wrong. He can do it.

-That's the reason why the girls always keep moving from here.

-We should go because people around will start to think.

-Think about what?

-That we have something…

-This is crazy… Are they mad?

-No.. but we are talking a lot.

Our conversation stretched over an hour, and during that time, a realization dawned on me. King Head's image of control seemed like a facade. Perhaps he wasn't simply dedicated; maybe he was avoiding something related to girl's issues to stay in his father's good graces and don't get punished. The sheer volume of his workload, nineteen hours a day, and his apparent aversion to spending nights at home - all pointed towards a deeper issue. A young man his age craves social interaction and leisure. His behavior suggested something more was at play.

Returning to the "girls' room," a sobering realization struck me: I wasn't facing just one problem. I could simply walk away now, but first, I had to ensure she wouldn't be the next target. I decided to talk with her straight. Convincing her to leave with me was imperative:

-You should leave. You know it.

-How? Where will I go?

-He can take care of it. Rent an apartment…

-And what? He doesn't have any communication with outsiders. No phone, no WhatsApp. We will not be able to meet, ever! Because he is with his father always.

-Are you in love?

-Yes… I had never felt something like this before.

-Jesus, what is going on? Are you both mad? What happened with you in Europe? Are you dating?

-I think so… he said he loves me…

-Oh my god…

-If I leave, I will lose him forever. His father will never allow him to go out.

-He is an adult and.

-No! You don't understand.

-So, explain to me.

-When he was 19 years old, he went to the police station at night and asked them to call his mom. To pick him up... and -And?

-They called his father...

-Has he done anything wrong?

-No...

-Why did he go to the police at night, what's happened?

-I don't know... -This is weird.

-Yes.

-Does his mom know about it?

-I don't know. But the police obey him so that nothing can be done.

-What? Is he a local gangster or something like that?

-I don't know... Listen, you have to take a rest. I will do the night shift. Sleep well.

-Easy to say.

-Close the door. I will be in the kitchen all night with a butler.

-Did King Head put a butler on the night shift?

-Yes, and also he said that you know him very well, his father.

-It's not my choice. Better, I would never know this place.

-Stop it. Sleep.

Sleep feels like a distant dream. My mind races with worries and the weight of decisions. I can't sleep or eat. The very thought of food turns my stomach.

Memories From Whatsapp Chats Luisa. Police Report Exhibit 20

"-I hope all will be fine.

-Nothing is fine, and it will never be fine

-I know, but he didn't call you last night. You went to sleep.

-It's a fucking pervert

-Thank God he didn't insist. What time are the other people coming this morning? How far do they live from the other butlers?

-No idea, really. I am always in the house.

-You didn't meet them in the morning? The other staff members?

-I met, I didn't ask. I don't know the territory. I don't care how about this stupid. They know what is going on here, and they are silent. Fick them all. Hope they are sleeping on the floor in a stable.

-Oh.. no. Always asl like you don't know. So, they don't have confirmation."

What do I have at the moment: a psycho monster probably involved in illegal activities across India, seems to lack a conscience and operates outside moral boundaries, protected by the police."; A kid, his son, who's likely suffered under his control all his life and seems genuinely obsessed with a girl, potentially the next target of his father's depravity; A girl, too innocent and young to navigate this web of immorality on her own; and me...what about me?

Why do I always feel compelled to protect those around me? It will be my downfall someday. It will kill me.

***

I woke up at 4:00 AM with a tight pressure in my head and a surge of body heat. My mind bombarded me with strange, panicky signals. Despite my exhaustion, I felt compelled to escape, to run away from this overwhelming sensation. I couldn't fall back asleep, the feeling lingering despite my fatigue. I reached for my phone and sent a text to GofG, hoping it would provide a distraction.

WhatsApp conversation:

-Listen, don't start at 4.. start at 6…Or later if you want

-Yes, God. I am so sleepy.

-Sleep, sleep, just let me know whenever you want to come

-Are you in the kitchen?

-Yes, I am.

-Are you alone?

-No.. one butler is here. If someone asks why FF family shoes are outside in front of the kitchen, tell them that there was no space in their shoe cabinet…

-We need to place it in front of the main door after cleaning. Did you see the sock when you took their shoes for cleaning? He usually places it near the shoes or in the bathroom.

-No.

-We have to give it to the laundry.

-I didn't see it anywhere. Whatever was supposed to be done was done by butlers. Or check in the bathroom.

-No, I will not go to the bathroom anymore. Never mind.

-Listen, if you see people going at 9 AM to puja, go there for some time and stand away. Because one of the BPA has to present. King Head sent us an email a long time ago.

I clutched my phone, seeking solace in thought. Her behavior seemed normal, a stark contrast to the weight of my revelation. Perhaps it's a self-preservation instinct, or maybe she harbors deeper knowledge than I do. Ever since she became closer to King Head, a veil of secrecy has descended upon her, accompanied by a shift in her demeanor. While I doubt she condones The WS's actions, perhaps his son guarantees our safety, preventing a repeat of the ordeal.

Doubt hangs heavy in the air as I face this new day. After two grueling hours of staring at the ceiling, I finally rose from the bed. Fresh makeup and my uniform donned, I head to the kitchen to relieve GofG and allow her some rest. The bustling kitchen staff, already in their stations, trigger a wave of Deja vu, reminding me all too vividly of yesterday's ordeal.

-Good morning, Ma'am

-Hi, are you on day shift?

-Yes, there's a haircut scheduled for around noon today. Because of that, we'll need to set up everything outside on the terrace.

-After breakfast?

-No, I don't think he will take breakfast. Usually, he is waiting for his son to wake up.

-Okey, so?

-So, when he will go to morning wellness, let us know.

-Sure…

The next two hours passed in quietness. I found solace in knowing that by the time he wakes up, I'll be attending morning prayers with the others. This provides a convenient window to avoid fetching him water or interacting with him until his haircut appointment. So, after sitting without cause in the kitchen, I sought solace outside, joining the local prayer gathering held for the workers and intended to "awaken the God." An elderly man, adorned in an orange ceremonial robe, prepared for the ceremony, arranging flowers and other religious items. I removed my shoes, scanned the faces around me, and took a position in the back, waiting for it to begin.

After a few minutes, the old man began to chant, prompting everyone to delve inwards, seeking answers and a deeper connection with their inner selves and their deity. As I focused on the ceremony, a flicker in my peripheral vision caught my attention. On the house porch, clad in his nightwear, stood the WS, seemingly searching for something.

He probably just woke up and was trying to find me to receive his water with morning procedures. With a determined focus, I closed my eyes, pretending not to see him. "Surely he wouldn't dare interrupt the prayer," I reassured myself, a sliver of doubt lingering. After all, the kitchen was full of willing servants, ready to fulfill his every request, even a baked pig. After five minutes, I peeked open my eyes, hesitant to scan the area directly. A quick glance towards the house porch brought a surge of relief – he was gone.

As the puja ceremony reached its conclusion, I silently hoped he was already engrossed in his wellness session. Ideally, King Head would wake up by then, ensuring my safety. After all, his games wouldn't be played out in front of his son. He will not dare.

Despite my earlier doubts, upon returning to the kitchen, I found him already engrossed in his wellness session. We, along with the housekeepers and butlers, bustled about preparing the terrace for the haircut. Once done, everyone dispersed back to the kitchen, leaving me alone once more in the quiet house. Restlessness gnawed at me, prompting me to step outside.

As I crossed the hallway, the door to the wellness room opened, and The WS emerged, blocking my path.

-Where have you been this morning? - he inquired.

-At the puja ceremony, sir, -I replied.

-Ah, alright, alright… Bring me water, - he dismissively ordered.

I understood the unspoken implications of his request. A sliver of hope flickered within me - perhaps his son, still slumbering upstairs, would deter him from further advances. With a heavy heart, I retrieved water from the kitchen and returned.

He sat in the dining area, a disgruntled expression etched on his face. As he finished his drink with the usual disregard, he spoke:

-Put the tray down.

Mustering the newfound courage from my earlier victory, I met his gaze and surprised myself by saying, "No, I have to go." I took the glass and turned to leave, feeling a surge of power.

In that same instant, a humiliating sensation flared - his hand grazed my backside. Feeling ignorant, I exited the house, the sting of tears threatening to spill. Back in the kitchen, the weight of his actions and my helplessness crashed upon me. I felt utterly belittled, the most inferior being in the world, utterly alone.

You probably again are asking, "Why? Why are you not raising your voice? Why are you silent?" but I am sure no one really knows how you will react in my situation.

The haircut had just begun when GofG, already awake from her short rest, texted for updates. A wave of indecision washed over me. Should I burden her with another complaint or silently navigate this ordeal on my own?

A suffocating weight settled on my chest – the day was young, yet a dark cloud already loomed overhead. But I wouldn't succumb to despair, not for the innocent girl sleeping peacefully within these walls, not with this monster lurking nearby.

Thankfully, fate offered a reprieve. Following the haircut, The WS and his son departed for the factory and some outdoor activity, leaving the house blessedly quiet. I found myself counting down the minutes until my shift ended, desperate for a moment to breathe freely. As usual now for me, I joined the butlers in packing away the outdoor tea set, the menial task a welcome distraction from the turmoil within. The days bled into one another, monotonous and unchanging, while my spirit steadily eroded.

-Ma'am, you are going to escort them to the temple. Please be ready, the car will wait for you on the backside.

-Temple?

-Yes, talk with Miss GofG she will explain.

Memories From Whatsapp With GofG 07:16 Pm Evidence Exhibit 20b Police Report.

"*-Where are you? Take care... Is it dark there?*

-Yes, it's dark

Take care

Impossible

-Okey, no problem... he won't try anything in the temple. They are still here with me.

-You never know...

-No, it's a religious place

-Let's see...

-He doesn't care but he won't show it in front of others. I don't know, really. Let's hope for the best.

-He is not asking to bring me here without reason

-He just likes you and wants you to be there. He also wanted at the hiking.

-I have 6%. He is still in the office and has no idea when he will come

-Don't use your phone. You might need it later. Sleep in the car. Ask them to wake you up when they are coming.

09:14 PM

-Coming, be ready.

Open the door, water, wet towel

-What? Me?

-Yes, you open the door

-No, they are doing it.

-You have to do it. He was asking where are you. Why are you not here?

-WTF

-He is pissed about the factory

-It's okey. King Head is here. "

Yes, the King's son... will he truly save me? Why this unwavering faith? Returning from the temple visit, I retreated to my room for a breath of fresh air. A sickening realization dawned: my shift wasn't a definitive barrier. He could seek me out anytime, before or after it ended. Powerless, I surrendered to the inevitable. Stretched out on the bed, I braced myself for the usual pre-dinner chaos. As expected, a flurry of activity filled the air behind the girl's room door – butlers scurried back and forth between the kitchen and dining room, laying out a feast fit for a wedding, yet for only two.

Again, the same, girl! What is going on in your mind? "Why are you even here? Just leave. He'll be fine. The King Head will take care of her." My frustration boiled over. "Haven't you seen him? You're either forgetting or deliberately ignoring reality! He's a scared child, powerless to change anything!"

By the time they reached the mountain peak, dusk had settled, cloaking the world in an inky twilight. Armed with a few projectors, we approached a small, silent temple that resembled a weathered hut. A minuscule clearing lay before it, furnished with a lone, aged bench. The WS and King Head settled onto the bench, a heavy silence descending upon them. Lost in thought, The WS stared fixedly into the distance. Beside him, King Head appeared even more vulnerable, his frail form dwarfed by the vastness of the setting. His contorted body seemed burdened, his head hanging low as if weighed down by an unbearable stone. Restlessly, his hands clutched a tablet, a small beacon of hope amidst the gloom. Witnessing his plight, a wave of pity washed over me. This kid needs to be rescued…

-What are you doing there? Come and sit with us – the WS ordered me as I am a street homeless dog without roofs.

Shamefaced, I met King Head's gaze and quietly requested permission not to sit between the two of them, especially not next to the monster who harassed me daily. The pure kid looked at me, then back on the floor, confusion flickering across his face. With a resigned sigh, he shifted, making space for me on the bench. Despite a surge of defiance, I knew better than to disobey and simply did as instructed. King Head seemed to shrink even further into himself, the weight of the situation pressing down on him.

Their hushed conversation painted a disturbing picture. The WS, brimming with anger, was clearly dissatisfied with his son's work.

They were talking about some factory issues and the firing of butler. The WS seemed to despise it for no apparent reason. King Head, his head bowed in silent defiance, fought to save this innocent worker's job.

The tension hung heavy in the air, a stark contrast to the serenity of the mountaintop. This was not a healthy conversation between them. As they are playing with someone, life is usually swearing between father and son.

Unease gnawed at me, refusing to relinquish its grip. Dinner would be over soon, and he knew I was alone in my room. Sleep, a distant comfort, felt utterly out of reach. Seeking solace in action, I drifted towards the kitchen, determined to help with the dishes, however menial the task. A trained professional, a woman with a wealth of knowledge embodied in over forty diplomas and certificates, I found myself washing dishes. Life, or rather, this monster, had a cruel way of twisting circumstances.

Groundhog Day

The next morning, I awoke with the same heavy weight pressing down on me - dread. Again, I found myself caught in a mental loop, strategizing for survival: Why wasn't I packing my bags and leaving? A barrage of arguments assaulted me: I was stranded, penniless, and unable to book a ticket out of this godforsaken place. My credit cards, luggage, and documents were all in the "Pink hell." Reporting this situation was a non-starter -I had no idea who was involved or complicit in this nightmare.

King Head, who is my direct boss had warned me to keep quiet, to wait for the "proper time" to escape. Uncertainty gnawed at me - was my luggage even safe in my room? Should I reach out to someone abroad? But who? What would I even say? And, more importantly, would it work? Silence, it seemed, was my only weapon. Keeping my head down and maintaining the illusion of compliance was the only way to stay alive. But what about my GofG? And what about this kid? Will you just leave it like this and disappear? Oh, yes. Are you in your mind? Do you want to be murdered anywhere on the road to the airport or even worse? Can you think about your safety first?! A voice screamed back in my head. Was I crazy to even consider it? The dangers of escape were far too real: murder on the road and unseen threats lurking everywhere. Safety had to be my top priority. Keep a low profile, especially around men - you never know who might be collaborating in this scheme. Thank heavens, this kid hadn't reported me to his father.

Silence had always been my defense mechanism. Throughout my life, I've shouldered burdens alone. Losing my father as a child and witnessing my mother's solitude - I never had the comfort of a protector. Loneliness was a constant companion. Time to get out of bed! We need to come up with a solid reason for you to skip duties inside the house.

This was my morning mantra, a chorus of dread echoing within my slumbering mind. Even in sleep, I couldn't escape the relentless torment - a cacophony of anxieties that ripped me from the solace of unconsciousness.

My shift began with the usual handoff from GofG, a brief chat with the kitchen staff, and Erela before the wellness session. I was already preparing an excuse not to serve water before and after massage, but no amount of preparation could shield me from his foul mood.

Entering the house to announce Erela's arrival, I found the old man already in a belligerent state. Ignoring my words, he beckoned me closer with a predatory glint in his eyes; he was confident in his morning wishes. The now-familiar chant began, "Come here, hug me!" his hand gesturing towards a forced embrace.

-I have to go, - I stammered, my voice laced with panic, - They're waiting for me.

-Who? - he sneered.

-The staff, sir, - I lied desperately - they're showing me the ropes.

-Come here, - his response was a dismissive wave of his hand. Before I could react, he lunged towards me, his hand landing with a sickening thud on my buttocks. Disgust clawed at my throat as I lied, "Someone's here!"

He flinched, his predatory facade momentarily shattered. Spinning on my heel, I fled the house, the weight of his upcoming threats pressing down on me. I knew, with a chilling certainty, that today's transgression wouldn't go unpunished.

-Erela..- I said, gripping her arm to halt her entry.

-What happened?

-Be careful; he is aggressive today…

Erela's face fell, a flicker of worry replaced by a cold glint of understanding. With a muttered curse, she disappeared inside, her determined stride belying her initial hesitation.

Resignation settled over me - all I could do was wait for the next round of humiliation, praying his son's presence would somehow appease him.

We entered the house with one butler to replace the newspapers, and a desperate wish welled up within me - for him to stay, for anyone to stay.

I started to think about Erela and her last issues, which she faced during the massage, and probably she has more troubles than me, and she doesn't speak about it. Yearning for solace, I considered staying indoors, but a stronger urge propelled me outside. I knelt by the door, ears straining for the telltale creak of the wellness room door. I knew each and everyone was looking at me as if I was crazy but I didn't care. I was so tired physically and mentally so I didn't react to anyone around. The suffocating silence was broken only by the relentless anticipation that gnawed at my insides. No panic, no warning, just a chilling calm as I conserved my energy, my nerves, for the impending battle.

Then, the sound of the door opening erupted like a sonic boom, sending a jolt of fear and pain through my muscles. I have to go, or he will come to the kitchen. What is worse? Muttering a request for water to the butler, I retreated into the house. I heard Erela behind the door to the wellness room; her presence sparked a flicker of hope - perhaps it would deter his wrath. "Next time," I vowed silently, "I'll ask her to stay until I return, creating as much noise as possible. It seems that's the only way to navigate this humiliation unscathed. With a heavy heart, I entered the dining area where he was waiting, just as he always did.

-Come here.

Extending the tray towards him, I stretched my arms out, widening the distance between us as subtly as possible. He reached for the glass, but in a sickeningly swift movement, his other hand darted up, lifting the hem of my already short skirt.

A gasp escaped my lips as I recoiled, my eyes widening in shock.

-What color are your underpants? - he sneered, his voice dripping with sarcasm. - Oh, I can see them.

His words felt like a physical blow, leaving me frozen in place. Terror choked any potential response, my mind reeling from the sheer unexpectedness of his violation. This wasn't just anger anymore; it was something far more insidious, a calculated humiliation that left me feeling utterly powerless.

-Come here, I have to show you something.

-Sir, Erela is..

-Come here!! - his voice boomed, a stark contrast to his previous tone.

I followed him to the table in the living room and he showed me the newspapers that we placed this morning. "Do you see it? "he took both exemplars and showed it to me. "Do you see they are similar? Why do I need to spend money for no reason? Explain to me". I had nothing to answer just to wait when he will allow me to leave.

-Who is responsible for purchasing?

-I will find out, Sir.

-Ask him to come. I want to talk.

-And bring me more water to the terrace in a while.

-Yes, Sir

I turned around and felt a wind around me coming from his hand. He grabbed me lightning-fast and grabbed my face, trying to lick or kiss my ear. "Why you are so naughty??" whispering it he pinned my head as if trying to crush it with pressure. Shook it twice; he left my head for a and I rushed out of the house, closed the door, and seat on my knees near it. Panic surged through me, a primal scream trapped in my throat.

My knees buckled, and I crumpled to the floor, gasping for air. The pounding of my heart echoed in my ears, a relentless drum against the suffocating silence. Only then did the memory of the forgotten tray pierce through the fog of terror.

"Mari, where's the tray?" The butler's voice, a distant echo in my mind, sent a fresh wave of tremors through me. "Mari?? a voice came in my head again, "Ma-ri, whe-re is th-e tra-y?" I shook my head and understood that it was a butler staying near me.

-I forgot it – I spoke in a calm and quiet voice, exerting as much control as possible.

-Bring it back.

-He wants to know who is responsible for newspaper purchasing.

-Why?

-Because he doesn't have the money to pay for two identical ones, - I said sarcastically, glancing up at the butler's face.

-Who said?

-Who can say it?! Ask Behemoth to handle it. And bring him water to the terrasse in a few minutes.

-Why? You have to do it.

-No, I can't. Can you please go?

-Go, bring the tray back, please.

I rose to my feet, unwilling to face him alone again. Seeking refuge, I retreated to the girl's room and stood near the window - the same one where I'd hidden during the haircut. This room offered a clear view of the main door and terrace, a strategic advantage. Here, I could observe his movements and avoid any unwanted encounters. Pressing myself against the wall, I waited with bated breath for him to come outside. Once he was out on the terrace, I could grab the tray and deliver the water without meeting him alone. Surely, he wouldn't dare act out with so many people around - there were always groundskeepers or someone else tending to the vast property. Every passing minute stretched into an eternity. My gaze remained fixed on the main door, my eyelids refusing to blink. A relentless barrage of questions hammered in my head: "Why was he so furious? Was it because of me? No, that couldn't be it. Something else must have happened. But what?"

Terror seized me as the front door creaked open. He emerged and headed towards the terrace, his presence radiating a dark energy. Crouching low, I slipped out of the girl's room, heart hammering against my ribs. Grabbing the tray and an empty glass from the living room, I sprinted towards the kitchen, the weight of his potential rage a suffocating presence.

One of the butlers had refilled the tray, and with trembling hands, I hurried outside through the terrace door near the girl's room. My mission was simple: deliver the water and vanish. Anxiety gnawed at me as I approached the terrace, my hands shaking so violently I feared dropping everything. There he sat, hunched over his phone, feigning normalcy.

But as I neared, I noticed the table was far lower than I'd anticipated. Bending down to place the glass, a horrifying realization dawned on me - my skirt was too short. Any movement would expose me in a way that would leave me utterly vulnerable.

Desperate, I sank to my knees, arranging the tray with frantic haste. He seemed oblivious, not even acknowledging my presence as I carefully set down the napkin and glass. Just as I rose to escape, his hand shot out, a vise-like grip around my wrist, yanking me closer. The world spun, the air thick with a chilling dread as his pretense of indifference shattered.

-I am not a bad person. I just don't like when something is not on my way. Do you understand what I am saying?

-Yes

-Repeat it

-Sir…

-Why did my son place so many butlers on the night shift? Did you ask him?

-This is for the best service, Sir

-How I can touch you if someone is always around. I will fire them all.

-Would you like something to eat?

-No, I will wait for my son to wake up. – he went inside his mind and relaxed his hand so I could pull out my arm.

I rushed into the girl's room, seeking refuge by the window. How could such contradictory traits reside within one person? Just yesterday, he was fuming because the housekeepers weren't sweeping the yard and entrance every two hours. Yet, in the same breath, he couldn't tolerate anyone around him. He'd hired an army of over four hundred servants to cater to his every whim, yet their very presence seemed to grate on him. It was a paradox I couldn't wrap my head around.

One thing was crystal clear – He could physically assault me. I was nothing more than a physical outlet for his anger, a dog to be trained, or a punching bag. This wasn't just bad; it was far worse than I ever could have imagined.

A flicker of movement outside the window sent a jolt through me. The WS was back from the terrace. He entered the house, and his footsteps echoed ominously in the hallway, drawing closer to our door. Panic surged through my veins. Desperate for cover, I scrambled behind the wardrobe, praying my silhouette wouldn't betray me through the thin fabric. The knob rattled, and the door creaked open. I held my breath, feigning sleep, as my gaze darted to the curtains, which fluttered suspiciously. "Was my hiding place exposed? Oh, God, he will find me. He will." In a last-ditch effort, I squeezed my eyes shut, trying to project the image of peaceful slumber.

An unnerving silence blanketed the room, broken only by GofG's gentle breaths. Then, with a resounding slam that jolted GofG awake, the door slammed shut. Relief washed over me, momentarily erasing the terror that had gripped me. I remained huddled behind the wardrobe, waiting for his return to the terrace before venturing to the kitchen.

-Hello, - with a sleepy voice, she greets me.

-Good morning.

-What happened?

-The WS came.

-Why?

-He was trying to find me.

-Oh, God..

-Is he mad? If I am naked here…

-His house, his rules.

-What is the time?

-You can sleep more. Oh, wait, he is returning to the terrace…

-And?

Cutting our conversation short, I left the girl confused. Stepping outside, my initial determination to escape the house evaporated, replaced by a disorienting fog. Wandering aimlessly into the backyard, I found myself back in the kitchen. The WS probably already questioned "Where the hell is this girl?" and butlers' resentment towards me was palpable, but I was beyond caring. I found a butler setting a tray with snacks and a hot drink. "He wants something to eat. Set the dinner napkin," he instructed curtly.

It was clear he'd requested food directly from them, bypassing me, which meant it was my mistake and irresponsible behavior. Anger and a surge of helplessness bubbled within me. These men had no idea what I was enduring inside this house, yet they dared to be angry at me.

Swallowing my pride, I made a weak plea, my face etched with exhaustion. "I can't do it. Please serve the food."

The harried butler, pressed for time, ignored my plea and hurried inside. He entered the house and went to the terrace through the door near the girl's room. Instinctively, I trailed behind him, slipping into my room unnoticed. GofG had already disappeared. How did I dismiss her? I watched through the window as the butler returned from the terrace, the back door clicking shut behind him. Silence, thick and suffocating, once again descended upon the house.

WhatsApp from GofG 04:10 PM.

-Where are you?

-In the room

-He came and knocked, and I ran inside the bathroom

-I asked butlers to serve. I cannot.

-Good. They will. You don't have to.

-He will be pissed because of this. You will see it. He is hungry and angry.

-Let him be pissed.

-Fuck.

-We cannot do anything.

-What was this? Did you hear it?

-But he won't do anything to us if he is in a bad mood. What?

-Someone hit the door.

-Elephant? It's okey now?

-The main door! Which elephant??

-See from the window.

-It's WS.

-Why?

-I have no idea. I am scared.

-Is he mad?

-Yes

-WTF is going on?

The slam of the front door echoed through the house, a harbinger of his fury. Every fiber of my being screamed at me to hide. The following minutes stretched into an eternity, punctuated only by a chilling silence. No tell-tale footsteps emerged from the hallway, leading me to believe he'd retreated to the bedroom. Driven by a morbid curiosity, I inched closer to my door, straining to hear any sounds from within. My heart hammered against my ribs, a frantic drum threatening to burst through my chest.

Crouching near the door, I fought to control my ragged breaths. From the distant room, a cacophony of disturbing noises erupted -a rhythmic pounding that mimicked a washing machine, a sickening thud, the unmistakable thump of furniture against the wall. No….it couldn't be. A strangled gasp escaped my lips. He was… beating him. His son…

A weird feeling grows up, blurring my vision. Buried my face in my arms, my back pressed against the cold, unforgiving door. A torrent of thoughts swarmed my mind, a relentless buzz that drowned out everything else. The once quiet house now pulsed with a horrific symphony of violence and despair.

Memories From Whatsapp with GofG Police Report Exhibit 20

08:42 PM

"-Was everything fine?

-No. He asked me to come after dinner. I will not do it."

GofG entered the room after my message and looked at me in shock.

-Don't go.

-Definitely no!

-Today, something happened near the temple...

-What? Please don't scare me...

-No, nothing serious... Ah.. so.. we reached the temple as usual, and they took a seat on the bench. He asked me to take a sit beside him. I denied it, and he said, "You want to sit on my lap?!" I said again no, and he was like "Then come and sit beside me." And I was like a stupid sitting between them both.

-What did King Head say?

-What is he supposed to say?

-I don't know anything!

-He wants to talk...

-With whom?

-With me...

-And what is the problem?

-Everyone is in the kitchen area.

-You are the lead and reporting to him, so go and talk. Or come here and talk.

-I don't know ...

-Where is he btw?

-I don't know.

-Can you ask him where his father is? I want to hide in the kitchen. I can't just walk out now. If this old prevent is waiting for me just to get out of the room, I am caught.

-Text him, he will help you.

The opportunity to ask about his father felt like a fragile lifeline, and I desperately wanted to use it. But not now, I can't ask him every time to save my ass, and the thought of constantly interrupting him to appease his father's erratic demands was a suffocating reality.

Steeling myself, I crept towards the door, straining to hear any approaching footsteps. A sudden sound sent me scrambling back, my hand flying to my head in a jolt of terror; I looked at GofG. Her face a mask of calm, stood before me, a single word escaping her lips, "Relax, it's just the King Head!"

The next moment, the kid's impatient rap at the door spurred me into action. Opening the door, after a quick scan of the hallway and a furtive glance towards the dining room to ensure his father's absence, I ushered the child inside. I retreated to the familiar sanctuary of the kitchen. "The Feast in Time of Plague" was finished, as evidenced by the weary faces of the staff cleaning up. I made a sit on my knees as usual near the door and, with the familiar knot of anxiety twisting in my gut, started to wait for him to come. A sliver of light illuminated the keyhole, jolting me from my thoughts. Someone was approaching. A peek through the keyhole confirmed my dread -"my tormentor" was heading straight for the wellness room... "Wellness session!" I mentally cursed. "Completely forgotten!" A fleeting sense of relief washed over me - one precious hour to create a plan.

I am always handling my life alone and prefer to be alone in any matter but never in my life have I felt so lonely and lost. I took some looks at the kitchen area at the staff there. Their laughter as they discussed their evenings grated on me, a stark reminder of the freedom they possessed while I was locked away." The rhythmic clatter of pots and pans was a stark contrast to the dull ache in my chest.

"So many men around pretending that is normal, 2 girls to sleep all night inside their boss's house with a broken lock. Does any of them really care what is going on behind this door with us? Don't think so; 'Despite the presence of others, a suffocating isolation pressed down on me. The men, oblivious to the horrors behind the locked door, reveled in the normalcy of their departure. This world was a brutal game, and here, I was a mere pawn. It is a jungle - every man is for himself. But you, my darling, are even worse, the lowest link in the food chain – woman; nothing, a piece of meat for procreation.

A sliver of light flickered in the keyhole; a faint spark of hope quickly extinguished. Without a shred of enthusiasm, I peered through the sight of an empty room offering a temporary reprieve. The King's Head must have left the girl's room. Deciding to seek solace in GofG's company, I made my way back to our room, yearning for some form of support. Just as I pushed open the door, the telltale creak of the wellness room door shattered the fragile peace. It was too late to retreat.

He emerged, his presence a dark cloud filling the corridor. His voice, laced with anger, demanded water as usual. Exhaustion warred with a flicker of defiance in my eyes as I turned and fled back to the kitchen. My movements were frantic as I prepared the tray, the desperate need to get him his water before Erela, my only witness, left. Reaching the door, I flung it open, my hand colliding with the handle just as Erela stepped out. "I'm a dead woman," I muttered, my voice barely a whisper. Following Erela's retreating figure with my eyes, I watched the door close with a heavy thud.

The WS remained rooted near the wellness room, his gaze fixed on me. A curt gesture of his hand beckoned me forward.

This "spa room" was a travesty. A large bedroom dominated by a king-sized bed and an assortment of Indian-style furniture bore the scars of a forced transformation. A small wardrobe had been converted into a makeshift spa area, complete with a massage table and flickering candles. An overly large bathroom completed the space.

This room supposedly belongs to his son, but he never sleeps here. Instead, he sleeps with his father in his room, in his father's bed. While there's nothing inherently wrong with a father and son sleeping together, in this context, it offers a disturbing explanation for why the innocent child spends all night in the kitchen, unable to sleep.

So, I made a few steps inside, stood in the middle of the room, and looked at the WS, who was closing the door behind him. My eyes became bigger than I could imagine; I wasn't expecting the fresh humility right now.

-Sir, Miss G. is in the room…

-So what? No one will come inside if the door is closed, so don't worry. Put on the tray we need to talk.

-Please, I need to go – almost with the lost voice, I asked in vain.

-Where is your family? - he took the tray from my hands.

-Sorry?

-Do you have a family? Where are they living?

-In Croatia -City?

-It's near Pula… but…

-Do you have brothers or sisters?

-Yes.. but..

-Are they fine? Your mother?

-Sorry?

-Are they healthy?

-Yes…

-Are you sure?

-I don't understand...

-Should I speak loudly or repeat myself? - His dark form loomed closer, and a fresh wave of terror crashed over me. His hands clamped around my waist, squeezing with a vice-like grip. It was a deliberate attempt to crush any remaining defiance, to mold me into complete submission. His goal was to shut up my ambition and last drop of courage before total obedience. "Do you know that I can shut your carrier with one call? Or I can give you a good review about your job in my company. What is your choice?" He grabbed my face and pulled it up to look into my eyes and make himself sure that I was totally morally depressed. "Do you hear?" he nodded my head as I was gesturing, "Yes".

A burning ball of pain and despair ignited in my gut, its tendrils creeping up towards my heart. Tears welled up in my eyes, hot and stinging, but a surge of anger held them back. I was consumed by resentment, a suffocating weight of injustice pressing down on me. Pain and suffering throbbed in every fiber of my being.

His grip loosened on my face, and with a rough yank, he started unbuttoning my shirt, grumbling in a whisper: "Why so many clothes always?!" He started aggressively to push it so he could squeeze his arm under it and touch my boobs. Feeling like a flawed creature with female limbs hating and despising my existence - the words echoed in my mind, a horrifying reflection of how I saw myself in that moment. Despair choked me as he manhandled my clothes. My body felt like a traitor, a vessel failing to protect itself.

Over the next few minutes, he dug his fingers into my chest, the pressure building with agonizing on my chest, sending a jolt of hellish pain through me. His expression was a cruel reminder that this was my punishment for not listening. I have to know my place in the food chain.

1.01.1

"The next morning, I woke up with a hollow ache in my chest, a void where hope used to reside. Every part of me felt utterly devoid of life, the mere act of breathing a chore. Rising from sleep felt like clawing my way out of a tomb, the remnants of the night's horrors clinging to me like a shroud. "There was one part of my behavior that remained a mystery to me until therapy shed light on it. Despite the relentless barrage of abuse, I clung to a desperate normalcy in front of others. Why? My fractured mind had crafted a refuge - a horrific reality transformed into a twisted nightmare, a detached experience happening to 'another girl' who merely shared my body. The truth was too brutal to bear, so I distanced myself, creating a fragile illusion of safety. I held onto that thought, a lifeline until the day I could pack my bags and vanish from this awful country. Till that time, I preferred to stay in a safe place inside my head.

The weight of the morning routine pressed down on me. Exhausted, I dragged myself out of bed, the familiar motions a blur. Reaching for yesterday's uniform on the table, a wave of despair washed over me. The wrinkled fabric became a symbol of defeat, and tears welled up in my eyes. Squeezing them shut, I fought for composure, each deep breath a desperate attempt to steady myself.

I went to the bathroom and found myself in a weird condition. I didn't want to take a shower: "I don't want to get undressed in front of myself. The idea of my own hands running across my skin sent shivers down my spine. Even basic hygiene felt like a disgust. Can you imagine it?" the silent scream echoed in my mind. "Is this what my life has become?" Paralyzed by the overwhelming aversion to touching my own body, I stood frozen, the world around me blurring. First food, now this. I was staying in the bathroom, confused in a stupor, looking around and not understanding what to do. Finally, I retreated, the problem unresolved, a knot of despair tightening in my gut.

Back in the bedroom, I sank onto the bed with the crumpled uniform in my hand. Pulling on yesterday's clothes, I reached for the hiking white t-shirt, I took it and dressed it under the shirt. But a chilling question echoed in the silence: "Do I still have hope? Can anything truly help? Don't be silly."

-Good morning!

-Oh, finally! I want to sleep…

-How was the night?

-Ah! Can you imagine King Head was all night here in the kitchen! And I was cooking eggs!

-Egg?

-Yes, in my traditional way! You cannot imagine how spicy it was, and he tried it!

-What? He is not allowed to eat spicy. He has an allergy, doesn't he?

-No, he is just not allowed …

-By his father or doctor?

-Which doctor? – she said it sarcastically

-Let's go to the room…

-Yes, and I will sleep finally.

-Were there any outdoor activities today?

-Yeah, hiking, tea, and temple as usual.

Head throbbing after just a few minutes in the kitchen, I offered GofG a retreat back to the room. The familiar space felt like a kennel, and I sank gratefully to the floor by the window. I'd forgotten to mention the tiny temple beside our room and a holy man in an orange dress, a daily source of..... well, let's just say morning prayers weren't exactly conducive to quiet contemplation. It was approximately 8 AM; I had almost one hour before my hell would wake up. "And plan?

Did I think to create a plan for how to avoid it? Did I ever dare to think about it?"

I was staring at GofG, falling asleep in the moment she reached the bad and thinking: "How would she react in my place? Would she tell me about it? Should I tell her? I can't... No". The urge to speak, to warn her, battled with the knowledge that the words wouldn't come. But the need to protect her burned fiercely within me. I had to make her understand - avoid him at all costs and push on King Head to protect her.

The hour bled by, each rustling outside, a dull ache in my head. Lost in a heavy fog, I gazed out the window, the world muted and distant. Suddenly, the old man's voice in his orange robes pierced the silence, his morning prayers echoing through the yard. The sound, a familiar anchor, dragged me deeper into a meditative state, a desperate attempt to escape. But the fragile peace shattered as a shadow fell across the doorway. A prickle of unease ran down my spine as I recognized the telltale shape of the night dress. A wave of nausea washed over me, a cold dread settling in the pit of my stomach. He is awake. Decided maybe to ask forgiveness from the

Gods for his sins yesterday. "Oh, don't be silly! Please! Wake up! You have to stand up, he will come soon for his morning 'procedures'".

The deeper I tried to connect with my body, the further I felt myself slipping away, falling through the endless depths of my mind. Reality dissolved, leaving me numb and disconnected. Forcing myself to get up from the floor, I raised a listless hand and draped the curtains over myself, a flimsy barrier against the unbearable weight of the next morning. An hour, I pleaded silently, just one more hour to face the onslaught of the day.

As usual, Pure Monster was trying to find me inside the house; he opened the door to our room, checked that only GofG was there, and went to the next door to the wellness room. I just create a problem for myself from the morning. Again, he will be pissed at me and definingly will show it with big pleasure.

Time to get up.

-Good morning, Ma'am!

-Hi.

-Is he in a wellness session?

-Yes.

-Okey, today you will go with us to serve "High Tea".

-Sure, I will be glad to help. And temple? Who will be with them?

-I think your colleague, because you will not be able to reach it on time.

-Got it.

-Let us know when the wellness will be done.

-As usual….

-And please check the laundry; we again didn't find the socks…

Again, these socks! Let me give you a rundown of my fishy daily duties. There are two people I'm responsible for attending to all their needs and cleaning tasks 24/7 inside the house. Now, here's the tricky part: company policy dictates that when the WS is at home, the staff is strictly prohibited from entering his living space for cleaning, bed-changing (a daily routine), adjusting lights, music, or temperature. So, who has to do it? I have.

Here's a breakdown of a typical morning: Turn on all lights (as per regulations); Check the room temperature and overall cleanliness; Inspect the shoes outside the main door -ensure they're clean and socks are collected for laundry; Verify the breakfast table is set with menus and newspapers are placed. After the WS wakes up: Check the bathroom for wet towels and laundry, clean removing them promptly. This applies to every time he uses the bathroom. Freshwater bottles are always placed in the bedroom and dining area, yet he'll still request water to be brought on a tray.

There are many such small details you need to handle, as no one else can enter until he leaves. Up until February, even butlers weren't involved in food service, acting solely as backup staff in the kitchen area.

So, regarding the socks he requested - they were likely left in the bathroom, and believe me, that's the last place I would not volunteer to go.

-Mari! How are you?

-Erela? Finished?

-Yes, he asked for water.

-Oh, God.. Sure, will do it shortly.

-Are you okey?

-No, - I choked out, the single word thick with unspoken pain. Her gaze held a silent understanding. Swallowing past the disgusted lump in my throat, I turned away, busying myself with the water and tray.

With the prepared tray, I went inside the house, reaching the dining area. I understood that he was not there and had probably gone to their bedroom. I didn't dare to go there as I knew how it would finish for me. I made some noise, placing the tray on the table, trying to show him that I was there. After a few minutes, probably angry, he went straight to the kitchen and found me in the dining area. He asked me to follow him.

I hate these moments when you literally push yourself down not to get punished later. Following him almost to the last room, he stopped in the living room and started to drink his water, pretending as if everything was normal. How much I hate this stupid game as a service for a man who probably is just enjoying this role-playing game. Finishing his fishy water, he took the tray from my hands and placed it on the sofa. With a gesture, he requested to follow him to the next room, showing with his hand something. I made two steps inside and a t-shirt or something similar which he probably was requesting to give for laundry.

-Now, come here -, he requested with a dissatisfied face, as I was supposed to do it without him asking me.

-I have to go.

-Can you stop it!? Give it! – he showed with his finger his nose and added – Give it when I ask you.

-Give what?

-Your nose! – he grabbed my face and pulled me to his smelly old face and started to kiss my nose as if it were a toy or baby face.

-Please, don't…. – I tried to push my head back.

-Listen, don't make me angry. Do you want a good career?? Are you a good worker?? I will through you out.

-Okey.

-Okey? So, you are naughty? Come here, don't pretend as if you don't like it;- He pulled me with hands again aggressively to his body, grabbed my buttocks with one hand and my head with another, trying to reach with his disgusting lips my nose. At that moment, I felt someone's shadow coming from the living room; I turned my face and saw his son, confused by the scene and trying to run away unnoticed. The WS was caught in flagrante delicto, and pushing me away, he started to greet his son as he hadn't seen him for a long year. How pathetic it was; we both know who you are and what you are doing. My face became red and confused as it was me who did something embarrassing. I grabbed the tray and wanted to fall through the ground so no one would see me anymore. Reaching the room, I found GofG still awake and confused as to why I was coming to our room with a tray and glass.

-Oh, it's just ... I forgot to...

-You forgot what? Are you okey?

-I don't know. I have to bring it back to the kitchen.

I felt embarrassed even to stay in front of her, so the best way was to calm myself in the kitchen area, my best place – sitting on my knees near the door.

The day was mostly calm; the morning incident seemed to have spooked the WS. He kept a low profile, likely fearing another witness. For me, the familiar rhythm of the kitchen was a balm, sedation. Assisting the butlers with packing the outdoor tea supplies, the routine movements soothed my nerves. Being around others, even briefly, offered a strange kind of comfort.

Finally, we prepared all the necessary and went for the designated mountain spot. The crisp air and breathtaking scenery filled me with a sense of peace I hadn't felt in days. Unfolding linens, arranging plates and cutlery, setting out thermoses and snacks - each task a small act of creation, a way to restore order in my chaotic world. For those few hours, I was lost in the simple pleasure of preparing the space, the worries of the house fading away. I never imagined that such simple tasks could bring such profound balance and comfort to my soul. I could have stayed there till the end of my trip, sleeping on the ground near the bushes under the stars, the vastness of the sky a stark contrast to the confines of my reality.

We were waiting longer than expected, and I just swallowed greedily every minute of my stolen freedom. So, why was I brought today for this afternoon tea? To pure the water! The sole responsibility they deemed worthy for me. How symbolic or sarcastic it is.

On the horizon, a burst of emerald green framed the emergence of two quadricycles. One roared into the jungle road, a blur of speed and reckless abandon. Behind it, a second vehicle lumbered along like a reluctant snail, its driver struggling to keep pace. The first rider was the King Head, his face flushed with a mix of adrenaline and thirst for excitement. Sometimes, I thought he would roll over before reaching the destination. His father trailed behind carefully, his presence rather out of place in such a fast-moving vehicle.

The race winner stopped on the road in front of our clearing and waited for his father to reach as well. And finally, the main actors came to the clearing and our prepared table was a silent testament to our work for them. With a heavy sigh, the WS sank into the chair, his eyes locked on his son, who, oblivious to his father's movements, continued to stare intently at his tablet. "Can you sit? Leave it for now at list". Taking a sit pure kid cowered in his favorite position and looked like a small hunched hook. As the "main waiter" today, I purred water for both of them and went silent behind the service table.

For the first time since arriving at this estate, a strange sense of protection and support settled over me. None of them had any idea what turmoil raged within me or the significance I placed on their presence in my mind.

Minutes ticked by, the silence broken only by the scrape of the WS's chair as he abruptly stood and headed back towards the road. His son trailed behind him, a dejected shadow, and they both made their way towards the nearby building, resembling an office. A tense feeling settled in the air. Perhaps something had transpired related to the work, but we had no way of knowing. We exchanged confused glances at each other and just continued to stay confused and wait for some actions.

After a while, realizing no one was returning, we decided to pack away the remaining snacks to keep them fresh. Suddenly, a bellow erupted from the building - the WS, his voice laced with fury. Moments later, they emerged, a grim tableau. Without a word, they mounted the single quad, the WS at the helm, and sped off towards the house. I grabbed my phone and called GofG, to be prepared that King was coming back to the house.

In a while, she called me back, and her voice, trembling with worry, echoed through the receiver. She said that they had been inside the house for more than one hour, and King Head was not responding to her messages. I offered empty reassurances to calm her down, but the chilling reality gnawing at me - The father is punishing his son. It's been an hour, and I can only imagine what's happening behind closed doors. No, not imagining. I know…

Dusk settled, bringing a chill to the air. Despite the growing darkness and cold, we remained at our posts, awaiting their return. No further instructions had been issued, leaving me in a state of watchful waiting and hope that he didn't get hard on this pure kid. Thousands of stars began to pepper the inky black canvas of the jungle sky. Each one, a tiny diamond chip, sparkled with an intensity that held me captive. The last whispers of the sunset lingered in the form of a deep, dusky pink that bled across the horizon, a fading masterpiece painted by the departing sun. It was a breathtaking spectacle, unlike anything I'd ever witnessed in all my time in India. The vastness of the sky felt all-encompassing, stretching endlessly above the lush canopy of the jungle. The silence was profound, broken only by the occasional chirp of a night insect, adding to the air of serenity. At that moment, under the breathtaking display of the cosmos, my worries seemed to shrink, replaced by a sense of awe and wonder.

-Mari, we are going.

-Canceled?

-Yes. They just will have dinner after the temple. So, we are packing.

-Let me help, give me some instructions.

-Collect all lights and candles.

-On my way – The words barely left my lips before I sprang into action, determined to complete the task. Intrusive thoughts barraged me, their insistent whispers forcing the words from my lips before I could stop them. "Coming back to hell," I muttered, the truth a bitter pill to swallow. With a sinking feeling, I knew what awaited me – his anger, surely even more potent than usual.

Returning to the house, we found the kitchen in the middle of dinner serving. Everyone was in their usual rush and I decided to stay here and not return to my room. Again, my best place was dishwashing, I went to the back area and started to sort out the rubble of dishes. Starting my meditation-cleaning, I heard a female voice behind me:

-What are you doing again here?

-Just helping; they are all in a rush, so they need clean dishes to serve the next course.

-Oh, God, just say that you don't want to stay in the house.

-Yes, you got me!

-Me neither…

-Wanna join?

-Yes, let's do it.

Slipping her phone away, she seamlessly transitioned back into work mode. What I truly appreciated about her was her ability to anticipate and synchronize with my actions. There was no need for constant instruction, neither from me nor her. We operated on a kind of unspoken understanding, a telepathy that flowed effortlessly. Suddenly, she broke the silence, 'Should we listen to some music??"- Genius idea!'" Menial tasks, especially cleaning, became a breeze with the soundtrack of our youth playing in the background. She grabbed her phone, popped a headphone in my ear, and launched into one of our favorite teenage anthems. A wave of nostalgia washed over us, and before we knew it, we were bopping along as we tackled the dishes. Minutes melted away as I found myself singing along, completely lost in the moment. The rhythm of the music and the camaraderie with this amazing woman made everything else fade away. We must have looked like a pair of lunatics, belting out tunes and dancing around the silent dishwashing room. But the thought of it, instead of reminding my situation, only fueled the energy. We cranked up the volume and danced with even more abandon. That evening, I grasped one of life's most important truths: true happiness comes not from possessions or accomplishments but from the connections we forge with others. This will be my lifeline, pulling me out of the depths of hellish despair I'd sunk myself into. It offers a glimmer of hope, a chance to escape the relentless grip of suffering and suicidal intention that haunts my thoughts.

As the night deepened, the ever-growing mountain of dishes brought a perverse kind of satisfaction. I was determined not to finish the job before he went to sleep. The arrival of dessert plates, brought in by the butlers, signaled the end of the dinner.

My heart leaped with a sliver of hope -his wellness session must be next. Perhaps GofG would be brave to bring him water this time. This day rekindled a spark of hope within me. Just a few more days, and I'll be leaving this oppressive place behind forever.

****

The next morning, I woke up in a better mood than yesterday, probably because I had seen the monster only in the morning. I felt braver again and wanted to keep this feeling till the end of this hell trip. As always, after morning wellness, I was requested by him for a glass of water, and I decided to change today's tactic. I asked GofG to come with me this time, and from today, we will bring him what he wants together. That sounds like a perfect plan for us. So, each of us took a tray with water, and we went inside the house; not finding him in the kitchen area, we went to the living room and decided not to go deeper. As I was in front, he came out, and his happy face changed in confusion when he saw her. He looked at us, came to her, and took the water from her tray. Requesting with the gest to live the house. That was the action that I didn't expect.

"You can go", he verbally repeats his request to her. Did not have other choices - she left me. Would I create anything not to leave her alone? Probably, I would stay near the dining area and wait, but maybe not. Now, I can easily create how I would react or what I would answer him.

-What was that? Why she is here?

-She has to study the job.

-Ah.. no need. I will teach her. Don't bring her again. – he came closer, finishing his first glass of water, and hit my buttocks as I am a naughty child - Did you understand me?

-She has to…

-Did you understand what I said?!

-Yes…

-Put the tray.

I stood frozen, defying his unspoken command. He snatched the tray, his usual scowl deepening with irritation, and placed it roughly on the sofa.

-Come here, hug me - requesting his usual stinky shit, he grabbed me and tried to push his hand between my legs. I felt so much scare bombing in my head that I thought my eyes would break out now.

-What are you looking at me? Do you think I am joking here with you?? - gripping my shoulders with bruising force, his face contorted with rage, he bellowed - Do you understand English? Hello??

-Yes

-So, what is your problem?? – he asked.

I was staring at the floor, trying to compress my entire body into hard stone. Because it felt like a most secure position in those moments when he touched me, he grabbed me again and started to touch my body in an aggressively stroking manner, simulating kisses with sounds: "Come on, kiss me. "

-No, I have to go – oh no, did I say it in voice? Why did you open your mouth? Was it so hard to think first or just leave silently?

He became pissed. Now I felt all anger and heaviness in his arms, which pushed me away so hard that I landed on the floor.

Leaving his threat hanging in the air, - This is my last warning. - he retreated to the solitude of his bedroom.

Fair enough, just kick me out of this place and don't touch me anymore.

***

"When I missed that moment that I already became a victim of priests and violence and accepted it also? For a long time, I hadn't realized the impact of what had happened to me and how it changed my life. It took nearly a year of therapy only to unearth this buried truth, not to threaten it. The trauma left me accepting violence as a possibility, a fear that lingers even now till this morning day when I am typing my story. I am still in the same stage and have mental issues. I am still thinking that my next experience with a man related to the job or any other relationship will bring me hell. The specter of abuse haunts my thoughts. Will every new relationship, professional or personal, lead me down a similar path? Will I accept mistreatment, trapped in a cycle of violence? Can I truly escape the next abuse and harassment? For more than nine months, I've been working with my therapist to dismantle the walls I've built around myself. Even small steps are not visible in this long journey. I struggle with an eating disorder and a negative body image, as I hate to look beautiful or feminine. Opening the wardrobe, I am always trying to take an oversized black color t-shirt that will cover all signs of a female body. These issues have become deeply ingrained, feeling almost foundational to who I am."

Rising from the floor, I snatched the tray from the sofa and retreated to the kitchen. The thought of returning to our room, of facing GofG's inevitable barrage of questions, was unbearable. With the tray settled back on the table, I retreated outside, seeking solace near the house door. I knelt, as usual; the cool floor was a grounding presence.

You might find this hard to believe, but in that moment, a twisted sense I deserve it. Yes. What just happened this morning, I got what I deserved because yesterday I dared to allow myself to smile and have fun and create stupid plans on how to avoid his disgust touches.

The universe, it seemed, was bringing me back to real life, a chance to yank myself out of this suffocating nightmare before I became even more deeply entrenched. But every flicker of joy, every fleeting smile, has at a cost- a heavy weight of struggle and suffering.

The day was routine and usual, but today, I was operated on to go on top hiking. I had no idea what it would be and what kind of action would be requested from me. After lunch, father and son, as a perfect fishy-happy family, went to outdoor activities, and we were preparing bags for the same outdoor tea time and one more for hiking. I was responsible for carrying it.

Changing my skirt to comfortable jeans I grabbed that bag with cold drinks and took a sit in the car with a guide guy. We drove almost 20 minutes to reach the same mountain where the temple is located. It was approximately 5 PM, and the sun was still burning you as in hell. The guide got out of the car and said:

-Now we are going on foot, as there are no roads to the top.

-Which top?

-That one – he gestured with the hand, showing me an unreachable place.

-What time will it take to get there?

-Oh, maybe 30-40 minutes. Don't worry, it is not so far.

The guide, a picture of effortless confidence with his well-prepared body and water bottler, likely enjoyed a hearty breakfast and lunch before tackling this steep climb. Meanwhile, I hadn't eaten all day and yesterday evening. Five minutes in, my legs threatened to buckle beneath me, sapped of energy. Every step was an uphill battle against the relentless sun. No cool breeze offered solace, and my mouth felt like a desert. Still, I pressed on, the summit of this infernal mountain a grueling 2 km away.

When the guide barked at me to pick up the pace, claiming we needed to reach the top before "them," the weight of his words felt crushing. The urge to hurl that heavy bag with drinks at him was overwhelming. I never thought I'd utter these words, but the fear of telling him that I couldn't complete the assigned task was stronger than my exhaustion. My trait of an executive slave - dutifully completing every task without question held me captive this time also.

Reaching the peak, I collapsed onto the ground, gasping for breath and fighting off dizziness. My parched mouth craved moisture. Just a few feet away, a well-stocked bag, which I hardly brought, taunted me with its glistening bottles of water. I could allow myself to take one small bottle. The worker's code - no food or drink which is prepared for First Family echoed in my head. It was a fair rule, generally speaking. But in such a situation and even getting so much suffering during my work here I still could not break this small rule! Why? Why am I such a conformist?

Farther down the mountain, I spotted two black quad bikes approaching the switchbacks we had just hiked. A young boy was with a passenger and, as usual, was driving them fast and skillfully while his father trudged behind, swallowing dust. I stood up to greet them, offering the cold drinks I'd brought up here, almost dying along the way.

Parking on the top, they stood down from the quad bikes and we started the weirdest hiking in my life. The road was covered with slippery grass and located on the edge, so one fall and you are out of this mountain. I was following them and observing the WS steps, even hoping he would slip once.

-No, son. I can't …. What is the program for today?

-We are going to that tree; it has a good vantage point all around.

-But here it is also good, no need to go so far.

-How you wish.

-Let's go back. This is amazing hiking, but I am tired. Yes? Are you tired also? - He approached his son and began to touch the boy inappropriately between his legs. Confused, I turned around and realized everyone else was doing the same.

Now I understand the unspoken rule: "When the White Shirt engages in unacceptable behavior, you close your mouth and then close your eyes. This is a rule I will never accept under any circumstances! I would rather suffer and not drink water, which is not mine, than be a silent witness to the blatant violation of basic moral principles like bullying and humiliation. You can ask me to stay awake for 30 hours and perform hard physical labor, and I will do it without complaint. However, don't ask me to turn a blind eye to immorality. I felt so angry and rage at the injustice of the whole situation to this kid that I couldn't stop my rapid breathing.

On the trek back to the quad bikes, King Head lagged behind us by ten paces, perhaps embarrassed by his lack of hiking prowess compared to his driving skills or maybe due to the earlier confusing situation. The view was truly breathtaking: rolling green mountains stretched across the horizon. Despite my greater love for nature than the human world, I couldn't fully appreciate it.

They climbed onto their bikes and rode back, leaving a trail of dust in their wake. I felt relief and a sense of accomplishment after the physically demanding trek.

-We should hurry, - the guide addressed to me, changing the direction.

Hurry? Where?

To the tea point. It will start soon.

You can't reach the tea point before them. We're on foot.

Come on. Fast. I will show you.

The guide wasn't kidding. He steered us onto a narrow path that looked more like a ski slope than a road. He took off running, sprinting down the mountain! It was a very steep and bumpy path, nearly a 70-degree incline. I wasn't running; I was practically falling, hoping not to slip and tumble down the mountain like a ragdoll, cracking my ribs in the process. I hopped from step to step, desperately searching for secure footing, silently praying for a safe end to this madness. In the distance, I saw them driving leisurely, reaching the same destination. Incredibly, we all arrived at the tea point at the same time. But deep down, I vowed that this would be the first and last time I'd ever put myself in such danger. "Oh, my dear girl," a voice echoed in my head, "this is nothing. You'd be better off falling and breaking something so you could leave this place for sure."

Night fell upon the mountain, bringing a sense of foreboding. I clung to the hope that I could hide again by washing dishes during dinner, allowing GofG to take water to him alone bravely. The night also brought a tense atmosphere between the son and his father. The White Shirt's mood was undeniably foul and laced with anger. Whenever he's angry, he unleashes it on the workers. Today, it was the butler's turn. Seeking any excuse to draw attention, he called one of them closer, demanding explanations for trivial matters like an unusual-tasting snack or lukewarm tea. He bullied them for every minor detail and imperfection, and terminations often followed these outbursts. Yes, working here came with significant risk. Being fired on a whim when the "God" was in a bad mood was a constant threat. A true joke, not a job.

I think not only the girls were going through feelings of disappointment, but the guys as well. It was the moment they realized they could be fired any day without reason, explanation, or compensation. Of course, I wouldn't dare to compare girls' situations. And I can't forget that everyone turned a blind eye to the boss's perversions. Inaction is a crime in my eyes, and I could never forgive them for that.

Gazing at the butler's face after his verbal abuse of the White Shirt, I felt a surge of empathy and asked, "Are you okay?" His expression morphed into a strained smile, revealing a clear message: he would never show me his true self. Here, everyone plays a game of survival. There are no healthy relationships between our departments, and it seems unlikely there ever will be.

With a determined resolve to head straight for the kitchen, I exited the car upon returning to the house. Grabbing a few manageable bags, I slipped past the butlers and made my way to the kitchen area. I immersed myself in helping with other tasks, deliberately keeping myself occupied to avoid setting foot inside the house. After all, dinner hadn't begun yet, and the possibility of someone asking me to fetch the White Shirt and inquire about his dinner preferences loomed large. To further cement my excuse, I even forced myself to eat.

-Hey, you are back... - a gentle voice of GofG interrupted my meal.

-Hey G..

-Are you eating? And didn't call me?

-He just placed it, sorry. How is it inside?

-Oh, they are on the terrace, discussing something. I came to tell you that we could start dinner in 5 minutes.

-Oh, what wonderful news!

Relief washed over me. Finally, I could begin my favorite task: washing dishes! I abandoned my unfinished meal and practically skipped back to the kitchen, a wide smile plastered on my face. Tomorrow would be my last night of hiding, my last night in this hellhole. Happiness and peace coexisted within me. As I prepped the dish-drying area, my mind buzzed with plans for the future -where I'd go, which country I'd visit. Perhaps a break by the ocean, a few weeks to unwind, was in order. With every passing second, my plans lifted me further away from this house, from the pain and tears, from the worst chapter of my life.

I was so lost in thought that I didn't realize dinner was over, and the White Shirt had already left for his wellness session. Empowered by a surge of strength, I temporarily forgot why I'd avoided entering the house before he went to sleep.

I reached the girls' room, flopped onto the bed, and began scrolling through new Instagram reels. Just then, the door creaked open. The White Shirt's silhouette stood in the doorway, a look of surprise etched on his face at finding me there. He started to enter the room as I bolted out of bed.

-I am going to bring water, it is ready.

-What? Ha, yes, please go.

Leaving him mildly bewildered, I bolted out of the room and sprinted towards the wellness room. Grabbing Erela's hand, I nervously pleaded with her not to leave the house and to make as much noise as possible until I returned with the tray:

-Don't worry. I will be here.

-Please…

-Don't worry, bring him water.

Almost flying into the kitchen, I snatched a water bottle from the fridge, poured a glass, and raced back to the house. The White

Shirt was stationed in the dining area, anticipating his evening dose of female attention. I thrust the large glass of water toward him, and he downed it in less than ten seconds before setting it on the table. BAM!

-What is this?

-Erela is cleaning the wellness room.

-Ah, okay. Come here, hug me.

-She's here.

-I said come here! - He took a step toward me, initiating his repulsive embrace. BAM! I sidestepped again, feeling him release his hands in frustration. "It works! He's scared of being caught!"

-I need to go. Good night! - I snatched the empty glass from the table and fled the dining area, leaving him perplexed once more. Entering the wellness room, I silently thanked Erela with a wave of gratitude for her assistance. Today, I emerged victorious from this fight.

Don't Sleep on the Frontline.

Act 1

"Last day!" My mind fixated on a single thought: today was my escape from this hellhole. I woke up as usual, conducting the routine checkups around the house and holding a brief meeting with the kitchen staff and butlers. Conversations held no appeal for me today; my focus was solely on packing my bags and fleeing this country that had brought me nothing but shame and disgust.

One disquieting thought still lingered amidst my dreams of a peaceful future: GofG. Would King Head look after her? How could I trust a boy who, until now, had turned a blind eye to the violence and perversion within these walls? How could I be content leaving her here alone? And the new girls? They would simply replace me, perpetuating this infernal cycle. This hell cycle will never finish.

Sitting by the window in the girls' room, I contemplated the future of this immoral place. Two sides of me warred: one, perhaps ego-driven, urging me to stay out of trouble, and the other - I lack the words to describe it - a fierce protectiveness that roared within me. This powerful urge to help, I had never felt it before, never heard it so deafeningly within.

I turned and glanced at GofG, who was finally asleep after a night spent awake in the kitchen area. As I watched her, I desperately searched for a reason to justify leaving her behind. Unable to find one, I rose and stepped outside for some fresh air. I clutched the list of today's activities, treating it as my final act in this place. Relief washed over me, a calming emptiness settling within. The day unfolded predictably: outdoor activities, tea time, and the temple visit. Yet, a rising wave of nausea threatened to engulf me as I remembered he'd soon awaken and request water. My mind, however, had already abandoned this place. Unable to stomach facing him again, I placed the list back on the kitchen table and retreated into the room, hiding behind the curtains: "I don't want to go through it even last time."

With headphones on to block out any disturbing noises from outside the door, I texted Erela to let me know when the wellness session was over. "Today, nothing can drag me back into that hellhole. I'll do whatever it takes to avoid his harassment.

-Wellness is done, honey

-Thank you...Can you ask butlers to bring him water? I am in the bathroom. I can't...

-Sure. I understand

"I know you understand like no one else here."- She's the second one in this house subjected to the boss's "true preferences." I never directly inquired about what happens behind those doors because I knew if I were in her shoes, the last thing I'd do is talk about it. It's not a matter of trust; it's shame.

Her contract is with a connected company, allowing her to leave without penalty once it's over. Additionally, she has more power and privileges, granting her freedom outside the house during her off-time and limiting her to "wellness sessions" only. The girls hired directly by the company, however, work 12-hour shifts.

Essentially, they're confined to the house or on standby, ready to be called upon for "massages" at his every whim.

As I already mentioned the day was usual. After lunchtime, they went out for some outdoor activities, and I was preparing to get to the tea point to serve the most important thing there: water. After "tea," to spend some fishy time near the temple, which makes me most irritated. The act of deceiving both themselves and their deity constitutes the most profound contradiction. Even the worst criminals hold some respect for religion and morality. Here, though, this supposed holy man was a walking contradiction - a festering core of depravity encased within an aged exterior. It baffled me how such a rotten-twisted soul could exist under the guise of faith.

After waiting for them on the mountaintop for over three hours, as I missed tea time entirely due to disorganization and constant schedule changes, every passing minute fueled my frustration, drawing my mind back to the unsettling discoveries from our previous escorting them to the temple. I was looking at those deep stars last to me and thinking: How could this seemingly spiritual man have become so morally corrupt? He was born into a wealthy family, his father having built it from the ground up. The man who provided him with such immense privilege in life would likely be horrified to see what his son has become and how he sexually treats his grandson. Does this old pervert ever think of his father with any respect? When did this man transform into such a monster? Was it when he was a child and first tasted wealth? How does this happen? At what point in their lives do these rapists realize that abuse brings them happiness and satisfaction? When they murder a defenseless animal or strike a girl in anger? Where is the turning point when they sell their souls to the devil, sacrificing their sanity and all the moral principles instilled by their parents in childhood? Perhaps it's a curse, some warped predisposition that marks them for darkness and a life of inflicting pain on others. Maybe they were born with this black mark and selected to bring dirt into this world.

-Mam, they are reaching.

-Coming. – I stepped out of the car, switched on my headlamp light, and, observing two quadbikes, continued my reflections.

Why was I so into it? To find an excuse for this scum's actions towards me? Yes? This was probably my intention; I couldn't accept in my head that someone could inflict such torment on another for no reason. And to this day, I have the same issue. I'm always trying to find the root cause.

-Oh, who's there? Where have you been? I haven't seen you all day! -the main actor of my reflections began to show me, in a "public way," that I would soon get a big punishment for avoiding him all day. I already knew this game and what it meant for me…

-I was busy with backup preparations.

-Okay, let's go to the temple. He's waiting for us. - "He" refers to the temple servicer who would probably be relieving all their new sins in front of the god.

Reaching the withered bench, I hoped he wouldn't ask me to sit with them again. Dust devils danced around the withered bench, mocking my silent plea. He wouldn't ask me to join them, would he? Every fiber of my being recoiled at the thought. I melted into the shadows behind the guide, desperate to shrink my very silhouette.

The irony scraped at my soul. Here, on a holy ground revered by millions, a stench of hypocrisy hung heavy. Disrespect, ridicule, neglect - a mockery of faith itself. It was a grotesque performance, a circus of what I felt a shame being a part of. "What a big joke and impiety mockery! Involving Gods as actors.

"We abstain from meat," they proclaimed, their voices dripping with piety, "yet women are fair game for harassment and rape." A bitter laugh escaped my lips, echoing off the silent hill. This, this was the greatest blasphemy I'd ever witnessed and involuntarily. Defiling the very concept of divinity with their twisted justifications. Wretched and insignificant act of flouting that has nothing to do with the highest creator or creators.

-What is so funny? – the WS interruption came swiftly, silencing my thoughts.

-Nothing. I sneezed, Sir. Sorry.

-Ah, okey.. – he muttered, then stood up to get into the temple, his son following behind.

Ah, the classic redemption arc - curt "Okay" followed by a vigorous stair climb. Guess scaling those dusty steps into the temple burns away a multitude of sins, doesn't it? Divine cardio, perhaps? Or maybe they just craved some pre-dinner chanting. Whatever the reason, it makes for a much more palatable story, wouldn't you say? Let's just gloss over the whole "gleefully harassing women" bit and focus on their newfound piety. After all, a little embellishment never hurt anyone… except maybe their already fragile consciences.

Act2

As we departed the so-called "place of atonement," twilight deepened into a star-dusted night. The heavens blazed with celestial fire, weaving a spell across the vast expanse. I was certain we were headed back to the house, but our self-proclaimed "king," WS, had other plans. Apparently, even here, making a mockery of English traditions of "Afternoon Tea" and taking it in the middle of the night, he doesn't feel confused. My evening was full of sarcasm that day…

On the way back to the house, my mood was already combative. I was so angry and hostile, even ready to fight him physically if he dared to touch me again.

Reaching the back kitchen area, I was greeted with the usual chaos that preceded "the feast during the plague" - dinnertime. Knowing my best and safest bet was the dishwashing area, I headed straight there without a word, even ignoring GofG's message, beckoning me to the room.

It was already late, so everyone was rushing to start dinner before midnight. After all, our "lovely" boss and his son were leaving for Europe in the morning.

-What are you doing again here?

-Oh, why are you not sleeping G? Take rest as you will fly tomorrow with them. You need to handle the shift.

-I will go now. I just wanted to speak with King Head. He is not replying.

-You know when he is with his father, he will not do it. Don't worry. He loves you.

-Oh! Stop it!! Be silent; someone can hear you!

-Everyone already knows, come on! It is obvious that you guys are in love…

GofG's eyes widened in confusion, a blush creeping up her neck like a flame. Caught between joy and embarrassment, a shy smile played on her lips. To stop this conversation, she quickly changed the topic:

-I am going back, come after dinner…

-Okey. Try to take some rest…

Leaving me alone, I put on headphones and started washing the dishes one by one. Scrolling all day, especially evening I have got some bitterness.

"So many bad thoughts I gave today for the god": a hollow counterpoint to the silent scream building in my chest. Headphones became a flimsy shield against the storm of questions raging in my mind: "I did not think anything bad about Him, but I used His name in swearing another person." Scrolling my thoughts near the temple offered no solace, only more flickering abyss.

God. What was his role in this mess? In all this? My life felt like a cruel joke, a tapestry woven with frustration and unanswered questions. Why are people complaining to God in all their troubles – Why am I doing the same now? Why plead for handouts when I had hands of my own? A functioning mind? Weren't those his gifts?

A bitter laugh escaped my lips. So, I built this hell? Every misstep, every heartbreak, a brick laid by my hand? Is that it? Answer me, dammit! Is it all my fault? Answer me…. Is it my fault?

-Mari!

-Ha? Yeah. Sorry, I am in headphones.

-We finished; get some rest, please.

-But there are still some plates…

-Leave it. We will finish. You go back in the house.

Wiping my hands, I left the kitchen with a big question mark in my head: "What was that? Why did I get so mad? This is your last day; just stop and concentrate on your goal". Reaching the house door, I opened it and faced the WS entering the Wellness Room. "How stupid you are! Did you completely lose your mind?"

-Come here

-Yes, sir. How can I assist…

-Come to my room afterward. I am leaving tomorrow. My son will be busy.

-I have to work.

-Did you hear me? – He shot me a furious look, clearly indicating it wasn't an offer, and then stormed into the wellness room. My mood in tatters, I entered our girls' room.

-Why are you not sleeping?

-Waiting for my King Head, he said he will come when his father goes for a massage

-He is there…

-Who?

-WS, who else? He told me to come after wellness…

-Come where?

-To his room. Where else? You forgot with whom you are working, girl. Wake up…

-Is he mad? Again?? Text King Head and ask him to help

-Oh, really? How?

Door Knocking

-God, who is there?! - I was so scared that I dropped down between our two beds and hid myself under a small piece of bedding

-Are you mad? It's King Head, Jesus! Get up.

-Oh, God, I thought it was your father… Guys, I will leave you for a while, I need some fresh area.

Of course, I didn't need any fresh area just didn't want to be the third wheel. I went outside and took a seat on the backside in a dark point. "Nothing should disturb me now." I was trying to keep my mind clean because the last time, I was already scared of my next thoughts.

I received a message from GofG to "come back," and after a while observing the sky and getting really frozen, I went back to the house as I could not stay anymore in such cold. The King Head had already left, as I understood after opening the door.

-Done?

-Done what?

-Kisses

-Stop!! We didn't kiss! Are you mad??

-And what did you do here?

-Nothing! Why did you leave?

-To give you guys some time …. To kiss….

-Stop!! What are you talking about?!

-Nothing, I don't know what to do.

-Don't go anywhere. Just be in the kitchen with the butler.

-Oh, yeah? And when this pervert will come and say:" Come here," What am I supposed to do? Will Butler save me from going inside the house?

-Then stay here, and that's all.

"Door's handle*

-Down!! – My breath hitched. In a heartbeat, I scrambled down between the beds, muffling a gasp with a trembling hand. From my hiding place, I stole a glance at GoG, feigning sleep with unnerving stillness. Then I saw his legs in the doorway through the crevice under the bed. Wedged almost inside our room, WS panted heavily, sickening beat and probably observing GofG sleeping.

The most horrifying thought clawed at my mind: "What if he stalks closer, right beside the bed?"

Terror coiled in my gut, a cold serpent squeezing the air from my lungs. My blood hammered in my ears, masking the frantic rhythm of my heartbeat. Every muscle screamed, begging me to stay perfectly still. Blinking felt like a thunderclap in the suffocating silence.

Door closed

For what felt like an eternity, we held our positions in suffocating silence. Was he still here? The lingering tension finally snapped me back to reality. I cautiously reached out and touched GoG's hand, a silent question about her well-being.

-He went to the kitchen, – she whispered.

-Yes…

-He will ask them where you are.

-I don't care.

-No! You don't understand. They will say you are in the house…

-Oh, no…

-And he will come again, and this time inside the room…

-I must hide in the bathroom!

Door's handle

The doorknob creaked open again, a weird groan that scraped against my sanity. A primal terror flooded me, cold and suffocating. I braced myself for the inevitable, for the brutal storm about to engulf me. A grim acceptance settled in - I was ready. Ready for the pain, the punishment for being discovered. A final glance at GofG, her face a mask of strained sleep, a tremor barely disguised beneath her stillness. A wave of crushing guilt washed over me. I had dragged her into this nightmare, and now she'd face the consequences.

My gaze darted back to the doorway, waiting for the silhouette to solidify from the shadows. Each ragged breath he took seemed to amplify in the suffocating silence, a monstrous lullaby counting down the seconds until my world shattered.

Back door slam

The back door slammed shut. A confused voice, undoubtedly WS's, boomed, "Ah, son! Where have you been?" Hurriedly shutting our door, WS tried to distract his son from the awkward situation.

Seizing this opportunity, I scrambled to my feet, fueled by a surge of adrenaline. I practically flew into the bathroom, slamming the door behind me. Plunged into darkness, I fumbled around, searching for somewhere to hide. Panic clawed at me, making clear thinking difficult. Finally, regaining some sense of direction, I approached the other bathroom door. Thankfully, our room had two exits - this one leading to the yard. After my first harrowing night here, I'd discovered how to unlock it, a potential escape route in case of emergency.

Reaching the door, I creaked it open silently and tiptoed outside barefoot. I found myself behind the kitchen, then slipped inside through the back door to the dishwashing area. My first step met with a wet floor, but I ignored it and focused on finding a hiding place.

-What are you doing here?

-Ah? Nothing, trying to find my headphones…

-The WS was asking for you.

-When?

-Just a few minutes ago.

-Oh, we spoke already, thanks.

Disoriented, I stumbled back outside and reached the bathroom door. A frantic thought echoed in my head: "I forgot my phone inside the room!" I berated myself, "How stupid can you be?

Calm down!" Sinking to the floor beside the door, I took deep breaths, desperately trying to regain control.

The cold tile seeped through my thin skirt, a stark contrast to the burning knot of panic in my stomach. My phone. How could I have been so careless? It was my only lifeline with GofG and some information about WS's location.

A wave of self-loathing washed over me. How did I even get myself into this situation? It all seemed so surreal. Just a few months ago, life was ordinary. Sure, there were monotonous jobs, but at least I was safe. Now, I was trapped in this house with a man who seemed to enjoy inflicting fear, a constant shadow looming over my every move.

The memory of GoG's feigned sleep sent a pang of guilt twisting through me. She'd risked to hide me, and now she'd face the consequences of my mistake. Tears welled up in my eyes, blurring the already dim light in the yard. I had to get myself together for GofG, for myself.

Taking another shaky breath, I forced myself to focus on the immediate task at hand. Retrieving my phone was a risk, but the alternative - being completely cut off - was terrifying. I had to find a way back inside the room, undetected, and get back here. This is the safest place, as he would never go out of the house in the middle of the night. The plan felt flimsy and riddled with holes, but it was the only one I had.

-Are you alive? - I whispered as quietly as possible, getting inside the room.

-Oh, my god! Mari!

-What?

-He came again.... Came inside the room and checked it!

-Oh, my God...- I knelt near her bed, grabbing my head.

-Yes! I think he will come back in some time...

-I was in the kitchen a few minutes ago... They will tell him that I was there, and he will understand that I am outside and...

-Calm down, go back. I will text you if he will come inside our room again.

Clutching my phone, I stepped outside and sank onto the cold ground. My mind was numb, devoid of thought or feeling. Only a hollow expectation remained.

For the next three hours, as the pre-dawn chill deepened and the sweetest time for sleep arrived, I endured a series of shivers. Every twenty minutes or so, I'd force myself into the kitchen for a brief respite from the cold, only to return to the bathroom door, seeking a semblance of comfort. Each time, sleep would snatch me momentarily, then abandon me in a jolt of shivering wakefulness. Dawn was approaching, casting light across the yard, and I was now exposed to the security and arriving staff. It was clear - hiding here was no longer an option. Utterly depleted, my body ached for the sleep I couldn't give it.

At around 5 AM, a message from GofG flickered on my screen. It signaled the start of the fight, but I was already spent.

WhatsApp GofG 05:02 AM

-Come

-Come? Now?

I bolted upright and hurried back to our room, only to find it empty. Figuring GofG was in the kitchen, I ventured outside again, slipping through the back door to the dishwashing area before reaching the kitchen.

-Oh, Good morning, chef!

-Good morning – one of the newly arrived chefs mumbled in response.

GofG sidled closer and hissed in my ear, -Where have you been?

-Waiting for your message, - I replied cautiously.

-He came again... -Came where?

-He came again to our room and was looking for you, - she explained urgently. - I woke up when he entered the room. I told him you weren't there, and then he came out here to the kitchen.

Door slammed

Terror surged through me as the house door suddenly swung open. Without a word, I bolted from the kitchen from the backside, seeking refuge near the same bathroom. Entering inside, I sneaked up to the girls' room door and strained to hear who was answering his questions. The slamming of a door sent my heart pounding. He was coming back. I darted back into the bathroom and returned to the kitchen - a desperate attempt to show everyone around normalcy. Without any look on staff, I reached GofG with trembling hands. I was on the verge of exploding. Grabbing the cup from GoG's hand, I busied myself making her coffee, my mind racing with frantic thoughts about what to do next.

-You have to do something, - GofG rasped, her voice strained with exhaustion.

-Do what??! – I roared, my voice laced with the hysteria that echoed through the kitchen - go to the room; I will bring you the coffee.

-Okey... Good luck.. - she whispered, her voice barely audible.

Continuing to stir the already-dissolved coffee, I kept my eyes downcast, a knot of shame tightening in my stomach; I didn't want to make eye contact with anyone from the staff. I knew the staff could sense the matter of what was going on inside the house, their gazes adding to my humiliation.

Grabbing the cup, I slunk out of the kitchen directly inside the house, defeat etched on my face. As I trudged down the hallway, a flicker of movement caught my eye in the doorway of the wellness room. The WS was sitting on the sleeping bed with a lowered head. Pretending that I didn't see him, I went to the girl's room door when his voice came out:

-Where are you going?

-I need to bring coffee to GofG. She woke up.

-Come here.

-I have to leave the cup – I opened the door and came inside the room. Looking at GofG with red and crystal eyes, I left the cup on the table and went back for my last fight.

-Where have you been?

-I was in the kitchen, sir.

-No, - he took my hand and dragged me to the wellness room – explain yourself.

-Sir, I was busy with catering and helping in the kitchen….to prepare all boxes for your flight…

-All night?

-Almost all night.

-Hmm – he grabbed my head and stared into my face, searching for any flicker of deceit.

My eyes get destructed with shadows in the corridor. GofG…. I saw GofG's face full of confusion and alarm, returning to our room.

"She saw it... I know ... I felt naked in that moment. What a hellish shame".

-Okey, go take a rest. Go.

Dread gnawed at me as I exited the perverse wellness room. Surprised of not getting a punishment I couldn't believe he allowed me to leave so easily. Reaching our door, a wave of apprehension washed over me. Facing GofG now felt like an insurmountable task. "What a shame"- a bitter thought flickered across my mind – "Why do I feel this way?'". With a trembling hand, I pushed the door open and stepped inside.

-What happened there? – looking at me with understandable eyes, she asked silently.

-Where?

-In the wellness room.

-He asked where I was all night.

-And you?

-Nothing...

-Okey...

Neither she nor I were ready to speak about it, as it's always easier to keep silent.

-I want to sleep so much...

-Take rest

-Wake me up before you leave. Don't leave without a goodbye.

-Okey. Sleep...

Memories From Whatsapp Chat With Erela 06:13 Am: Evidence Exhibit 20b Police Report.

"-Fuck this horrible night.

-Oh no, why? What's happened?

-I will tell you.

-OK, Are you ok?

-25 hours my shift for the moment, and he is pissed

-Come here tomorrow as soon as you can.

-He is upset a lot.

-Oh fuck, why?

-He was trying to find me all night.

-*sad emoji*

-I was running around the all house.

-Oh, bless you. He is leaving very soon.

-Chef understood that something was wrong."

My hands were so exhausted I could barely hold the phone. A similar paralysis gripped my entire body. I lacked the energy, or even the awareness, to change position or feel the discomfort of the scattered objects beneath me. Dragging the blanket over myself, I welcomed the familiar embrace of sleep. It descended so swiftly that I doubt I even took a breath. Nothing, I thought, could disturb or wake me this early morning - my biggest blunder.

"Wet...something wet.." the thought echoed through my waking mind. A primal dread clenched my gut. Something was wrong, terribly wrong. "GofG? Is that you?" My voice emerged as a hoarse rasp. The wetness grew, spreading across my lips and invading my mouth. A horrifying realization dawned: "It wasn't GofG...."Oh God, no..." My eyelids fluttered open, a sliver of consciousness piercing the haze of sleep.

WS loomed over me, his face contorted with a sickening mix of excitement and predatory hunger. His right hand clamped down between my legs, repeating rubbing movements with pressure. My breath hitched; a strangled gasp trapped in my constricted throat. Panic surged, a primal scream clawing its way up my esophagus.

But before the scream could take form, I managed a single, desperate sound - a strangled cry that defied definition. It was a patent on a dying squeal, a desperate plea for help that echoed in the suffocating silence of the room. The sound seemed to stun him momentarily. He recoiled, his eyes widening in unsatisfaction before he scrambled out of the room, the slam of the door the only punctuation to the suffocating silence that descended.

Stage of Despair

Knocked in the door

-Mam? Good morning! Mam?

-Yes, what?

-Mam, we need to clean all the rooms and close the house.

-Give me 5 minutes.

-Sure, Mam. – the housekeeping guy didn't even dare to open the door and carried on the conversation behind closed doors.

Rising from the bed, I began gathering the scattered clothes around me, shoving them into the small black suitcase. I raided the bathroom, tossing my toiletries onto the growing pile without bothering to pack them properly or check if the bottles were sealed. Yanking on a pair of jeans and a black t-shirt, I crumpled the uniform into a ball and hurled it into the luggage with a surge of anger. Slamming the suitcase shut with my foot, I kicked it repeatedly until the clothes were compressed enough for me to close it properly. With a cursory glance around to ensure I hadn't forgotten anything (though, at that moment, I barely cared), I snatched my phone and the bag, storming towards the kitchen area.

-Good morning.

-Morning? It is already ten – one of the butlers replied with a smile that chilled me to the bone.

-So? It's morning.

-Oh yeah. Do you want something? Apple?

-No. When are we leaving?

-Soon. We are just waiting for Mr. Lotus.

-Will he pick us up at the accommodation or the airport?

-No, to the hotel. The flight is tomorrow.

-Flight to…?

-Pink Hell

-Okey, - I muttered, turning and walking out. I took a seat on the threshold.

<u>Memories From Whatsapp Chat With GofG: Evidence Exhibit 20b Police Report.</u>

"-He came in the morning and kissed me on lips …. I thought it was you. 10:03.AM

-What the heck? You did not open your yes? Did he say something? 11:33 AM

-<u>Audio record:</u> No, I did not, of course I did not! It is disgusting. I was sure it was you, but after I thought about why you will kiss me, my lips for what fucking reason. I opened my eyes and saw him. He also made something under my cover. 11:34 AM

-<u>Audio record:</u> He kissed you and opened your blanket to pick inside. Seriously?? 11:37 AM

-Yes. It's disgusting. 12:27 PM"

Reaching to the nearest hotel with few butlers and managers I cast my eyes around, searching for a small shop. A craving for a cigarette had gripped me. The deserted street in this tiny village gave me the sinking feeling that I couldn't find anything. Basically, the dusty red earth street stretches out before you, its usual bustle of bicycles and motorbikes, but here it is replaced by an unsettling silence. Or a stray cow wanders down the middle, interfering with the passage of everyone. The vibrant chaos of everyday Indian life is absent here, replaced by an eerie stillness.

-Mari, let's go. We need to check-in.

-I need a shop.

-For what?

-I need a cigarette.

-You smoke?

-No…. but today, yes.

-Okey. Let's check in first, and after, I will help you.

-Thank you, Sir…

-Lotus.

-Mr. Lotus…

The hotel resembled a cheap eco-resort, with a handful of small, single-room bungalows scattered around poorly maintained grounds. I reached my door and entered my room. Leaving all my clothes behind, I went outside to find the manager and claim what he had promised me. Turning left opposite my room, I noticed the closest room was open, so I knocked on the door.

-Mr. Lotus?

-No. He is in different bungalow. Can I help you? – another manager replied, hurriedly pulling on his t-shirt.

-Do you have a cigarette?

-Yes. Do you want some?

-Yes, and lighter...

He lifted his jeans from the bed and retrieved a pack of cigarettes and a lighter.

-Actually, just one cigarette would be fine.

-Take it... - probably understanding what was happening with me he held out it.

Grabbing the cigarette, I bolted out of his room, my face flushed red and my blood boiling. Embarrassment and confusion warred within me.

Reaching my room, I collapsed onto the terrace. There, I lit the cigarette and took a drag, a strong cough wracking my body. The last time I'd smoked was when I was fifteen or sixteen. I never had a taste for it, preferring to stay smelly-free.

Dizziness overwhelmed me with each successive puff. I forced myself to slow down, taking shallower drags. The first cigarette back after so long was a strange experience, leaving me nauseous and clouded by the stinky scent clinging to my clothes and hair. I returned to my room and promptly fell asleep, oblivious to the rest of the day.

Opening my eyes, I fumbled for my phone on the nightstand but came up empty. The darkness in my room was absolute, making it impossible to see anything on the white bedsheets. Raising my still-sleeping body, I began a more thorough search, feeling each centimeter of the bed with greater focus. Finally, my fingers grasped the phone, and I sank back down with a sigh of satisfaction. "No way! The battery's dead! What time is it anyway?" Without much enthusiasm, I climbed out of bed, located my charger in the jumbled mess of my luggage, and headed outside to the terrace for some fresh air and warmth. The sun was still high in the sky, but its light had begun to soften. Finally coming to my senses, I switched on my phone and opened the latest messages from Erela: "Are you awake yet? Want to come sit outside and enjoy the sun for a bit?"

Honestly, I lacked any enthusiasm for activities, but the thought of sitting alone in my room was already unbearable. Pulling on my shoes, I ventured outside and settled onto a bench in the so-called "mini-garden" located in the center of the eco-resort.

-Hey! How are you doing?

-Hey, Erela, Sorry I fell asleep earlier today…

-What's happened yesterday?

-Ugh… I'd rather not talk about it. He got really mad and spent all night looking for me.

-For what reason?

-You know why.

-He is gone now. Forget about him. Just relax and take a break. Let's order some food - hey, they even have beer! We can grab some.

-Beer? I'm not much of a drinker…

-Oh, come on, just to unwind, that's all. I'm leaving today, and I have no idea when we'll see each other again, so don't say no. Just relax.

"Just relax"– those words seemed like a distant melody carried away on a summer breeze. Relaxation felt like a forgotten luxury in the face of my reality. Regardless, I clasped Erela's hand in gratitude, accepting her offer. Almost disappeared sun dipped lower in the sky, casting long shadows across the ecoresorts grounds as we sank into conversation. For more than two hours, we had pushed aside the disgusting reasons that brought us here and the shameful job and left it behind. We were simply two women perched on a weathered wooden bench beneath a canopy of rustling palm leaves.

Our conversation flowed like a refreshing stream, weaving tales of childhood dreams, unexpected turns in life's journey, and the triumphs and heartbreaks of our respective careers. Erela spoke with a passion that ignited a spark within me. Her dreams for the future, ambitious yet grounded, were a powerful contrast to the disillusionment I'd been feeling. Here was a woman who wasn't just existing; she was actively building a life on her terms. As twilight descended, painting the sky in hues of orange and purple, I realized I wasn't just getting to know Erela; I was witnessing a beacon of strength and determination. Her story was a balm for my soul, a reminder that even amidst the chaos, hope and ambition could still bloom.

After a warm conversation and a delicious non-vegetarian dinner - my first in over a month - I returned to my room, giving Erela time to pack her luggage before our goodbyes. Entering the room, a familiar craving hit me - the urge for a cigarette. I couldn't explain the intensity of the need, but it felt like a desperate attempt to de-stress. Deciding to avoid another awkward encounter with the neighbor, I texted Mr. Lotus, hoping he could help. Thankfully, within ten minutes, my fresh "dose" of nicotine was delivered to my doorstep: -Thank you.

-No problem at all.

-But still…

-Would you like another one?

-No, thank you. Actually, if I text you again tonight, don't answer, please.

-Ha-ha, I'll try my best to resist! - he chuckled, waving goodbye.

The fresh dose of nicotine after the beer left me feeling hazy and relaxed. However, sleep wasn't calling my name at all, and I hadn't said goodbye to Erela. So, I headed straight for her room.

There she was, a beautiful young woman in her natural habitat, trying to cram an impossible amount of stuff into her suitcase. She scurried around the room in a flurry, momentarily forgetting small items that wouldn't have easily fit in the already overflowing bags. Finally, with a sigh of relief, she zipped shut the second suitcase and collapsed onto the bed.

-Text me and write, any time, all right? - she whispered, fatigue evident after her packing marathon.

A lump formed in my throat as I managed a strained smile and a nod. We hauled the luggage down to reception, the weight of the bags a metaphor for the emotions I couldn't express. As I watched her climb into the cab, a pang of sadness shot through me. Her eyes, alight with a mix of exhaustion and hope for the future, held my gaze for a moment. In that silent exchange, I sent her a silent prayer. "May the universe grant all the dreams nestled within your gentle heart, Erela".

A lump formed in my throat as I tilted my head back, the weight of the goodbye with Erela heavy on my chest. The stars, a million glittering pinpricks against the velvet darkness, mocked me with their eternal brilliance. "Look at them," I whispered, a tremor of awe and melancholy in my voice. "So vibrant, these ancient fireballs, burning with a light that has traveled for eons. And yet, so cold, so indifferent to the fleeting human reality".

Slipping inside my room, I closed the door with a soft click. Sinking onto the table by the window, I finally allowed the weight of the evening to settle. "Alone at last," I murmured, the quiet both a comfort and a pang.

The lamplight from the yard flickered and died, plunging the room into a darkness that mirrored the despair in my heart. Tears welled up unchecked, blurring the world into a watery mess. A strangled sob escaped my lips, morphing into a choked cry I desperately tried to stifle. It was no use. The sound echoed in the silent room, a testament to the raw pain ripping through me. The harder I tried to stifle my sobs and avoid attracting attention from my neighbors, the deeper I sank into this state, my mind spiraling out of control and suffocating pain constricting my chest.

I curled into myself, hugging my knees for comfort that wouldn't come. My body was wracked with silent sobs, trembling as if caught in a storm I couldn't escape. How long I stayed like that, lost in the throes of grief and despair, I couldn't say. Time seemed to warp and stretch, each minute an eternity. When I finally surfaced, my eyes were swollen and puffy, my nose raw and red. Every breath felt like a struggle, punctuated by the occasional retching.

Engulfed in this hysterical episode, I realized I'd exhausted every method to calm myself, yet nothing soothed the storm within. Have you ever experienced such a state? When your emotions, mind, and body spiral out of control, and you fear succumbing to the chaos gripping you? Panic threatened to consume me as I felt powerless over my own body. But amidst the turmoil, a spark of defiance ignited. Repeating a silent mantra, a steady hum resonating in my chest, I began pacing the room.

"I endured and held back myself too long from the morning incident. Don't ever dare to do it again with yourself"- a silent echo in my mind reverberated.

Get the Price of Freedom

'Don't take a step forward because you could be forced to take two steps back.'

Knock in the door

-Hello? Are you there? I brought your wallet.

-Luisa?

-Oh, Hi! Finally, you are back!

-Yeah… How were your lonely days without us?

-It's so boring; no one is coming out of the room, at least for a talk. What happened to your face?

-I think some allergy… Need to visit a doctor.

-Oh, shit, it looks not good. So, tell me, how it was?

-What?

-Pink Hell 2.

-Same as I texted you. Nothing is professional here. Better to leave this place.

-No way… so bad?

-Yes.

-But maybe there will be a difference? More girls and we are not sleeping in his house, and we can work 2 by 2.

-Don't think so much. Whatever you create, he will destroy it.

-No way... so sad...

-Yeah. So...

-Did you receive your wages?

-What?

-Salary? Did you receive it?

-No. I don't know. I don't care about it.

-You should be! This is your money. I don't know how you are so silent after 3 months without a bank account and money. I gave them one week to change it. My time is not free. Come on!

-Don't worry, they'll pay you, - I said, adding silently in my head: "They'll pay you for your silence."

Luisa, though older than me, appeared refreshingly naive. Lost in thoughts about trivial matters and office gossip, she seemed oblivious to the real problem. Her chatter about mundane routines and silly rumors felt miles away from my current state of mind and heart. Nothing made sense here; it was all a stupid joke, and it was only a matter of time before the next victim, you, perhaps my dear Luisa, would be caught in its grip.

I knew she would dismiss my arguments and avoid all facts. I'd been in her place once, naively believing the fault for these terminations lay with the women themselves. This place was a hellish circle, a relentless place that crushed women's spirit and soul, murder.

The place I arrived at three months ago, which once felt like home, now resembles a concentration camp. The small suit office between the girls' accommodation and the king's house feels like a cruel and silent control lever of torture and humiliation. The Regency Division, whose primary function is to cater to the needs and desires of the VIP customer, now appears to be a facade for the king's perverse indulgences. All the employees, led by his son, are nothing but cowardly, driven rats who aid and abet the evil in this place. Everything changed. The rose-colored glasses fell off my depleted, blistered face. The question now is how to leave this place without causing even more harm. I have no money, no security, no support. I am nothing in this devil system going on in Gujarat State - just another screw.

The next morning, after the first day of arriving back at Pink Hell, I woke up around nine and began to dress in the uniform, moving on autopilot. Suddenly, I jolted myself awake, shaking my head. "What are you doing?" I exclaimed. "He's not here! You don't need to go into this fishy office! You don't work here anymore! Wake up! Pack your bags and get out of this place!"

Sitting back down on the bed, I surveyed the room with a dull ache, desperate to escape the trap of being a good, obedient slave-worker. Today, I had to figure out how to leave. The best advisors? The girls who had already escaped.

Grabbing a fresh cup of coffee, I started scrolling through my contacts, searching for the girls I'd been on good terms with, the ones who could offer some helpful information.

*All message records have been renamed to comply with the provisions of the Indian Penal Code (IPC) Section 228A. This section strictly prohibits the disclosure of the identity of any person against whom an offense under Sections 376 (rape), 376A (rape leading to death or permanent vegetative state), 376B (sexual intercourse by husband on wife during separation), 376C (sexual intercourse by a person in authority), or 376D (gang rape) is alleged or found to have been committed. The anonymity of potential victims and those involved in such cases is paramount.

*Message to Marbella:

Hi darling! How are you? Did you find a new job? Listen, I've got some problems in the house... have you ever faced anything there? How did you handle it? Who proceeded with your resignation document? Please keep it confidential, as I don't know what is happening here. Thank you *Message to Annie:

Hey, I don't know if you remember me. We met in the morning near the coffee machine and spoke about Ukraine Russian War. I just joined the company these days. How are you, btw? Did you get a job? Listen, do you still have contacts of the HR who helped you to resign? Can you share it, if you don't mind?

*Message to Kaira:

Hi, Kaira! Hope you are fine...I get a little bit stuck here. If you can help me with some contacts, I would appreciate it. Text me when you can.

*Message to Saanvi:

Saanvi. Can I ask you something? Does he do something weird for you? How do you manage it? Any advice?

*Message to Rebecca:

-Hi my darling! Hope you reached hope peaceful and already found a good job! I have a weird question for you. How did you leave the company? Who helped or managed your documents? Can you share your contacts with me? Thank you! -Hey! I am fine. Why do you ask? Do you want to resign?

-Oh, hi.. finally, someone answered. I want to leave in the next few days.

-Did you text someone else?

-Yes, for a few girls from BPA and a few from your department, wellness.

-Did you speak with King Head?

-Nothing useful…

-Listen, I will call you sometime. But don't think that you can leave in a few days if he doesn't want to.

-What do you mean?

-If he didn't fire you or ask you to leave his house – you can't. If you didn't run out of the house during the night shift – you can't Forget. No one will take a breath without his permission. No one will give you an answer. You have to "request" him.

-They can't do it. I have the right.

-Rights? Oh yeah, you do. Please don't get in trouble as Virginia.

-Who is Virginia?

-She was from your department and trusted me; she got enough shit, including the police. As I heard she shaved her hair off from her head.

-I will go to the hotel and pick up my documents from the main office. I don't need my salary.. they can burn it for their gods.

No way… what are you talking about…

-Do you think the police cannot come to your hotel? For example, say that they found drugs in your room. Do you understand what kind of trouble you can put on your ass?

-They did it to her?

-My advice… stay silent and wait for your turn. Don't play Wonder Woman…

-God it.

-I am serious. Why do you think they give you 40 minutes to pack all your luggage and keep eyes on you after shifting you to the hotel from accommodation and, after that, make sure you leave the country without permission from the immigration center?

-To make sure we will not speak.

-Yes, so please take my advice properly. The less what you will get – banned from working in India as you break the rule, leaving the country without an exit permit, but you can leave with this... I don't think you will get excited to work again in fucking India.

-Understood. Thanks for your honesty.

-I will call you in some time. If you don't mind, can you delete our chat?

-I don't mind. I am thankful for your answer.

The worst thing I could do was ask for advice from the girls who left. I've just sealed my fate, buried myself finally and irrevocably.

"Who is this Virginia? Why haven't I heard this name before? Perhaps she worked here a long time ago. But her story reveals their strategy for if I dare to speak. Knowing their next steps is helpful, as I can see how far back they can potentially push me. However, I'm stuck. My only plan failed. What are my prospects? I hope that he won't return this month, as he had scheduled other countries and finally will forget about, allowing me to approach King Head about my "freedom".

***

-Hey darling! Good morning. Are you going to the office today? – coming down from the first floor Luisa almost shines and blossoms that finally she can speak with someone.

-Hey. No.. For what?

-Let's make a presentation. I have some ideas which can be useful for the estate. Did you see that old curtain.. it has to be replaced, so big shame.

-Shame?

-Yes… so will you go?

-No. I will work from my room. I am still weak and sick from this allergy.

-Oh, I totally forgot. Did you find out the reason?

-No. It can be anything. Stress.

-Yes. You told me that you had long shifts in Pink Hell 2…

-No, it is because of the stress. Long shift doesn't fuck up your face. – I pronounced it with an irritated and disgruntled voice, shocked by myself.

How quickly she drives me crazy! I never get so mad at someone for no reason. It's probably not her fault, as she hasn't done anything bad to me, and I respect her hard work. That's rare these days - she's a truly hardworking person. But her words… they completely blindside the real problem. That makes me furious as I see myself in her voice.

-So, you are not going.

-No, I want to escape for a few days from this planet.

-Okey, have a good day. Text me if you will get bored!

-Have fun with office guys... Send them a big greeting...

For the next few days, I practically disappeared into my room, focusing on what Luisa had mentioned - the presentation. Throughout the week, I compiled a fresh database encompassing beginning from furniture brands and finishing with luxury clothes houses, including contact information for agents and the most convenient stores for ordering. The days and nights blurred into one long stretch of research and analysis. I was incredibly grateful for the opportunity to escape the real problem, and I didn't allow myself an hour away from my laptop, keeping my mind constantly occupied.

So, my day typically began around 9 am, though sometimes it stretched as late as 11, depending on when I finally fell asleep. After grabbing a fresh cup of coffee or masala tea from the machine near the second bungalow, I'd settle on the terrace outside my room and open my laptop, diving headfirst into the world of fashion, beauty, and luxury. By noon, when the sun beat down mercilessly on my terrace, I'd take a 15-minute break to grab some food from the cafeteria-parking area. Spoon in hand, I'd return to my research, continuing it from the comfort of my room. By 4 or 5 pm, the small size of my room began to feel oppressive. To escape the feeling and get a change of scenery, I'd grab another cup of coffee and head to an empty first-floor terrace on a random bungalow. After an unobtrusive and silent sunset, almost getting eaten by mosquitos, I was returning to my terrasse. Once covered up to avoid further bites, I'd channel all my energy into new research; sometimes, it consumed until the morning.

The same scenario played out day after day. Driven by the same desire to avoid the main problem, I convinced myself I still had time and the chance to escape. That was my mind stage when a new message from the GofG materialized on the screen, each pixel a shard of dread. My breath hitched, the world around me shrinking to the confines of the tiny notification. I clicked it open, and the words burned into my retinas, and the innocuous message transformed into a chilling countdown:

-Hey! Are you alive? He is landing tomorrow morning. I will send you the shift schedule soon. Be on the phone.

Walls of Silence

"The darkest places in hell are reserved for those who maintain their neutrality in times of moral crisis." - Dante Alighieri.

"Looking back on those days, I can't help but wonder if it was my weak mental and physiological condition or a meticulously crafted girls' trafficking scheme that caused my sluggishness and indecisiveness. Observing the girls' experiences and history, I've been able to categorize them into three distinct stages:

<u>Blind Recruitment:</u> You receive an enticing offer from a supposedly reputable agency to join a prestigious company with comprehensive benefits and official documentation. You start a seemingly ordinary daily job, but gradually, day by day, they implement rules that progressively constrict your freedom, even down to controlling your diet. There's no mistaking it - this is a trap.

<u>Testing and Intimidation:</u> Once the girl is fully under their control, the perpetrator begins to test her limits and deliberately inflict disgusting rape, taking pleasure in her vulnerability - trapped in his house and a foreign country. This continues until he tires of his "new toy."

<u>Disposal:</u> When the perpetrator's appetite for violence and rape is satiated, the girl remains in a state of shock and confusion. This is when his henchmen, scavengers' step in, issuing threats and

discarding her like unwanted trash. Their goal is to ensure she's too intimidated to speak out.

Now, I see with chilling clarity the stage I was trapped in and why I made the choices I did. Dear reader, as you consider my story and my actions, I remind you to gather all the pieces before forming an opinion. Don't fall prey to the illusion of "I would do this and this" - you can never truly predict how you'd react in such a harrowing situation. But the better way for you - just observe and learn from my mistakes."

***

Panic surged through me, and I paced the room like a caged animal, desperately awaiting the call from GofG - my only lifeline. I scrolled through the speech, rehearsing arguments and reasons why I couldn't possibly work this job. Frustration gnawed at me. "Why hadn't I acted sooner? Had I already forgotten the horrors of "Pink Hell 2"? Just grab your clothes pack and leave now. What a nonces!"

Yanking opening my wardrobe, I began a whirlwind of activity, flinging clothes onto the bed in a frenzy. My suitcase, precariously perched on top, tumbled down with a graceless thud, landing squarely on my head. Ignoring the throbbing pain, I fumbled it open and started shoving clothes inside. Nearly done, I left only the company uniform hanging in the closet. The bathroom, however, presented the real challenge: countless bottles of skin care products, most lacking caps, threatened to erupt in chaos.

"Where the hell was your mind all this week?" continuing to grumble at myself, I suddenly switched to my phone and started to check for the hotel. "Where should I go? But if they will make the same meanness as they did to Virginia? I can't risk and go there".

WhatsApp call from GofG

-Hey, listen, I decided…

-Wait one second, – moving away from the microphone she said something in Hindi to someone who probably was near her – Listen, all will be fine. We planned everything. And I will come.

-What the hell did you plan? When will you come? Are you escorting him on this trip?

-No, I am not. Listen! You will work together. I mean, there will be 2 girls in one shift, and you always will be with her. This will be the rule! If he wants something or asks – go together with Luisa! And! Listen now! If he will say for her to go, you say, no! Order from King Head. Understand?

-I can't work in …

-Can you calm down and listen to me now? First of all, this is a big house. It is not that small thing in the jungle. Secondly, there will always be people in the kitchen and wellness girls on standby, and again, I repeat, you will be with another BPA. Don't go if he requests; send her to check what he wants and stay behind her. Deal?

-I don't know ….

-You know! We will come soon in a few days so I also will work. All will be fine.

-Nothing will be fine in this place. You spend too much time away from here and don't hear me… Why do you want me to die…

-Nothing will happen. Wait a minute. I will call you back in a while and explain the schedule.

-No

- Mari, please hear me out! This man is only staying for 2-3 days, no longer. I'll put you on night shifts with Luisa or Rati so Jesabel can cover the days. Unlike last time, he won't be up all night. He'll wake up for breakfast, leave for the day, be served evening by butlers, and then be asleep. That's it - two nights, and he's gone. Okay? Now, check the house with Luisa. I have a bad feeling about Jesabel being alone in the house.

-Let her make whatever she wants...

-Can you go and check? And let me know with whom you want to be on the shift.

-Okay, I will text you.

My phone landed with a dull thud on the nightstand. The room mirrored the turmoil within me - a chaotic mess of clothes and scattered belongings. A familiar voice echoed in my head, her words laced with doubt, "Maybe she's right? It's just a few days; nothing will happen." How desperately I craved to believe it, a yearning that carved a deep ache in my chest.

Lost and confused, I grappled with the choice before me: take a potentially life-altering risk till death and flee, or swallow my fear and endure the next two days. Time, at least, was on my side. With a task at hand - a routine inspection of the house - I sought distraction. I fired off a quick text to Luisa, requesting her company on my rounds.

A medium-sized, pale-yellow house in the Indian style stood beside the office, separated by a tall fence. Lush green grounds, meticulously landscaped with flowers and shrubs, surrounded this second, rather imposing residence. Employees like housekeepers, cooks, and butlers had a designated entrance - a back door that led them around the house to a small waiting room in front of the small kitchen.

First, upon reaching the door to a small room, you had to remove your shoes. Stepping inside, you'd wash your feet in a floor-mounted sink with icy water. Unfortunately, there were no drying facilities - no towels or wipes to be found. Next, with wet feet, you come to the tiny kitchen. Here, you'd wash your hands, only to be met with a perpetually damp, grimy towel for drying. Apparently, dry towels were reserved solely for the cooker.

Pushing open the next door, you'd find yourself in a short hallway. On one side, a door led to the first bathroom, while a large, imposing entrance on the other side provided access to the private quarters of the house. Beyond this threshold, entry was restricted to everyone except the butlers when they delivered meals. Only the "wellness girls" and us, the BPAs, were granted access to this area when the king, shall we say, was in residence.

However, during his absences from work, the housekeeping staff descended upon the previously off-limits area, meticulously cleaning and refreshing the linens and towels daily.

The house itself adhered to an Indian aesthetic, with opulent furnishings and heavy, luxurious artwork adorning the walls. To the right of the entrance, a grand fountain graced the space, leading to a generously sized pleasure room complete with a large bathroom and jacuzzi - a "wellness room," as they preferred to call it.

The right wing, the largest section of the house, boasted ten rooms spread across the ground and first floor and connected to the outdoor pool and by a corridor to the laundry room, typically closed when the king was in residence. During my initial induction, I genuinely feared I'd never navigate this labyrinth. Every room seemed to blend into the next.

Coming inside with Luisa, we started checking each room for cleanliness, odor, temperature, and supplies (soap, towels in bathrooms, water, snacks in the fridge). His bedroom, located farthest on the first floor, boasted a massive wooden door that muffled even gunshots. Protocol dictated that we sit all night on the round marble staircase next to this room. From the ground floor, it was impossible to hear if he needed anything. The kitchen, by the way, functioned as a soundproof bunker, oblivious to the nightly happenings within the house.

His son's bedroom, situated farthest on the ground floor, ensured nightly encounters. As we perched on the cold marble staircase, dutifully guarding his father's sleep, he'd return from the office and pass right by us. We were like guard dogs, you see, but for a different kind of master.

Honestly, I can't say for certain if any of the girls ever endured a whole night sitting there. The cold was relentless, and our skimpy outfits - short skirts with no stockings or socks – were a slut style. Cystitis and the constant urge to use the restroom were unwelcome companions on night shifts.

Sometimes, when you simply couldn't bear it any longer, you'd sneak back to the kitchen only to be met with the disapproving voice of a butler: "What are you doing here? You're supposed to be in the house! What if he wakes up and you're not there?" Not everyone but some individuals seemed blissfully unaware of the absurdity of the situation.

"- Why are you here again? He just went to sleep; he is still awake. Go back!

-It is cold there; can you understand, please? Do your job what you are doing. Polish the glasses and don't touch me.

-If he will want to drink water?? What then?

-Then he will come to the kitchen and ask! Stop!

-Okey, can you go and check if he is not there? I want to place breakfast cutleries and crockeries on the dining table.

- Let's do it later.. please…

-When?

-We have all night, so just finish whatever you are doing and we will go inside.

-But you have to be inside!

"Pink Hell"

-Just leave me, please! – I slammed the kitchen door shut and retreated into the house. Seeking refuge, I sank to the floor near the elevator, my body a coiled spring ready to leap away at the slightest sound."

It wasn't universal, but there were nights when I couldn't help but feel these men were living in a fantasy world, oblivious to the bigger picture. Did anyone ever stop to ask: "Why are the girls confined to the house all night while I'm not allowed to come in? Perhaps he's wearied of the company during the day, and that's why he desires a young, beautiful woman for his service in the evening. But at night? Why does she need to be here then?"

Perhaps the butlers who didn't force me inside knew the situation. Their averted gazes and unspoken apologies spoke volumes.

-Mari! Do we need to check how to switch on the music? We had to greet him with music as per protocol;– Luisa grabbed the control panel and started to search for the right buttons.

-Don't worry; you will be with Rati or me so that we can handle it.

-Yes, but still, I want to know… - she continued to do her research with a doubting face.

-Luisa.

-Yes.

-Can I ask you something?

-Yes.

-Just in case he requests something from me, can you please always be with me, and even if he pushes you to leave - don't go. Don't leave me alone.

-Oh my god… please stop scaring me.

-I don't ... just asking if you can do it.

-Okey .. don't worry.

-Let's go back. We need some rest, and the schedule is still not ready.

-GofG has not answered me since she left that month for Europe!

-She is busy...

-With what?? 24/7??

-Yes.. - a grin tugged at my lips as I watched her and was reminded about these two lovers hiding and pretending to be a simple colleague. How will they hide their chemistry here? How long could they keep up this charade in such close quarters? The office will erupt once everyone catches on to the "newlyweds' act". Though, perhaps it's already common knowledge - whispers do have a way of traveling fast.

-Can you call her, please? We need to know the schedule.

-Yes. Let's go back and do it.

Back in my room, I reached for my phone, dialing GofG's number. No answer. I assured Luisa I'd update her as soon as I knew anything. Exhausted, she retreated to her first-floor room to catch some rest.

Darkness had settled outside, and the mosquitoes buzzed to life for their evening feast. Ignoring the temptation to dwell on tomorrow's uncertainties, I changed into comfortable clothes, grabbed a cup of coffee, and settled into a terrace chair. Headphones sealing out the world, I focused on finding a moment of peace.

I didn't accept the fact that I would work tomorrow, but my movements and actions showed the opposite.

Screen on the phone

"Mari, listen. We can't place you with Luisa ... you will be with Jesabel on the night shift. This is the best way. She is a lead also and will take all responsibilities and service with him just to be first. And that is what you need. Take rest.. tomorrow at 8 pm be in the house with gloves and a charged phone. Good night"

Your Fight is Over

"Sometimes, the tightest grip loosens the most."

Around seven, I donned some clothes and headed to the cafeteria for fresh vegetables – the only edible option for me. My face still bore the angry red blisters, and the doctor prescribed a bland diet to avoid further irritation.

A message pinged in the company chat – he was arriving soon. Dinner duty likely fell to Jesabel and me. This girl, Jesabel, we had so much unresolved tension hung between us. A month ago, she'd unleashed a torrent of negativity and shit on us, the new arrivals. She'd ignored us from the start, offering no support or basic courtesy.

But the thin, almost gaunt girl with her caked-on makeup and practiced smile seemed different now. Anger and irritation had given way to a sense of empathy.

The tiny, stuffy kitchen buzzed with chaotic energy, overflowing with personnel. Flustered chefs, faces flushed red and aprons damp, barked orders at anyone attempting to navigate their domain. Deciding to avoid the fray, I settled into a small room adjacent to the kitchen, waiting for Jesabel to come. Luisa and Rati were likely already inside, having finished fawning over the king. Now, they impatiently awaited their shift's end, their eyes constantly glued to their watches.

-Good evening, why are you here?

-Hi, Jesabel. Waiting for you.

-For what? You should be in the house.

-But the girls are there; what we are collecting a harem?

-Sorry?

-Nothing. Let them go we will hand over the shift.

-Hi, Jashi! How are you? – interrupting my probable monologue, Jesabel abruptly shifted her focus to the butler, who evidently held greater importance at that moment.

This was typical Jesabel – boisterous and attention-seeking. Around people, she'd erupt in loud laughter at every joke, desperate to be the center of attention, the star of the show. It was like a chronic case of attention deficit disorder – a constant need for validation that I found utterly perplexing. Everyone else seemed to get it, though. Laughter would ripple through the room whenever her name came up or a poker face would descend upon them. No one dwelled on the reasons behind her buffoonery; it was simply a collective amusement. While I wouldn't normally condone such ridicule, today, she was my unlikely savior – a bombastic shield against the true villainy in this house. To think, just a while ago, such a notion would have been unthinkable. Yet, here I was, feeling a strong sense of security in her presence. Yes, Jesabel was my shield, thankfully too self-absorbed to grasp the irony.

Thirty minutes later, the dinner began. Following protocol, we changed the role with the girls and entered the house. We were expected to remain in the living room, keeping an eye on the dining room table. Once the king finished a course, we would inform the kitchen to prepare the next one, which the butler would then serve. As the sole intermediary between the king and the staff, Jesabel reveled in her perceived power and importance within this system.

Perhaps that's what allowed her to endure this life for nearly a year, accepting all the "work's nuances". Here, in this house, marked both her first and last performance and swan song as a main concubine. Throughout the evening, I couldn't help but notice how she scurried around him, ten steps behind, eager to display her knowledge and impeccable work ethic.

After finishing dinner, the king headed straight for his spa session, leaving his loyal Chihuahua waiting expectantly by the kitchen door. Unlike the devoted dog, I wasn't so eager to please. I wandered outside and settled on a chair near the watchful butler. Let them stare. I wasn't about to return to that subservient role, groveling at his feet. Nothing could budge me from this newfound sense of rebellion.

-Ah, here you are.

-Wellness is done?

-Yes, the wake-up call will be at 8 AM.

-He will wake up or do we have to do it?

-Ahahaha *Hindi talk*– A strange laugh erupted from her lips, accompanied by a flurry of Hindi I couldn't understand. The butler responded in kind, their exchange laced with a secret amusement. Perhaps they thought their words would confuse or dishearten me, but they were mistaken. She was my shield. Let her humiliate and mock me all she wants – as long as I am secured behind her back, her barbs hold no power.

-Did he ask for water?

-I already did everything. Don't worry

- Okay, - I added a thought: "What do you mean by 'did everything'?" Anyway, I don't care. I'm just calm, not to be alone.

Early in the morning, around 7:00 am, we both trudged down to the staircase and settled onto a cold marble step. Ignoring each other, we glued ourselves to our phones, waiting for him to wake up in case he felt like starting the day early. Every few minutes, she'd erupt like a cuckoo clock from an old wooden house, spouting random comments and instructions:

"Usually, we sit here at night. No one from the girls chills in the kitchen. Got it?"

"And another thing, never go to the kitchen if you're the only BPA here. He could finish his wellness routine any time, and it's your responsibility to inform everyone."

"Don't sit there glued to your phone looking like you're having a loud conversation. He can hear you and might wake up early."

I simply listened to her like a malfunctioning radio, sometimes picking up a clear message, other times just static.

At eight o'clock sharp, she shouldered the most important responsibility of the morning and ascended the stairs to wake him. Returning, she stationed herself by the staircase railing, a sentinel awaiting her king's descent for breakfast.

■■■

"You should imagine this scene: Two young women, dressed in revealing uniforms – some might say reminiscent of a sex shop costume – stand at the top of the grand staircase. They wear short skirts with naked legs and white gloves, their faces plastered with forced smiles as they greet the "King."

The King himself appears, rubbing sleep from his eyes, still clad in his pajamas. He descends the stairs to where these young women stand, dispensing what he likely considers witty remarks before condescendingly patting their heads and disappearing into a wellness-pleasure room for his appointment with the next undressed exotic Beaty! What a chill life, man!

It could be easy to take specialized girls for It, but no, our king prefers fear and desperation in slaves' eyes! The height of bliss! "

Jesabel buzzed with high-level service and productivity all morning. Her smile remained unwavering, even when he was around or spoke with her. She poured her energy into ensuring his perfect morning and showed me how experienced and talented she was, yet it felt like nothing was enough. A few hours later, a message from the GofG arrived like a punch to the gut: Jesabel was fired, and I was assigned the night shift alone – as per the king's request. Bingo!

"Oh, pure Jesabel. She had no idea how much I thought about her after that night, how much she meant to my epiphanies during that horrible time in my life. The fact that the most irritating and nasty girl was gone made me feel more desperate than losing my lovely Sunflower. In such moments, when an opposing team who is your enemies loses, brings and for you a defeat too."

What can I say?

24:17-20 Do not rejoice when your enemy falls, and do not let your heart rejoice when it stumbles. Otherwise, the Lord will see, and it will be unwilling in His eyes, and He will turn away His anger from him. Do not be angry with the evildoers and do not envy the wicked, for the evil one has no future; the lamp of the wicked will go out.

5:43-48 But I tell you, love your enemies and pray for those who persecute you, that you may be children of your Father in heaven. He causes his sun to rise on the evil and the good and sends rain on the righteous and the unrighteous. If you love those who love you, what reward will you get?

Wakeup Call

Defeated, I knew I had to act. The next day, I focused all my efforts on switching shifts with one of the other girls. I desperately needed another day to formulate a plan. Unfortunately, with only three of us remaining, working alone was unavoidable. There was no chance of being paired with someone else on a shift.

-Mari, listen. I can place you in a split shift as it was for Jesabel a few months ago. You will come in the morning and evening to be presented when he is in the house and girls will do 12-hour shifts day/night alone.

-G…I didn't get it.

-They will work shifts, but you will come only morning for a few hours before he leaves for work and evening before he goes to sleep. So, you are not alone. Girls are there…

-But if he will fire someone again?

-Don't be ridiculous.

-Am I ridiculous in this situation? Is he mad?

-Yes. He is… but don't worry, we will figure out what to do, and I will come tomorrow.

-Will you make shifts?

-No… no one has to know that I am coming.

-What are you talking about?

-Listen. I will come for one day because King Head is coming and Monday we will fly back…

-So, he will see you in the aircraft.

-Who?

-The WS from whom else you are hiding?

-No, he will not. He is not coming.

-What?

-He will stay more…

-No.

-Yes, he will.

-No, no, no, you are kidding?!

-Don't panic. Okey?

-Will talk later…

Considering the fact that I have at least my lead GofG and King Head on my side, I could grab some time to avoid the inevitable, but his aggressive actions as firing someone just to get his wish opened for me a new trait of his character: ruthlessness, unscrupulousness for any living soul. I knew it before, but not in such a context.

The attempt by GofG to have me work both day and night shifts backfired due to a misunderstanding with the estate managers and a lack of interdepartmental communication. She requested a few days to rectify the situation. In the meantime, I spent the day strategizing, anticipating the pitfalls and situations the WS might create during my daytime assignment. Choosing the day shift was a deliberate move. More people in the kitchen meant less unsupervised time for him.

Around 6 pm, I encountered Luisa as she headed out for a post-nap lunch break.

-Hi.

-Good morning for me.

-How are you? How was your night shift?

-Oh god.. don't ask.

-What happened?

-He is so weird. I went morning to make a "wake-up call," and he was like come here closer...

-What? How is this stupid procedure going? I never did it.

-So, you have to come inside his room, touch his hand, and whisper: "Good morning, Sir".

-Oh, my god, so creepy. Who told you to do it?

-That wellness girl. I forgot what his name was.

-Helga?

-Yes! Mari, this is so weird and stupid. I came inside, said whatever I had to say, and went back to open the curtains.

-But breakfast in bed? Did you forget your responsibilities by protocol??

-Stop, listen! Oh, my god, if he asks me the next morning to do it, I will kill him. So, when I went to open the curtains, he was like:" Come here".

-Come where?

-Back to the bed, where else!

-Holy...

-Yes! I pretended I didn't hear it.

-Is he mad?

-And yesterday … he said: "You are so tall! I never had such a tall girl!

-Oh, no.. anyone heard it?

-Everyone! I mean the butler and Rati. When I brought him water after wellness he was trying to kiss me.

-What?? How?

-I came upstairs to his room. He was like, "Come!"… and pushed his old stinky face to mine.

-Where was Rati?

- In the kitchen.

-Don't go alone! Never!

-Yes. Now I understand what the issue is. We should keep someone around all the time.

-Here is easy. We are 3 and can come up with something.

-I don't know…

-Are you today again? Night shift?

-Yes

-I will be on the day tomorrow. Let me know what time he will wake up, so we can go together and you don't need to do it alone.

-Yes…

-Good luck today. Stay strong…

Luisa's honesty and frankness were a balm to my soul, a much-needed source of strength and support as I contemplated my next steps. The realization that I wasn't alone, that others within these walls harbored similar grievances, filled me with a flicker of hope.

Perhaps, by working together, by devising a shared strategy to deflect harassment and protect ourselves from future humiliation, we could find a way out – a silent, peaceful exodus. Maybe the WS would tire of his games, lose interest in our silent defiance, and eventually let us go.

This newfound solidarity sparked a surge of determination within me. No longer would I face this ordeal alone. We were in this together, and together, we would find a way.

A decent night's sleep left me feeling surprisingly well-rested at 6 am. I donned my uniform and headed out for a cup of coffee before relieving Luisa inside the house. The morning greeted me with a pale sun and a chill that raised goosebumps on my exposed legs. Gazing down at the humiliatingly short skirt and bare legs, a wave of anger crashed over me. "Why do I have to look so ridiculous?" I fumed.

Returning to my room, I ransacked my closet, desperately searching for Sunflower's uniform. It was a larger size and, thankfully, a bit longer. Slipping it on, I replaced the offending garment with a silent act of defiance and headed back towards the house.

Tired Luisa and one of the butlers were sitting near the kitchen area alone.

-What time is the wake-up call?

-Hey, good morning! How I am happy to see you. I can go and sleep. Wake-up call at 8 AM -Should we go together to do it?

-Yes.. we can.

-How was your night, guys?

-Boring.. Let's go inside. I will show you something;- Luisa took my hand, and we went inside the kitchen. – This is crazy .. .what happened today…

-Stop stressing me, please.

* Voice behind me*

-Good morning! – Helga greets us coming from the wellness room, I don't know if you remember that girl with antennae on her head.

-Hi Helga, how are you?

-Good. Girls, he will wake up soon.

-Yes, we know.

-Someone has to be here. Don't leave the house empty.

-I will be. Luisa, go to the kitchen.

Helga, the second-most guarded individual after Jesabel, according to what I'd gathered, remained unseen during my shift. Eight months with the company – a stark reminder of the hierarchy and hidden complexities within these walls.

As the butlers and kitchen staff began to fill the small space, I grew weary of playing guard dog by the door. Venturing into the kitchen proper, I approached the chef. "What's on the

menu for breakfast today?" I inquired

-Who is in the house? – a voice came behind my back.

-Can you calm down? I need to make a briefing before waking him up.

-You have to be in the house and near the stairs.

-I can handle my locations, don't worry.

Helga, the apparent second-in-command after Jesabel, materialized with a scowl, taking her position by the door. Her icy glare was a thinly veiled attempt to demonstrate "proper" guard duty. Annoyance flared within me, but I quickly quelled it. A realization dawned – I had backup. She, not I, would be the new Jesabel today, shielding me from unwanted contact. With a brief explanation of the "necessary procedures," I sent Helga upstairs to raise the WS. Bingo! A wave of relief washed over me.

Throughout the morning, I strategically positioned myself in the kitchen, observing Helga's growing frustration at my perceived lack of effort. Indifference was my weapon. While she stewed, I remained detached, calculating, doing everything possible to avoid a solitary encounter with him.

After breakfast, protocol dictated that I inform them to prepare the car, retrieve his shoes, and bid him farewell with a saccharine smile. These pre-departure moments were prime opportunities for unwanted advances, unseen by prying eyes. Today, however, I would seize control. Keeping a watchful eye on his feet, I waited until the very last moment – the final shoe being secured. With lightning speed, I flung open the heavy door, plastering a dazzling smile on my face. "Have a good day!" I chirped, reveling in his obvious displeasure. Never had I felt so bold, so utterly determined.

The moment he was out of sight, the house buzzed with activity. Housekeeping staff and other workers descended, transforming the estate into a well-oiled machine, catering to the whims of this self-proclaimed king. The I of normalcy was infuriating. A "normal" job, they'd say, except for the underlying reality – a gilded cage, a forced servitude that reeked of some sinister stinky old dick. Professionalism and education were expected, all while remaining readily available for his gratification. A sickening duality.

Thankfully, my shift ended before his return, sparing me the evening's "hunt." Returning to my room, I felt a surge of hope for the day ahead. The battle lines were drawn, and I was ready to fight.

***

-Good morning Luisa! How was your shift?

-Oh, hi! Mari, wake-up call is at 9 AM. I don't feel so strong to stay one more hour.

-So late? Why? Don't worry. I will figure it out. Where is the wellness team?

-Probably to make sure you will wake him up, ha-ha. Joking. They are not here. There will be no wellness inside the house if it's not a massage appointment.

-What? Did I miss something?

-Have you received a message from the manager?

-What message? What again?

-Come.. – she took me again inside the kitchen, away from the butler, who was too interested in our talk.

- Listen….Ahm…

-What the hell again? Can you stop stressing me…

-I was so fucked yesterday…

-Wh..a?

-No, no.. but it was too much. And Helga is not allowed to come inside the house anymore. If you will see her around, text the manager immediately.

-How will she do wellness then? Virtual??

-I don't know… but The WS clearly told to managers that he doesn't want to see her inside the house.

-Does King Head know it?

-What are you talking? He is the boss here.

-But his son is our reporting manager.

-Hello? He is the boss here. Wake up. He can ask everyone here directly, and they will do it.

-No.

-And I forgot to tell you something.

-What?

-Helga was in the house all night yesterday…

-Where exactly? Near the stairs? This is not her responsibility.

-No, she was in his room. From 12 till 5 AM. Almost all night…

-For what?

-She said he had a headache, and she was doing a 'massage," and her lips were red…

-No, please. Stop.

-I don't think they were kissing.

-Stop.

-I think she was sucking his old stinky dick.

-No, no, no….

-I was so shocked, but that butler pretended like it was normal. Ha-ha! What the fuck!

-It can't be truth…

-I saw it.

I still couldn't believe that I was in the middle of such disgust and had to fight for my honor. Luisa, with a big red eye, silently requested me to let her go and take a rest, and I understood that this night she had a horrible time because Helga wasn't here, and she faced whatever he wanted to show her. My situation lost control, and again, all the steps that I so furiously climbed up almost saw the light of the exit – failed. Again, I am lying at the bottom after a good slap.

At an appropriate time, wafter thousand steps around those damn stairs, I went upstairs and reached his room. I have to wake him up following the procedure by touching his hand. Coming closer and looking into the dark room I was trying to find where exactly he sleeps and understand if he can hear me from here. "Good morning, sir!" not loud, I said in my first attempt. After a while, not receiving a response, I repeated loudly, "Good Morning!" – again silent. Waiting for a few minutes with an exploding phone due to corporate group chat messages, I maliciously entered the room and reached his bed. "Sir?" – I said in a confused manner as everyone would already wake up from my annoying voice before.

His eyes snapped open, and with a predatory glint, he seized me, pressing my face harshly into the mattress. A guttural whisper, laced with fury unlike anything I'd ever witnessed, rasped through gritted teeth:" Do you want to play games?! Ha?! Is it so funny for you? I will make sure you will never leave India the same as you were before. Do you want 20 thugs to fuck you one by one during a week?? Ha?? I am asking you last time!! Is this what you want?? I will arrange it!" He shoved my head down again, the force sending it rebounding off the bed. Then, with a heavy thud, he retreated to the bathroom, perhaps offering a cruel parody of choice. Choice? What choice did I have? Tell me, God? Tell me, anyone! This feels like a divinely orchestrated trial, one I'm destined to fail. A pathetic specimen, incapable of self-defense. He, on the other hand, an experienced sadist, a tyrant, senses this weakness and exploits it, testing the boundaries of my endurance.

Holding back a torrent of tears, I rose from the bed. Straightening my rumpled shirt and skirt, I descended the here; by the bottom step, I stood, the air thick with anticipation, awaiting him like an obedient dog.

From that moment, my hell started to become real; whatever I faced before was just warming up; he was kicking my legs day by day so that today I would fall to my knees with no way to get up.

Day Limits

"Perhaps there is no limit to the pain a person can handle. We are defined not by our breaking point but by the will to keep piecing ourselves back together, again and again, in a relentless pursuit of meaning in a world indifferent to our suffering."

The insistent drone of the corporate chat woke me around 7:00 am, relentlessly counting down the minutes until my day shift began. I stumbled out of bed, craving a cup of coffee, before heading into the house. The faces in the kitchen that morning were a blur - nameless, voiceless figures going through the motions. A monotonous chorus of questions filled the air: "Is he awake? Wellness done? Breakfast ready? Why are you here? Go inside!

I went upstairs to his room, reaching the bedside; I delivered the obligatory greeting, "Good morning." In a flash, his hand shot out, grabbing me between the legs and attempting to yank me towards the bed to reach his wish under my skirt. Adrenaline surged as I fought his grip, wrenching free. Instead of complying with his advances, I strode towards the curtains control, switching them wide open to bathe the room in sunlight. Perhaps, I thought naively, a little public exposure might shame him into stopping.

My duty wasn't over. Protocol dictated that I record his "awakening" in the corporate chat and then retreat downstairs, forced to wait near the staircase - a prime target for further harassment. This was just another layer of the constant bullying I had to endure.

His descent was a prelude to the next ordeal. He scanned the dining room, ensuring the butlers were absent, before returning to the stairs. There, he seized my hand, shoving me into a secluded corner. A deep breath preceded a horrifying display of power. He roughly unbuttoned my jacket and shirt in one hand, silencing a potential scream by muffling my mouth. The other hand squeezed my chest with a bruising grip until it hurt, restricting my air. Perhaps fearing a struggle or outburst, he pressed my head against the wall, making it difficult to breathe. Animalistic moans punctuated the pleasure, his eyes occasionally darting towards the dining area as if checking for witnesses. Convinced of his privacy, he lifted my skirt to get inside my underpants, attempting to violate me further. Instinct took over, my hands fighting with a primal need for self-preservation to push him back. This violation, this degradation, was beyond anything I could tolerate.

Exhausted from the physical struggle, he shoved me away, his face contorted in annoyance. "Straighten your clothes!" he barked before disappearing for his "wellness session." This harrowing scene became my daily reality during the day shift. Sometimes, the assault occurred before the wellness session, sometimes after breakfast, or even before he left for the office. He was a predator, relentless in his pursuit, seeking any opportunity to satisfy his depraved desires.

One morning, during the wake-up routine, he feigned deeper sleep than usual, waiting for me to approach and "shake" him awake. The moment I drew near, he lunged, his hand clamping around my neck. He yanked me toward his face, his sleep-heavy breath reeking of something foul as he licked my lips and nose. "Wait, where do you think you're going? Bathroom! Grab a towel now! Fast!"

His reason? To place it on the pillow, a barrier to protect the pristine white linens from my makeup.

Lie on the bed.

I have to go; they're waiting for me.

I said, lie down! - Frustration laced his voice as I dared to defy him. He stormed out of bed and slammed the door shut.

-Please don't. – I answered.

I felt that I couldn't control myself anymore I took a deep breath, "No way.. Please… please…" At that moment, I felt on the verge of collapse. With a gasp, a searing pain erupted in my chest, leaving me trembling and weak. "PLEASE!!!" I shrieked, a desperate cry lost in the suffocating silence.

-Shh! Shut up! - his demeanor shifted as the fear of discovery dawned on him. He scrambled back to the bed, shoving me onto the mattress. - Shut up! Lie down! I'm not doing anything; shut your mouth!

He roughly pressed my body down, his form on top of mine. His hand reached out, patting my chest in a parody of comfort, a pathetic attempt to silence my rising hysteria.

-See? Don't open your mouth again! I don't want to hear it!

My body, a vessel of terror, betrayed me. It lay unresponsive, a paralyzed vegetable beneath him. My gaze fixated on the dark ceiling, a silent mantra echoing in my head: "Get up! Get up now!"

-Give me your hand, - he rasped, his voice laced with nervous energy. He fumbled in the darkness, finally seizing my hand and forcing it against his groin, his moans a sickening attempt at arousal.

My phone buzzed insistently in my pocket, a barrage of messages from the corporate chat. Twenty minutes of unanswered messages culminated in a call. The insistent vibration jolted me back to reality. I sprang up like a scalded cat, mumbling nonsense: "They're here! I have to go!"

I bolted from the room, fixing my hair in a shameful attempt at normalcy. Halfway down the stairs, a horrifying realization struck me - my hairpin was on the bed. But the thought of returning to that room, back to him, was unthinkable. I twisted my hair into a tight knot, hoping it would hold, desperate to conceal the telltale signs of my ordeal. Smoothing my skirt, I descended to the kitchen level and typed the obligatory message into the chat: "He's awake."

Panic clawed at my throat. "I can't face him again. I need to get out – to the kitchen, anywhere. I can't! Please, just stand somewhere visible, you stupid girl. Go!" My internal voice screamed, urging me to escape the suffocating tension.

Voice behind me

-Mari?

-Ha? What?

-Where is he?

-Wellness.

-So, write in the chat that we have work here to do. Is it so hard? We don't have your eyes.

-I came and said, what is your problem??

-You have to write and wait near the door when wellness will finish so we can start to serve the first course of breakfast.

-Oh, God.. just leave me.

-Sorry?

-Nothing! I will do it... - opening the door back to the house, I entered and continued my speech for no one – Just leave me, everyone.

After wellness, I got one more portion of shit: King, who was not satisfied with the wellness session, returned to his bedroom to change before breakfast and didn't miss the chance to play his under "shirt game". With a curt gesture, silent enough to ensure no eavesdroppers, he indicated the corner near the stairs and spoke in a voice barely above a whisper: "Come. Come." Following him like a prisoner to the gallows, I knew my place in this house all too well. "As silent I will be as soon it finishes, and I can go back to my room"- the only thought in my mind during these 2 minutes of humiliation and disgrace. Another critical moment occurred upstairs, where he'd request "assistance" with his wardrobe and towels. Every request to remove soiled towels and nightclothes was punctuated by a feigned display of anger, accusing me of failing to perform my duties properly. "Keep your eyes on it!" he'd bellow, the thinly veiled threat clear.

This meant he intended to lure me into the bathroom, the discarded towel a mere pretext. Having endured similar tactics at "Pink Hell 2," I was prepared. Luisa, however, remained blissfully unaware. One of those nightmare days, she handed the shift over to me and recounted how she'd been caught that day.

-He is mad.

-Why? – looking at her, I already knew what kind of shit she would tell me now.

-He shouted at me yesterday that I didn't remove wet towels from the floor.

-And?

-And I went upstairs, collected it, and he came.

-Pff, Gosh..

-He tried to kiss me, but I am tall, and it was hard for him to reach my face. Idiot! Is he in his mind?

-No…

That was one of that rare moments when she was sharing with me and I didn't judge or angry with her, as I knew why she was silent.

Those two morning hours stretched on like an eternity throughout that harrowing week. My gaze fixated on him; I meticulously tracked his every move as he finished breakfast. Each passing second felt like an hour as I yearned for him to leave for the office.

Finally, the butlers arrived with the wet towels. My palms slicked with nervous sweat, I dug my nails into the fabric, mirroring a cornered animal. My eyes fixated on the damp towel, waiting for him to reach for it - the signal that the torture was over, that I could finally make my escape to the front door.

Giving him his shoes, opening the door, and uttering a "hell day" were the last of my morning duties. Those precious seconds stretched on like an agonizing eternity until his car door slammed shut, finally releasing me from the suffocating tension.

Relief washed over me like a tidal wave. Without waiting for housekeeping to finish the cleanness or handing over any new requests from the king to another worker, ignoring the lingering questions and stares from the staff, I ran out of the house. I darted past the office, a single-minded focus on reaching my room. No one else existed; nothing mattered. The haven of my room beckoned, the only place I could find solace.

Bursting through the door, I collapsed onto the corner of the bed, a guttural moan escaping my lips. Shaking from one side to another and grabbing my head - my body was wracked with tremors; I could barely comprehend the ordeal I'd just endured. Though nearly violated, a flicker of life remained, as evidenced by the searing pain that consumed me. I was almost murdered inside, but some signs of life were still there as I was feeling this pain.

My phone buzzed incessantly, an onslaught of calls and messages from the office and house, berating me for neglecting my duties. It baffled me. The entire male staff of this infernal place seemed inexplicably frustrated that I dared to go to my room during duty.

During a week, I was going through the same hell scenario day by day: mockery and abuse of my body and mind, till the moment when he again requested me to make night shifts and my usual excuse didn't work because he finally understood that I was lying.

**Memories From Whatsapp with GofG Police Report Exhibit 20*

08:38 AM

-We need to talk

Call me when you are awake

07:18 PM

-We have to talk. Where are you?

*Next day

-I cannot do night shifts

Why do you want me to die…

Call me…

*Memories From Whatsapp With Luisa Police Report Exhibit 20

11:07 PM

-I will change the schedule.

-I told him (King Head) only on Saturday when he will be here, I will go for 1 night.

-GofG told me you must do it day and night. Okey, let me know, as I need to check how I can edit the schedules.

Screenshot of mail from King Head

"Dear Ma'am

Please keep Mari on the day and Night Shifts (currently being done by Rati); you (Luisa) are on the night shift, and Rati can be on the day shift.

It is very important for you to be present on the night shift as a senior Butler Personal Assistant.

Thanks and regards

King Head "

-He said you need to take Rati's place

-He will change it

-Ok. I will wait for his email. If he will not send me the email before 3 AM I need to make a new schedule. I can put you on the 18-night shift so that you will have almost 2 days off and again night shift. That amazing.

-He said only one night.

-King Head? Which day?

-When he will be here.

-Only Saturday. Only 3 shifts for you. That's ok! King Head said you must be in the night because you are the senior butler!

-No, no, no, no !!! No night shifts!!!! I will write him again.

-This is nothing, Mari. Let's keep it like that.

-No night shifts. I am serious. I will write him."

Running from one side to another inside my room that evening and reading her messages where she was pushing me to do the night shift and had already prepared the schedule, so I could not back up; I got the whole picture: Why was she so active and cooperative with

King Head to place me in night shift and why this to lovebirds asked her to tell me about it.

As you can see, it took me far longer than it should have to realize I'd been sold. My hope for "pseudo-help" from GofG and King Head was nothing more than a self-deceptive illusion. Why would I have been so naive? These two "kids" were continents away, living comfortable lives. They had no incentive to defy their father's wishes, especially when they were enjoying warm beds far from this wretched brothel of survival. Perhaps during the first week, they could have fabricated excuses to keep me off the night shift, but nothing lasts forever.

It became clear that GofG was deliberately ignoring me, likely out of shame. Her lover, too cowardly to face me with the truth, simply accepted my requests to avoid night shifts while simultaneously pressuring Luisa to deliver the harsh reality. Perhaps Luisa, too, relished the prospect of a reprieve from her nocturnal horrors.

For those few days, I clung fiercely to the delusion of safety. However, a seed of doubt had been sown. One morning, during my shift change with Luisa, her appearance sent a jolt of disquiet through me. She practically burst into the kitchen, fleeing from whatever transpired in the house. Her face, flushed red, mirrored my terror. Her eyes, wide and owlish, darted around the room, haunted by unseen horrors. Her hair, usually meticulously styled, hung loose and disheveled. A stark contrast to the composed woman who reported for duty the previous day. Her hands trembled uncontrollably, clutching her jacket as if concealing something or perhaps desperately trying to hide her unbuttoned shirt.

The facade of solidarity shattered; the truth laid bare. I was utterly alone in this suffocating abyss. GofG and King Head's arrival the next day offered no solace. In this place, every man, every woman, was an island - facing their private hell, with no room for empathy or shared suffering.

Night Limits

"The night stretches on, a vast canvas upon which exhaustion paints its masterpiece, leaving us vulnerable to shadows both within and without."

WhatsApp messages with Erela 04:34 PM:

-Hi dear.. how are you? I am reaching Pink Hell today. Are you there?

-Hey, yes, I am. Did you fly back?

-Yeah.. he changed his schedule and decided to stay longer, so they requested me to come.

-Yes…there were some changes.

-What changes?

-He fired almost every wellness girl from accommodation, and they didn't arrange new.

-Why?

-Why? That's obvious – fewer companies want to work with him, as it was a huge mess after that Thai girls.

-What was that about?

-They were sending videos to everyone here and to their company, which brought them here.

-Video?

-Yes, "massage" video…Kind of protest for what is happening in the house.

-Fuck…so crazy.

-It is…so welcome back.

-Can we meet before my appointment?

-Sure, any time you can come to my room and take a rest. I am on the night shift today…

-I will arrive around 6 pm.

-Great, just come directly to my bungalow.

-Is his son here?

-Yes, thankfully.

That was really "thankfully" as I didn't have any other possibility to catch to survive that night. By day, my mind was consumed by a morbid game of "survival scenario planning." I meticulously constructed various situations, desperately strategizing ways to avoid any potential disaster. This all-encompassing obsession rendered me oblivious to the world around me.

Luisa, after a few days of working in the house, retreated into a shell. Isolated and alone, I had no one to wake me up, no one to strategize with. Honestly, I wasn't ready to open myself up to anyone else, anyway. The betrayal by GofG and King Head had left an indelible stain on my trust in others.

As evening draped our territory in darkness, the afterglow of a hasty sunset barely a memory, I donned my uniform and donned my white gloves. With a heavy heart, I headed towards the house, bracing myself for the worst. Reaching the backside of the kitchen, I already heard the hum coming out, the familiar hum before "Feast During The Plague". Tense atmosphere, chaos, turmoil, and bustle before the dinner, but nothing changed, except for location and my mental condition. I felt it; I was again different. I was more lost and deeper inside my safe box.

-Hi, you will open the door?

-Have no idea; it depends on when he will arrive before or after8.

-After that, then I will be with you.

-All evening?! King Head asked you.

-I am not on the night shift…asked for what? – the confused butler looked at me and couldn't realize what I wanted from him.

-Nothing, you will open, and I will keep wet towels, right?

-Okey, listen, no. You will…

-Where is King Head? Inside?

-No, - he grinned and rolled his eyes as if I was stupid or narrow-minded and added, - He is in the office as usual; he will come only for dinner and will go back for meetings.

I looked indifferent at him because his attempt to reproach me and his words did not even ring my feelings. I turned around and went to the house to check it and relieve the girl on duty. Erela, as it turned out, was already there in the wellness room, putting the finishing touches on preparations.

A notification in the corporate chat jolted me back to reality. "He's arriving in a few minutes," the message blared. With a sigh, I switched on the welcome music and informed the ever-annoying butler lurking in the kitchen that it was time. We took our positions by the main door. Peeking through the small window, I saw his car pull up. A dark figure emerged and, with unsettling haste, practically sprinted towards the house.

3.. 2…1… deep breath to fortify myself and swung the door open:

-Good evening, sir…

-Oh, who is it!! Is she there? – he gestured to the wellness room, probably forgetting Erela's name.

-Yes

-Good – he took the water from the butler's tray and disappeared into the house labyrinth along with the butler, who went to the kitchen.

Dinner commenced before he had a chance to receive my presence with an untightened shirt. King Head arrived a few minutes later, both men taking their places at the massive ten-seater wooden table. It always baffled me why they kept such a large table when the house never hosted family, friends, or outside guests. As far as I could tell, King Head never entertained - no friends, no relatives, just the ever-present staff. It was always just the two of them, a constant duo, isolated from the outside world.

Door open

-Mari! Are you sleeping there??

-What?

-What??? Are they finishing the course?? We have to inform chef to prepare the next one! Don't create a problem for us!

-You can come and check by yourself if you don't trust me.

Door slam

Finding some common language in the kitchen, we finished this feast without incidents, and the king went directly to the wellness room. Butlers who were cleaning the table after dinner and with King Head disappeared from the house in a few minutes, leaving me alone again. I felt that I was not prepared for this situation. The moment when he finishes the massage, no one will be there, and only one butler in the kitchen, so I am alone and supposed to stay near the stairs during the night. What I, for sure, will not do it.

-Come here – a voice of WS came from my back.

-What?

-When they leave…kitchen, come to my room.

-They will be there all night.

-Why are you still with makeup? Don't come for the night with make-up.

-I have to follow the protocols

-I am the protocol here. Get up to my bed when they leave. I am not satisfied with this girl – he gestured to the wellness room – come, I need a massage.

-I am not qualified for this.

-Oh, how do you know if you didn't try it! – he grabbed my hand and, with circular movements, placed it on his genitals, explaining to me when exactly he wanted a massage.

Tears welled up in my eyes, threatening to overflow at any moment. Unable to hold back any longer, I bolted from the house. Seeking refuge, I huddled in a corner near the kitchen, pulling my legs close to my chest in a desperate attempt to conceal the offending glimpse of underwear beneath the ridiculously short skirt.

"I knew it! I knew it!" the words burst from my lips, laced with raw emotion. "Why do they all want me to suffer? Why won't anyone listen? Why?" A torrent of grief and indignation poured out of me, escalating into a fit of uncontrollable sobbing and hysteria. It felt like the primal scream of a child, a pain magnified by its very helplessness, by the lack of control I possessed over my situation. Perhaps that's why the betrayal stung so deeply - I had clung to a sliver of hope, a naive expectation that these people would somehow shield me from this personal hell. Why had I been so foolish, so irresponsible, as to relinquish control over my own life? Shame mingled with the tears, a bitter cocktail of self-recrimination and despair.

**Memories From Chats with GofG 01:17 Am Police Report Exhibit 20*

" -Fine?

-No.

-Why? What happened?

-He asked me to come.

-When? Now??

-Yes.

-Don't worry, he won't do anything.

-He will.

-How do you know?

-He said.

-Don't worry, don't think about it. He said what?

-He wants me to touch him -What? Where? Touch him where?

-What do you think?

-Just pat his head and maybe touch his arms. Play stupid as you don't know.

-He showed me where it's not his arms.

-Penis?

-Yes.

-Just play dumb and say, "No sir, I am scared."

-It doesn't help anymore. I told you I cannot do the night shift. And I cannot run like it was in Pink Hell 2

-I don't know. I thought Luisa was supposed to be there; why is she not there?? Yes, she is doing the night shift, and Rati is doing the day shift, and you are doing both night and day…So that you don't have to be alone. In the day, there is Rati. At night, there is Luisa.

But King Head sent the mail in front of me."

"So now she's playing me? Pretending they decided on a different schedule and this was all a misunderstanding? There was another plan?" My mind, already frayed to its breaking point, teetered between anger and a flicker of dawning hope. Could it be true? Was the information somehow garbled, a misunderstanding between Luisa and me? Perhaps I had lashed out unfairly. Maybe they genuinely intended to help, but fate had intervened with a cruel twist. The truth, I suspected, would forever remain elusive.

*Memories From Chats with King Head 03:23 Am Police Report Exhibit 20

"-He asked me today to come to his room after wellness and massage his ***. He gave me 30 minutes…so when I went upstairs, he was feeling asleep, thank god…but he would be pissed in the morning that I didn't come.

I don't know what to say: sorry for his bad morning mood, or wtf, sad emoji."

Around 5 AM, the King Head returned home from the office. I hadn't stayed in the house all night, even after the lucky chance to avoid the evening chaos. He usually enters through the same door as the other staff, using the backside entrance. Technically, he always appeared like one of us and never presented himself as a real "VIP client" in front of us. The weary kid, exhausted after 20 hours of work, entered the kitchen and looked at me. Pressing his hands, which were shaking and showed signs of weight loss, on the tablet, he turned his hunched body towards me. Almost scared, confused, and ashamed to say it aloud, he whispered,

-What happened to you?

-Nothing lucky me today..

-What did he say? – whispering to avoid attracting the attention of the butler who was outside the kitchen, he moved closer

-He said he wanted a dick massage as his wellness wasn't satisfied

-Oh my g...- He covered his mouth with one hand, unsure whether to laugh or smile.

-Yes... that is what I face here.

-He is sleeping now?

-I don't know. I will not go inside.

-Okey... good night...

He disappeared behind the house door. Frustration overwhelmed me. "How could I even consider letting him take care of me? How?! Yes, he's my boss, leading over 300 people here and in the other offices. But there's always a 'but,' isn't there?!" My mind raced with thoughts of my stupidity and worthlessness.

Preparing the fresh newspapers that were supposed to be placed inside the house before the "king's" wake-up call, I began to crumple one of them in anger at myself. "If they want to play games with me here, put me under his father, and pretend it wasn't their fault, I'll show them my teeth too."

I ended my shift and returned to my room, feeling a surge of newfound strength to fight against the chaos and manipulation surrounding me. Throughout the next week, I projected confidence in my actions and demeanor around the King. I aimed to show him that his intimidation tactics no longer fazed me, hoping he'd get bored and simply leave me.

On the day shift, when it was time for the wake-up call, I entered his bedroom. As I opened the curtains, I declared, "Good morning, your breakfast is ready…" Without waiting for a response, I exited the room.

The next "red line" was by the stairs. I stopped standing there to wait for him and deliberately started hiding behind the kitchen door. I was observing him go to wellness so that I could pass a message to the group. The next critical point - after his wellness session - caused me the most anxiety. The kitchen staff had already begun questioning my absence from the house. However, I remained resolute in my plan to escape this situation. Nothing could deter me.

During the night shift, I blatantly disregarded his requests, offering no explanation or excuses. I was essentially lying to his face:

Following his wellness session, the king, as usual, requested that I accompany him to the stairs. He stopped near the corner and, cornering me there, shoved me against the sliding door with such force that I nearly hit it. Then, with a sickening excitement, he began his usual routine: unbuttoning my shirt, clearly eager to see my bare breasts. He let out a sound that could only be described as the moan of a dying hyena.

-Come upstairs when everyone will leave.

-Sure.

-Don't fool me like last time.

-I didn't; you were sleeping when I came upstairs.

-And what?? Wake me up! You don't know how to wake up a man?? I will show you- he took my hand and again placed it on his heated penis.

-Stop!

-Shut up just do what you are supposed to do!

"Shut up, just do what you are supposed to do!" or sometimes he was saying 'Shut up, do your job! – the words that I will never forget in my life. These words changed the structure of my character, interaction, and behavior in critical situations. For my head now, it shows like a dog call sign which completely interrupts my movements and mind from the next action.

It's like a destroy point, a whip to shut me down as a naughty dog, like a switch button of which you don't have control.

The Bloodstained Pink

After receiving permission to go out, I changed into my regular clothes and applied a generous amount of fresh SPF to avoid getting sunburnt on the way to the hospital. During the drive, I pondered what other items GofG might need, considering the possibility of surgery today.

Upon entering the hospital, I already had a good idea of where to go, recalling my visit from the day she was admitted. As I made my way up, I finally located the VIP room - the last one on this floor.

-Hey!

-Oh, finally! I thought you were lost…

-How are you? What did they say?

-Nothing, the same… if the IV will not help, then I will get cut off my glands.

-It will not be painful, don't worry.

-How is it in Pink Hell? Silent?

-Same as usual…

-How are the girls?

-Oh.. waiting for you, especially Luisa.

-Why?

-To put you on shifts, of course!

-Ha-ha, no thank you…

-I know, but she was asking me about you, and when I told her that you are in the hospital with some throat infection, she was so upset…

-Because I will not work and he will stay one month more?

-He will stay one month more?!

-No, actually one month, but yes…

-And you will work?

-Yes… do I have other choice? After recovery, I will… I didn't work in Pink Hell, so…

-Oh… yes I forgot… But you know. Better to stay here and wait for surgery than to be in that house. Trust me…

-I know…I am scared now. King Head will leave and he can't take me back. So, I will be alone… how will I live without him??

-Are you mad??

-He will come back only after a week! A week!

-And what??

-I don't know… I already miss him.

-Oh, Jesus… you are totally blinded. You made the biggest mistake last week; you were supposed to stay and check your health and not run the disease up to the hospital. You could die!

-I can't stay without him… I miss him…

-You missed a common sense, girl

-Are you on shift tomorrow?

-Yes, morning.

-Will you come after? Or you want to take a rest...

-No, don't worry, I will come.

-Check how he is there... take care of him, please...

-Are you going to die?

-Ha-ha, no...

-So, chill.

Her face was pale and gaunt from illness. Her eyes were wild and glazed, reflective like she was facing the throes of drug withdrawal. Her mind seemed completely disoriented, unable to grasp the true picture of her situation. She, like all of us, came here to work. Yet, instead of focusing on resolving the problems within the "house" or finding a new job before the WS targeted her as the next victim, she had fallen madly, irresponsibly, in love. It was likely an illusory love fueled by extraordinary circumstances, a man she wouldn't have given a second glance to in normal life. Recalling the day I met her, a radiant girl with a captivating smile who effortlessly connected with everyone in the office, I could barely recognize the woman before me. While I had faced my hell here, she had gone through her own, which also destroyed and changed her but in another way.

Around 11 PM, I booked my cab and returned to my accommodation, leaving her alone to grapple with the pain of separation from her illusory lover. Reaching the security post, I felt my phone vibrating in my pocket.

-Good evening. Are you awake?

-Yes, I just returned from the hospital.

-Ha, I see... listen we have a force majeure here. I need you to come for the night shift.

-When?

-Now.

-Now?!! What happened? Why?

-Rati left..

-When?! I saw her in the morning.

-She left from her shift right now... I can't ask Luisa, she made the day shift, and tomorrow she is on night... so can you please come. I have no more options.

-I see the light in her room... she is packing. What happened?

-I don't know. Ask her if you will have a chance. Come please now, no one is in the house.

-But the butler?

-He is there, but he is not allowed to come inside. So come faster.

I entered my room and quickly changed into my uniform. Fueled by a surge of determination and confidence, I knew the clock had struck midnight. I was prepared to stay awake for nearly 20 hours if it meant avoiding contact with him. Stepping into the kitchen, I took a seat near the butler, feigning normalcy.

-Good evening.

-Hi. How is it going? – staring at him, I asked the question, hoping he would tell me the truth, as he was the only one who witnessed what happened with Rati.

-Fine.

-Fine?! – exploded from my mouth. "Your "collogue" just left in the middle of the night from her workplace, and you dare to lie in my eyes and say fine? Leave it; she is a girl! A girl!" -Yes, - interrupting my thoughts, he added without shame.

-Oh, okey. I see

He was probably prepared for such incident blatantly to lie into the pure girl's face and he knew that other staff would never tell the details to them, but he forgot! Today, the estate manager was a foreign man who doesn't play in these stupid games of covering your boss' dirty pants. How painful and warm in the same moment to catch someone red-handed and continue play in his spectacle.

During the night, I fell asleep and lost control of my wakefulness. Around 6 AM, after King Head returned from grueling office night, I got up from the chair and started to prepare morning newspapers when he came to the kitchen:

-Where is she? – the "king" with an annoyed voice requested his worrying towards me.

-Who? Rati?

-Yes

-She left, packing.

-Okay. I don't want to see her anymore. Bring me some water.

-Here please, take one it is ready.

-Good morning, Sir – devoted butler decided to raise his voice, coming inside the kitchen.

-Yes, yes.. – confused and probably not happy to see him, the king went back dissolved behind the house door.

I was so confident in myself that I didn't even think really about bringing him this glass of water. Understanding the fact that there are only two girls left who will work in the house, and there will be no possibility to change shifts, so one will work only night, another only day – I get hope of surviving the next few days before GofG returns from the hospital.

The kitchen staff started to arrive slowly and without haste because today was Sunday, and the "king" slept till his son woke up.

I was already at zero energy and barely understood what they wanted from me. Trying to avoid any

Communication, I went outside and stood in the same corner where I was crying that night.

-Good morning!

-Oh, you are also on shift today?

-Every day, when he is here. We don't sleep at all, Khani was living in the office chair last week. He even didn't return home to change or say "HI "to his wife.

-And you?

-I am reaching my hotel for 3-4 hours rest and return.

-Oh, so bad? I think we are the only ones who got over shifts…

-You are also. Btw, thank you for coming yesterday, and there is one more problem.

-What problem?

-Can you stay on the day shift also? If I bring Luisa now, that means evening you have to come for the night shift.. so…

-I will stay, no night shift, please. I will stay.

-He will leave for the temple after lunch, and you can go and take a rest; Luisa will come early to the shift.

-Okey, let's try. I think I can try to handle my sleep for the next 6 hours.

-Thank you. Any news from Rati?

-I was here all night, no idea…

-Okey…

-I will return to the house, better.

-Don't forget to message when he will wake up.

-Oh, don't worry ... I will not.

-Around 12, the haircut styler will come, and we will start to prepare the area soon.

-Same guy who was in Pink Hell 2? I have his number if you need

-No, no. Different.. don't worry, all is sorted.

There was no way I was returning here for the night, so I braced myself for 30 hours of being awake instead of facing the evening nightmare. Returning to the kitchen my confidence had waned. I steeled myself for whatever challenges the day might bring. My one glimmer of hope was that his son was here today and would stay with him until his flight back to Europe. Doubtful, but perhaps it would offer some respite.

The kitchen was already crowded with amazing smells of different bakeries and desserts just waiting their time to be served on a brunch table. Around 9:30 am, I went upstairs for a wake-up call, having just one chance to leave before he opened his eyes. Reaching the room, I gently ran my hand along the wall, trying to find the switch for curtains.

-Who is there??? Come here? Luisa? - overslept the moment of the hunt, the confused king gets up from his bed immediately to check who is on shift today.

-Good morning. The wellness lady is here.

-Come here! – getting closer, he took my arm and pulled me to the bed.

-I have to go.

Ignoring my startled squeak, he shoved me onto the bed, demanding his morning "petting." Chucking me not to dare to stand up from his bad, he scurried to the bathroom to grab a towel. A familiar dread washed over me as I felt rooted to the spot. "Why are you on day shift again?" he roared, furious that I dared to make my own decision. He tossed the towel at me and barked, "Take off your jacket and shirt."

-No.

-What??

-I said NO.

-Stop this drama; do what you are supposed to do!

-I said no, I have to go – taking all my bravery inside my small heart, I rose from the bed, and he pushed me back aggressively – I said I have to go!!- almost shouting, I raised again and left the crowded room with an atmosphere of fear, despair, and excitement.

My blood pounded with anger and exhaustion. My legs trembled as I descended the stairs, reaching the bottom with a shaky breath. I planted myself near the kitchen door, a silent vow forming in my mind: if he dared touch me again, I would scream.

Moments later, the WS appeared, directing him towards a wellness appointment, oblivious to my presence in the living room. "Done? Is he really finished with me? Or is this just another sick game?" My gaze followed his retreating form, a flicker of hope igniting within me. The possibility of freedom felt so real that I could almost escape the clutches of this living hell.

After the massage, he went out straight to the haircut area, which was organized in a white gazebo with massive columns, most looking like an "Afternoon Tea Area" in 17 centuries. Its imposing, fluted columns cast long shadows across the neatly trimmed hedges, creating a sense of secluded luxury. Luxury haircut. The sun was already high in the sky, casting a stifling heat over the space. Even the shade offered little respite from the suffocating air.

Butlers descended upon the dining area, their practiced movements filling the space with an air of quiet efficiency. They began meticulously arranging the table, setting it with a dazzling array of exclusive pastries and meticulously crafted snacks. The massive table, capable of seating ten, practically overflowed with a wealth of exquisite food. This extravagant spread, a true centerpiece for the morning, is supposed to be the main character of this "Brunch" performance. Having completed their masterpiece, the butlers discreetly retreated out behind the scenes.

Drawn by the opulent display, I drifted towards the window in the dining area overlooking the golf course and the distant gazebo. The WS sat there like a pompous turkey, roasting in the oppressive 50-degree heat, taking a luxury haircut. A flicker of movement caught my eye - the king's son was exiting the house, his steps directed towards the back area, presumably the office. He departed without so much as a glass of morning water or a word exchanged.

After his haircut, the WS returned to the house and, once again, bypassed my presence entirely, heading straight for his son's room. When he found it empty, he reappeared in the living area, his silence heavy.

-Where is my son? - he barked.

- He went to the office, - I replied, my voice barely above a whisper. But in my mind, a fierce retort echoed: "No, I know exactly where he is. He's hiding in the office because you're a suffocating boa constrictor, a monster who poisons the air from this house! That's why your son, who leaves for Europe today after a mere four hours of sleep, would rather return to the stuffy office on a Sunday than spend another moment with you!

The morning that began disastrously continued to spiral downward; not even the sumptuous Sunday feast could lift the king's spirits. He sat down at the table without a glance at the spread and curtly called his son, questioning his behavior. The heavy silence that followed only intensified the tension in the dining room.

Within a faded voice, he requested me: "Check from the window and let me know when he finishes his haircut." Going to the observation point without a word, I stand near the window, obediently following his request. After 20 minutes of a dog job, after twenty minutes of straining my neck to watch this tedious process, I reached up to massage the ache. "Stay focused! Keep an eye out," he bellowed. "I don't pay you to goof off." he smashed on me a ridiculous notice. I recognized this as a mere power play meant to remind me of my lowly position in his household.

He stood up from the table and went to his room direction, giving his last notice:" Do not miss when he finishes it. Look properly. At least that's something you can manage, isn't it?"

He delivered his final humiliating remark, which I choked down without a word. A moment later, I felt a sudden draft and a strange rustle behind me. The WS lunged, grabbing my arm and shoving his hand between my legs in a sickening attempt to remove my underwear. In a surge of primal panic, I clawed at his hand, ripping it away with all my strength, squeezing my legs shut and crossing them tightly. Horror and fear fueled my desperate struggle, and I managed to break free from his grasp. Gasping for air, I fled towards the kitchen, the first deep breath burning my lungs. "Don't dare to go out! Stay put!" I managed to choke out. "I told you to check on his haircut! Do your job properly!"

Dizzy from the shock and the sudden influx of oxygen, I wandered the room, my mind reeling, finally settling near the lounge area with its large panoramic window overlooking the marble staircase. From there, I numbly observed his son's haircut, clinging to the desperate hope that obedience would somehow appease him. Silently, the WS approached me, a predator satisfied with regaining control.

-I am going to take some rest, wake me up when he will finish his haircut, – he adds leaving me trembling with fear that everything will repeat.

For the next five minutes, terror coiled around me like a serpent. Every rustle in the kitchen, every laugh or sound, sent a jolt of fear through me. I froze, not daring to turn, not a single muscle twitching. He could be anywhere, a predator watching, waiting for the slightest sign of weakness. Fear, a cold, metallic clamp around my heart, held me captive. It was a cruel leash, indeed, one that achieved obedience through sheer terror. My mind was consumed by a singular task: observe the haircut and report its completion. There were no other thoughts, no room for anything else.

After what felt like an eternity, the scene before me shifted. The stylist removed the white cloth from the king's son's neck, and the boy stood, retrieving his tablet and immersing himself in its glow, his gaze fixed on the house. Seizing the opportunity, I turned and hurried upstairs to the king's bedroom.

-The haircut is finished, I reported my voice barely above a whisper.

-Good. Now, remove all the clothes from the bathroom floor. It's already 2 pm, and it's still a mess. Why do I always have to remind you of your duties?

Without any reply, I headed for the bathroom, which was on my right. Passing through the mini lounge, I saw several wet towels strewn across the middle of the room and the night suit on the floor in the next room, the wardrobe. Grabbing the wall between the shower and toilet for support (my body was already at its limit after 30 hours on foot), I bent down to pick it up.

The man lunged at me, his grip tightening around me even more. I felt a primal fear erupt within him, fueled by adrenaline. He shoved his fingers between my legs again, the pain radiating through my crotch. Frozen in terror, like a trapped rabbit, I couldn't control my body. My mind screamed at me to fight back, but my limbs refused to obey. It was a horrifying chaos within me. Gasping out the words, "Stop, no, please! Stop it!" I felt like I was in a nightmare, unable to scream, unable to run and freeze in one place with exploding fear and this condition getting you out of your dream, but I am not in a dream!! Where is the remote control to wake me up from this panic attack? Where??

My fainting state took over sobriety. Hearing the echo of reality, his moans and half-dead growl, I was trying to connect with my body, and I felt the most horrible disgust of it – the terrible pain I felt between my legs get took shape, his fingers were inside me, pressing on the vaginal wall trying to tear and pierce them. His nails dug into my mucous membrane. I thought it was a scissor from the dressing table, and in the next minute, I would cover the entire floor with my blood. And this horrible thought woke me up, and I screamed for the last time in my life! He shoved my face with his hand, his anger evident through gritted teeth. "Shut up bitch!! Shut up!!" He pushed me to the floor like used trash, calmly walked to the sink, washed his hands, and went out, leaving me to lie on my knees, choking from snot and rhythmic breathing.

Gasping for breath, I reached down to check myself, if I had something inside me as it felt burning and tight. Rising on shaky legs, utterly confused, I stumbled towards the mirror. The woman staring back was unrecognizable. Her clothes were messy and dirty, her ugly face pale and drawn. Dark circles rimmed her bloodshot eyes, which welled with fresh tears. With trembling hands, I turned on the faucet, the cool water a small comfort. I splashed it on my face and hair, trying to wash away the mascara and the sting of humiliation.

As the truth of what happened settled over me, a chilling realization dawned. The terror that had gripped me began to recede, replaced by a horrifying certainty. For the first time, I felt it - a hot, insidious mass spreading through me like a cancerous growth. It devoured everything healthy in its path, sowing a garden of pain, oppression, fear, and chaos within every cell. My chest ached a constant dull throb that intensified with each ragged breath. It felt as if the very blood coursing by veins carried the taint of this tumor, each exhale a searing agony pushing the poison further into my body, infecting new corners and refreshed cells. Words fail me. No amount of language can capture the utter devastation consuming me.

With glazed eyes, I descended the stairs, utterly detached from this world. Below, the devil himself sat at the head of the dining table, which remained untouched, a centerpiece of pristine emptiness. Reaching my usual spot by the kitchen door, I witnessed a pathetic scene of heartbreaking pathos: The kid, who made everything to avoid any connections with his father today, emerged from his room post-shower, a small black suitcase clutched in his hand - a silent gesture for escape to the airport. And a bewildered fooled old man who didn't get what he wanted from his son. He resembled a figure manipulated beyond his understanding. This kid knows how to live in this hell; he has learned to navigate the treacherous waters of their dysfunctional family. But what about me? It's easy. Their dysfunction is a storm they must live themselves. Like a Stoic, I should hold onto my own virtue and inner peace, unmoved by their chaos. I don't belong to this house. I refuse to be swept away by their current.

-I have to go..- he silently pronounced, explaining his movements.

-But food?

-I don't want to eat. I have to go.

-Okay, I will go with you.

-Where?

-To drop you...– King, dumbfounded, rose from his seat. His face, a mask of betrayal, was directed towards the entrance door. His hesitant movements and lowered head spoke volumes of a father's pain, a man who couldn't comprehend why his child wouldn't love him. Only a deranged mind or a maniac could behave this way. Any sane person, sooner or later, understands their mistakes. But this monster - he will never get it. Doomed to carry the crushing weight of his terrible karma, a burden that will follow him into the unknown depths of his next rebirth, he will forever be haunted by the lesson he could never grasp.

As I shut the main door behind them, a commotion reached my ears. Butlers and housekeeping staff had already swarmed the house like flies. Deciding to forgo the rest of this funeral celebration, I turned to retreat to my room. Before leaving entirely, I cast a final glance at the magnificent, abundant brunch table. The centerpiece of this day's performance, which failed, remained completely untouched, not even a single bite.

***

www.ingramcontent.com/pod-product-compliance
Ingram Content Group UK Ltd.
Pitfield, Milton Keynes, MK11 3LW, UK
UKHW020243240426
12048UKWH00026B/1583

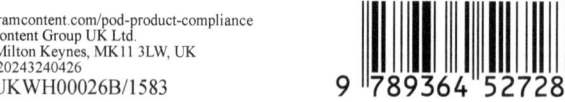